The Quality of Literature

Linguistic Approaches to Literature (LAL)

Linguistic Approaches to Literature (LAL) provides an international forum for researchers who believe that the application of linguistic methods leads to a deeper and more far-reaching understanding of many aspects of literature. The emphasis will be on pragmatic approaches intersecting with areas such as discourse analysis, sociolinguistics, ethnolinguistics, rhetoric, philosophy, cognitive linguistics, psycholinguistics and stylistics.

Volume 4

The Quality of Literature. Linguistic studies in literary evaluation
Edited by Willie van Peer

The Quality of Literature

Linguistic studies in literary evaluation

Edited by

Willie van Peer

Ludwig Maximilian University, Munich

John Benjamins Publishing Company

Amsterdam / Philadelphia

TM The paper used in this publication meets the minimum requirements of
American National Standard for Information Sciences – Permanence of
Paper for Printed Library Materials, ANSI z39.48-1984.

Library of Congress Cataloging-in-Publication Data

The quality of literature : linguistic studies in literary evaluation / edited by Willie van
    Peer.
    p.   cm. (Linguistic Approaches to Literature, ISSN 1569-3112 ; v. 4)
Includes bibliographical references and index.
1. Criticism. 2. Literature--History and criticism. 3. Discourse analysis, Literary. I. Peer,
    Willie van.
PN85.Q35   2008
801'.95--dc22
ISBN 978 90 272 3336 3 (Hb; alk. paper)   2007047268

John Benjamins Publishing Co. · P.O. Box 36224 · 1020 ME Amsterdam · The Netherlands
John Benjamins North America · P.O. Box 27519 · Philadelphia PA 19118-0519 · USA

Table of contents

Acknowledgments

Permission has kindly been granted by Oxford University Press to reprint the contributions by Stein Haugom Olsen and Willie van Peer. The permission is gratefully acknowledged here

In Chapter 4, William Empson's *Reflection from Anita Loos* is reproduced by kind permission of Chatto & Windus.

Foreword

In preparing this volume I have had the help and support of many people, first and foremost, of course, from the various contributors, whom I would like to thank for their kindness and their patience in the long road of preparing the volume for publication.

I would like to thank especially those colleagues who have provided me with extensive feedback in earlier stages of the book's preparation: Don Freeman, Elrud Ibsch, Gerard Steen, Peter Verdonk and Sonia Zyngier. I owe them my personal thanks for their keen criticism and their widening of my perspective.

The evaluation of literary texts

A new perspective

Willie van Peer

The evaluation of literary texts is something that readers almost always, automatically, and spontaneously, engage in. They judge the development of a plot and generate feelings of pleasure or dislike at particular events, they feel that the text does not yield what they had expected, or they find the author's style rewarding or awkward. All of this evaluation usually takes place as an integral part of the reading process. But also off-line judgments about the text are made: in conversations with spouses or friends, in a discussion with colleagues, or in writing an email to a student. And then there are, finally, the debates about the evaluation of texts by professionals: critics or academics who write reviews in the newspapers, in magazines, or in journals and books, or who may engage in public debate or in the mass media. Evaluation is a significant activity both for individual readers and for cultures at large. Evaluating a literary text is an instinctive practice in which we engage both routinely and with fervor.

Yet among this ubiquity of evaluative activities one must acknowledge that we have extremely little information as to how such judgmental processes and outcomes function. Theoretically one can conceive of three major features playing a role in the process: the text, the reader, and the context. We may assume that readers evaluate specific features of the text: whether it induces suspension in them or makes them laugh, whether it makes for easy reading or it employs elevated language, or whether its content is erotic or *risqué*. All these are linguistic elements of some kind or other that could influence a particular reader to make the text pleasant or unpleasant to read. But it seems intuitively clear that not only the text, but also features of the reader play a role: presumably readers differ in their tastes and preferences, so that the same linguistic ingredient may produce an agreeable feeling in one reader, but be boring or insulting to another. Readers' concrete goals and expectations, their past reading experiences and personal biography, or their knowledge of certain genre conventions, may all drive their evaluative process in one direction or another. But such readers do not live in a vacuum: they are surrounded by other people who equally evaluate texts, thus mutually influencing each other. It is easy to imagine how a particular reader may be receptive to the opinions of persons dear to him/her, or may be afraid of uttering his own opinion in a totalitarian state, or may let judgment be influenced by the prestige of the author. These three factors, the text, the reader, and the context, may all steer the evaluative processes in a particular direction. Moreover, they do not operate in isolation, but may interpenetrate, enhance, counteract, or neutralize each other. For instance, readers leading a daily life of routine in a Catholic surrounding (*context*) may welcome content that is of an adventurous or rebellious nature (*text*), because such semantic material provides them with the possibility of escapism (*reader*).

How are studies of these factors represented in literary studies? Surprisingly, there seems to be a strong bias in favor of contextual explanations, defined here as ideological contexts. Most literary scholars seem to believe that the judgment of literary texts occurs under a strong influence of readers' immediate surroundings, their gender, class, race, nationality or sexual and ideological inclinations, and so forth. That certainly is the opinion of Herrnstein Smith (1988), who asserted that the evaluative processes involved in canon formation are inherently biased toward existing power structures and their ideological legitimation. Most theoreticians, including scholars like Culler (1983), Eagleton (1983), Fish (1989), Guillory (1993), all emphasize the contextual determinacy of evaluative mechanisms. While it is certainly not to be denied that contextual factors are at play, and may under certain circumstances even impose powerful imperatives for the evaluation of literary texts, an over-emphasis on them could lead these authors into an awkward position.

For one thing, they thereby seem to assume that evaluating literary texts is driven by one factor only, thus presuming some kind of mono-causality. By denying that any influence from the reader's personal characteristics or particular linguistic features of the text play a role in the evaluative process, these authors claim that out of a range of potential explanations, only one applies. Such forms of mono-causality are, however, extremely rare in the social and cultural field, where usually several, if not dozens of factors are at play simultaneously, and interact with each other in highly complex ways. By denying the complexity of these processes, most literary theorists create a radically oversimplified picture of cultural processes and are thus involved in an extreme form of reductionism. True, some form of reductionism may be unavoidable in research, but one should at the same time be conscious of the reduction, and not forget the factors that one has factored out. In the case of the evaluation of literary texts, it seems highly implausible that only one of the three factors discussed earlier would be involved. There is also something strange in a position that explains cultural phenomena in a deterministic way. Given the nature of culture, it seems so much more probable to expect its phenomena to emerge in a highly dynamic rather than contextually predetermined way.

Defenders of the contextualist explanation do not provide any arguments why processes of literary evaluation should follow a mono-causal and deterministic path. Against this position, I claim that there are no reasons to expect that reader or text characteristics do not exert an influence in the evaluative processes either. The over-emphasis on contextual explanations has led to a situation, however, in which very few studies have been carried out of the influence of these factors. Granted, it is not always easy to find appropriate methods to disentangle the separate factors in a complex network of interactions. But difficulty is not impossibility. The present volume at least makes an attempt in this direction by investigating the role of textual factors. This is not to deny the importance of readers' characteristics, nor, indeed, of contextual factors. But for those of us who have a keen interest in the nature of literary texts themselves, the question in what way the formal and semantic elements of the text may contribute to positive or negative evaluations is an intriguing one.

The enterprise of bringing together the various contributions in this volume goes back to an essay that was published several years ago in *The British Journal of Aesthetics* (Vol. 36, No. 2, 1996:97–108). In this article, I made a detailed analysis of two texts that are identical in theme, and similar in content, and written at approximately the same time, one of which ended up in the literary canon, while the other did not. The texts selected were Shakespeare's *Romeo and Juliet* and Arthur Brooke's *The Tragicall Historye of Romeus and Juliet*, published in London some thirty years before Shakespeare's text. By taking a detailed look at the language of both works, I hoped to gather some degree of insight in possible textual factors that may have contributed to canonization in Shakespeare's case, and to virtual neglect in the case of Brooke. The results were interesting in at least two respects. On the one hand, the language of Shakespeare's play turned out – in comparison to Brooke's – to be substantially more complex and innovative, more varied and richer in style and register, while at the same time reverberating with multiple meanings. At the same time, while the plot lines of the two texts run almost completely parallel, the specific content, and especially the evaluative slant on the events from a narrative perspective differed remarkably. The point of view taken in Brooke's text is completely in line with contemporary power positions and their ideology in Elizabethan England, while Shakespeare's is at odds with them. Here then was a pair of texts showing the relative *un*importance of contextual elements, obviously falsifying Herrnstein Smith's thesis: Shakespeare's text clearly undermines the prevalent views of those in power during his time. In the course of history his text came to be valued more highly than that of Brooke, whose views were completely in line with the power structure of his time.

While this was interesting in itself, the enterprise was of limited value for an obvious reason: it concerns one case study only, and as is well-known, it is notoriously dangerous to draw conclusions from a single case. If other similar analyses could be carried out and compared with the present one, the case for gaining insight in the text's contribution to evaluation could be made stronger. In the course of time, favorable reactions to my article from several colleagues led to a collaborative effort at extending the data base of such textual comparisons. The present volume is the outcome of the various interactions and collaborative efforts that grew out of this idea. It contains a range of studies carried out by colleagues, making similar comparisons between pairs of comparable texts or genres by looking in a detailed way at the language employed in those texts, complemented by some theoretical reflections on the evaluative process.

The clearest verdict comes from Stein Haugom Olsen. The defenders of the view that literary value is essentially based on social power or influence suffer a significant defeat at the hands of Olsen: the assumptions underlying their claims are taken apart piece by piece. Yet the major force of his argument comes from his prediction about the works of Hugh MacColl (1837–1909), a now forgotten Scottish author of two novels which, so Olsen convincingly shows, are artistic failures, and will therefore never be part of a literary canon. While the ideology presented in both works is totally in agreement with the then prevailing ideas and attitudes in society, this did not prevent the author from disappearing altogether from the history of English literature. The reason for this becomes clear when one analyses the characters and their problems, the theme and the language of the novels, and contrasts them with comparable contemporaneous works, such as, for instance, Mrs. Humprey Ward's *Robert Elsmere* (1888), a work that still is remembered and read. Olsen writes: "One could continue aspect by aspect with MacColl's two novels and demonstrate this lack of imaginative realisation of events, situations, characters, and relationships, and how this is closely linked with an extensive use both of clichés in the language and of stock situations and characters."

I think Olsen is right in his claim that Hugh MacColl is not, nor will ever be, part of a literary canon. It is not simply the claim about this particular author, however, that makes his argument significant: it is that Olsen addresses the issue in the appropriate arena: that of empirical statements about reality. We would certainly advance more in our understanding of literary evaluation if more scholars were prepared to make such predictions about the future canon. I believe the example proves Olsen right: even if all his opponents were from this very moment to set out 'canonizing' Hugh MacColl, it is perfectly clear that they would not even remotely succeed.

A similar approach is taken by Jan Gorak. By setting Joseph Conrad's *The Secret Agent* in its context of production, by comparing it to the more popular (and commercially successful) spy novels of his days, Gorak is able to highlight how in Conrad's hands the generic material and conventions are systematically defamiliarized. As with Shakespeare / Brooke, the semantic material looks similar only at first sight. A closer analysis brings to light the extent to which entrenched ideological categories of the time are systematically undermined. As far as the correspondence with his publishers reveals, Conrad was an author who sought popularity (but much to his chagrin, never really attained it – and ended up in the literary canon instead). At first sight, *The Secret Agent* makes use of a popular genre, the spy novel. Yet, as Gorak demonstrates, Conrad uses the genre in a highly innovative way, namely to investigate the ruptures in national and cultural identity that presented a serious crisis sweeping through England and Europe at the time. "In Conrad, canonicity and popularity are interdependent," writes Gorak. By comparing Conrad's work with popular Edwardian spy novels like William Le Queux's *The Invasion of 1910* (1906), Erskine Childers' *Riddle of the Sands* (1903), and Edgar Wallace's *The Four Just Men* (1905), Gorak documents how in these works "the secret agent embodies the values of individuality, good breeding, and cool courage. The secret agent of the spy novel answers the fears of the invasion narratives that the national virtues have entered decline." Verloc, Conrad's character, by contrast, is the very opposite of these virtues, and the outcome is "inglorious disaster" rather than salvation.

Generic comparison is also the theme of Tom Barney's analysis. While Gorak's emphasis is on the semantic aspects of text-type, Barney concentrates on the linguistic *form* of a particular genre. His main thesis is that form plays a predominant role in literary evaluation: how well does the writer employ the possibilities of traditional form, and to what extent is s/he able to transcend these possibilities? The form selected by Barney for detailed study is the *villanelle*: one is Ernest Dowson's *Villanelle of Marguerites*, the other William Empson's *Reflection from Anita Loos*. "Is it possible for a poet to be defeated by a form," Barney asks – and after a meticulous analysis of both poems, concludes that Dowson's case is really that the formal requirements dictate the content of his poem, preventing coherence from emerging. In the case of William Empson's villanelle, by contrast, one observes how the risks involved in the formal constraints are successfully overcome in a virtuoso handling of semantic material tightly integrated into a formal pattern.

A similar enterprise is undertaken by Laurence Lerner. As a first test case, Lerner contrasts two poems he calls radical – in the sense that they voice outrage at social injustice; the poems chosen are Mary Robinson's *The Birth Day* and William Blake's *London*, both written in the 1790s. Lerner shows how Robinson establishes a *homology* between the poet's indignation and the poetic form chosen. In Blake's poem, by contrast, the indignation is cast in language that unsettles our craving for clarity by shifting its meaning constantly into something else. Does that make Blake's work less forceful as a political argument? Lerner thinks it does, while at the same time making it more successful as a literary event. What the analysis shows, according to Lerner, is that literary quality is independent of a political stand. If this is so in politically revolutionary poems, then, to complete the picture, one has to make a similar analysis of conservative poems; three are selected, all by Wordsworth. Again Lerner demonstrates how literary quality in the texts is irrespective of their political stand, and that the politics of the poems neither guarantee nor prohibit quality to stand out.

Working in the same historical period, David Miall compares two highly similar poems by Coleridge, "To the Rev. George Coleridge," written in May 1797, and "Frost at Midnight," dated February 1798. Although both commit a good sense of Coleridge's feelings, the former is hardly read nowadays, while the latter has acquired some kind of canonical status, having been reprinted in many anthologies. "Why has the fate of these two poems been so different?" Miall asks. The argument he provides is highly illuminating, as it casts light on the mechanisms authors may deploy to catch the reader's attention, thus locating their reading process at a deeper (and hence emotionally more involving) level. After assessing the language, structure and rhetoric of both poems, Miall comes to the conclusion that at each of these organizational levels both texts create an implied reader, but that one of these (the one in "To the Rev. George Coleridge") remains an outside observer, while the one in "Frost at Midnight" becomes a participant. In due course, we become "participants in the unfolding processes of the poem, having made those processes relevant to the fate of our own feelings" – and it is these processes that may be of paramount importance for the evaluation and canonization of literary texts. Where the language, structure, and rhetoric of the text do not facilitate such participatory processes, it may be discarded and forgotten.

A special opportunity to study the evaluation of literary texts offers itself when more than one version of the same text exists. Short and Semino take up this opportunity, by analyzing two extant versions of the first stanza of William Blake's *Tyger*, and then later (after having considered some evaluative issues with respect to Ted Hughes' *October Dawn* and T.S. Eliot's *Little Gidding*) the two versions of John Fowles's *The Magus* in their 1966 and 1977 editions. Since Fowles decided to make the changes in the 1977 edition, one may presume that he himself must have thought that the changes were an improvement. By making detailed linguistic analyses of comparable passages from both editions, Short and Semino are able to show that in the passages chosen from the first edition, the narrative point of view is much more from the 'I-as-character', providing an immediacy of the protagonist's thoughts and feelings, while in the same passages in the later edition this impression is diluted by an oscillation between the 'I-as-character' and the 'I-as-narrator' perspective, thereby presenting a less coherent and more detached point of view. Needless to say, such analysis concerns only brief passages, and therefore may not inform us about the processes that shape the evaluation of a whole, long, novel, and thus further work is needed on how such small-scale analyses can and should be integrated in the overall evaluation of literary works. The value of Short and Semino's contribution lies in the fact that they demonstrate the very possibility of explaining in detail a particular evaluation (not the one shared by Fowles, by the way) of such selected passages. Short and Semino's work also brings to the fore the intimate connections between evaluation and interpretation of texts, an issue taken up more concretely in the essay by von Heydebrand and Winko, who see socially mediated schemata as the interface between interpretation and evaluation.

Walter Nash has picked a poet who certainly was politically incorrect in his own times. Although Juvenal may from an establishment perspective be called ideologically dubious, his works survived for two millennia, making him an interesting test case for the claim that literary evaluation is inherently biased toward existing power structures. Indeed, the claim seems to forbid a satirical writer ever to enter into the canon. How could Swift ever have become so famous, having satirized about every power structure of his own age? Juvenal's reception in English literary history, however, mainly through Dryden and Johnson, betrays a serious misunderstanding of the Roman poet. Both translated Juvenal into English, and made him into an 18th century Christian poet, thus fundamentally misunderstanding and bypassing Juvenal's spirituality. This raises the issue of translation in the canonization process. To stay close to his spirit, Nash strongly recommends avoiding 'imitations' of the kind provided by Johnson, but instead aiming for a word-for-word faithfulness. While this may not look a translator's ultimate goal, it has all the advantages of conveying a sense of unfamiliarity, which is often present in the original as well. As such, it recognizes the defamiliarization of the literary language better than a smooth and elegant translation.

As Juvenal has been in the canon for a couple of millennia, it is appropriate to distinguish between fleeting, contemporary fame and permanent fame. Such a distinction is made by Colin Martindale in his essay. In a tongue-in-cheek mode, Martindale presents an impressive array of research that systematically correlates long-term eminence with other factors. Tongue-in-cheek the style of his chapter may be, the argument is not less powerful for it, as it spells out a number of rather objective measures that correlate with eminence over the long term - objective in the sense that they can be independently checked and replicated by other researchers. The number of anthology reprints is such an objective measure, but Martindale has himself developed a number of computer programs that measure various aspects of texts. In this way one can see what eminence is correlated with, and what it is *not* correlated with. For instance, on the basis of the analysis of a considerable sample of British poetry, it becomes clear that contemporary fame does not significantly correlate with 88 variables lined up by Martindale. Eminence, however, was negatively correlated to the expression of emotion and pleasure, and with secondary process content. On the other hand, eminence correlates positively with imagery and concreteness. Summarized, then, these data mean that great poetry deals with the depths of the human mind in a concrete and imagery-rich way, avoiding thought, action or emotion. Another mark of eminence is the variation in sentence length: great poets intermix short and long sentences. Martindale's finding should not, of course, be interpreted as prescriptions. It is not to be expected that one will become a famous poet by intermingling short and long sentences. Martindale does claim, however, that poets who do *not* abide by this rule have considerably fewer chances of ending up in the canon. His findings are therefore to be interpreted as necessary, not as sufficient, conditions to attain eminence over time.

In her chapter, Sonia Zyngier investigates how corpus linguistics can contribute to our understanding of literary evaluation. Shakespeare's *Macbeth* is contrasted with Holinshed's and other contemporary texts on two major dimensions: predictability and function. This has obvious limitations, but also advantages: it allows a more rigorous isolation of individual factors that may contribute to the canonization of Shakespeare's text as compared to Holinshed's, and in that way may deepen our grasp of how long-term evaluation works. It turns out, as in the analysis of Van Peer, that the computer analysis marks the superiority of Shakespeare's language over his source text again and again. As such, the chapter goes beyond the interpretative mode characteristic of other contributions in this volume. Zyngier also argues that such a corpus approach has evident pedagogical applications and advantages. She outlines a teaching program whereby students will arrive at their own conclusions about the language of the play by going through successive analytical steps using a corpus approach.

Like Olsen, Fricke wants to make evaluative statements *empirically predictive*. Obviously this is a courageous and important step in investigating literary evaluation. If we can make such valid predictions, we will have taken a giant leap forward. And if our predictions turn out not to be valid, we will have learned a good deal in the process anyway. Fricke tackles the problem head on, by proposing 'laws' that operate over the evaluation of literary texts. An example of such a law is that a text containing a deviation that serves one function in the text will be evaluated lower than when such a deviation may fulfill more than one function. Such laws should be understood as operating under the *ceteris paribus* principle. When we apply this principle (of *other things being equal*), however, we can start manipulating texts and testing their evaluation. Although Fricke stops short of testing, his proposals have wide implications, not in the least because he provides different manipulated versions of poetic texts, and makes concrete predictions about their evaluation.

The volume closes with two theoretical considerations that place the study of literary evaluation in a wider context. Livingston offers a current overview of the various positions concerning the problem of evaluation in present-day analytic philosophy. As such, it provides important information to literary scholars about the debates philosophers are currently involved in. Granted that such debates have become more technical over the past decades, Livingston's mapping of the various positions presents a valuable contribution: it allows literary scholars a possibility of orientation in the field.

I started this introduction by pointing to three components relevant to the evaluation of literature: the text, the reader, and the context in which the reading and evaluation take place. Von Heydebrand and Winko take up these different factors by offering a systematic reflection on the nature of evaluative activities in a pluralistic society. It incorporates theoretical reflection on values and the canon, but also research in social psychology and the psychology of cognition. The authors develop a balanced model for the study of literary evaluation, in which the various individual and social components, as well as the content and structure of texts, are given their due relevance. The authors conclude with a call for more empirical research on acts of evaluation, and outline a number of issues that should be investigated empirically.

What has been set out in this volume are not last words, but only beginnings in the study of literary evaluation. There are three kinds of criticisms however, that are likely to turn up in the debate, which I believe have to be addressed, albeit briefly. One relates to the issue of power, another to the subjective nature of evaluation, the third one to the pluralistic nature of modern societies. Let us look briefly at each of these arguments.

The first issue concerns the claim that evaluation is driven by the reproduction of unequal power structures in society. Could it not be that those in power cleverly subscribe to the high values of canonical works, even when these denounce or undermine the current power balance, as a cunning ruse – to let people think they are free to admire these works, while in actual fact, nothing will change? For instance, one could argue that the ruling groups in society are clever enough not to promote Brooke directly (at the expense of Shakespeare), because that would simply be too obvious. Therefore, they also admire Shakespeare, go to see his plays, but make sure that things stay the way they are. One could say that in that sense they are hypocritical.

What are we to make of this view? Even if we were to concede that it is realistic (which I think it is not), i.e., that ruling groups in society indeed act on this hypocritical scenario, that already would show some kind of progress: better to have ruling classes that at least in theory acknowledge the utopian view of the equality between the sexes. Hypocrites they may be in this sense, but there is an inherent danger in playing out this stratagem: as Taylor (1993: 228) has pointed out, once we are over this hub of acknowledging that this **is** a better model after all, then it may be only a matter of time before things will really start changing.

Hypocrisy is itself an attitude that results from sociological changes related to processes of civilization as described by Elias (1947). For a long time in medieval Europe, members of the aristocracy had no need to behave hypocritically: they could just do as they pleased. With ever longer interdependence chains (largely dictated by economical and political ties), they were gradually forced into playing things differently. It is in Elizabethan times indeed that these civilizing processes get under way in England, and thus, the argument of hypocrisy may carry some weight. Note, however, that hypocrisy does not explain the popularity of the play – the rulers of the time could have been embarrassed by it, and subsequently play the hypocrite, but it does not explain that they massively chose to go and see it. Anyone clever enough to speculate on the potential consequences of promoting the Romeo and Juliet scenario could have predicted the danger it involved in the long term. And precisely because of the danger involved, one must still explain the popularity of *Romeo and Juliet*. The danger in letting this utopian vision emerge certainly was serious enough, so that it should be explained adequately why the ruling classes let it pass in the first place – unless one believes that literature has absolutely no influence on the social world; but that seems obviously untrue; see the debate between Stolnitz (1991) and van Peer (1995). Some social revolutions have their origin in the theatre, and the many anti-theatrical movements show the acute awareness of the ruling classes of this danger; see Hjort (1994); see also the impressive research by Robert Darnton (1996), showing how popular literature on the eve of the French Revolution profoundly affected public opinion in France at the moment, thus contributing in part to the revolutionary mood. Thus the argument of a sly stratagem on the part of the powerful to accommodate works of art that are at odds with their own ideology leaves much to be answered.

A second criticism of the analyses in this volume could be that they remain somehow subjective. For instance, one claim that has been made is that complexity plays a role in evaluation. Shakespeare's text was deemed more complex than Brooke's and this contributed to its higher evaluation. But why pick complexity as a criterion, the critics may counter? Is that choice not purely subjective in itself?

I would argue that it is not, and that there are good reasons to employ the criterion of complexity in the evaluation of literature or art works. As Martindale has pointed out in his essay, the relation between evaluation and other factors is often non-monotonic, and usually takes the form of an inverted U-shape: if we plot a particular textual characteristic, such as complexity, on a horizontal axis, and readers' evaluations of the text on a vertical axis, one can observe that texts with minimal complexity get (other things being equal, of course) the lowest evaluation, and that with increasing complexity evaluation also increases, but only up to a certain point. Beyond that, further increases in complexity will lead to ever lower evaluations. This is the famous Wundt curve (after the founder of experimental psychology, Wilhelm Wundt) that has been demonstrated in dozens of studies, including art works; Berlyne (1971). This shows that we are cognitively wired to enjoy modest levels of complexity. Too little complexity leaves us bored, whereas too much complexity will baffle us. Therefore, complexity is not just a subjective choice of a few critics or scholars, but is part of our cognitive and emotional make-up. The choice even makes it clear why different groups of people may evaluate a literary work differently: because they have different thresholds from which further increases in complexity lower the evaluation. Canonical works, then, may be defined as those that have optimal levels of complexity for the largest number of (literate) people in a society. And historical fluctuations in the appreciation of particular works may be accounted for by different levels of literacy, or different ceilings of complexity toleration. One may see in the preference for complexity as an evaluative criterion a return to *New Criticism*, and indeed its notions of complexity and ambiguity played a considerable role in the work of the New Critics. One may see in their approach an intuitive appeal such notions have, which at the time were not yet well-understood. Today we have at least an inkling of the role such qualities play in cognition and emotion. That complexity levels certainly influence readers' reactions has meanwhile been demonstrated experimentally by Zyngier, van Peer and Hakemulder (2007).

Note, however, and this cannot be stressed enough, that complexity is only one of the presumably many criteria that are applied by readers in the evaluative process. We do not have as yet even an unordered list of such criteria; we do not even know how many there are: 10, 100, 1000? And presumably not all are of equal importance, so that one would need relative weightings for each of them in the evaluative process. As long as we do not devote ourselves to researching such criteria, but – as literary scholars often do – declare beforehand that such things are too complicated, or too difficult, or that they are simply 'subjective', we will thereby foreclose the very possibility of developing a better-informed view of the evaluative process, and by that act create a self-fulfilling prophecy (that has been quite successful so far).

This means then that when the level of complexity of a literary text is not optimal, the text may be less eligible for inclusion in the canon, *unless* it makes up for this deficiency by scoring better on several other criteria, for instance versification, narrative perspective, stanzaic structure, and so forth. Neither of these may by themselves promote a work into the canon, but as they add up, they will create better chances for a work to become canonical. This brings us to the important point that such criteria are **necessary**, not **sufficient** conditions for evaluation. To deny that such necessary conditions are at work comes close to saying that works in the canon are there by accident.

Suppose there are x parameters at play in evaluation. On each of these parameters one may establish the particular measure of a particular work of art. For the parameter of 'complexity' one could then establish fairly objectively that Shakespeare's work scores closer to the optimal level than Brooke's. Some other contemporary works (e.g. in Euphuistic style) may score higher than Shakespeare, but that would not automatically promote them into the canon, because complexity measures are not sufficient, but only necessary conditions, and also because they are only one of the many parameters at work. One could also wonder whether a eupheuistic style does not confront the reader with too much complexity, and hence elicit less positive evaluations, precisely because of its higher complexity. Thus, given the fact that many parameters are at work, it is the *overall* measure of all parameters together that is going to set a work's chances of getting into the canon, not the absolute score on any single parameter.

The model can also adequately account for historical variation. It may very well be that when, for instance, the demand for complexity goes down (e.g. in Wordsworth's poems such as 'I wander lonely as a cloud'), the requirements of other parameters goes up (e.g. the demand for 'authenticity' in the Romantic movement, as compared to the 18th century). So the overall picture of evaluation would remain constant, in spite of fluctuations with regard to specific parameters – which means that the model provides local variation with global equilibrium.

All in all then, the use and selection of criteria in the evaluative process need not remain subjective, but can be integrated into a complex model that allows one to describe at once some stability in the canon, even over longer periods of time (see Nash's essay on Juvenal, for instance), while at the same time allowing individual, cultural, and historical variability. It seems to me that the development of such a model is to be preferred over resignation or the non-explanation that it is all a matter of subjectivity.

A third criticism of the approaches in this book may be geared toward deep sociological changes that have taken place – and are still taking place – in most Western societies. The idea of a unified canon may have made more sense at a time when such societies were much more unitary than they are today. It is argued, for instance, that most Western societies are no longer unified through common values, but rather pluralistic societies, in which a multitude of values characterize many different groups and subgroups. It is further argued that, because of a lack of strong unifying value concepts, the discussion over the literary canon can no longer rest on consensus.

Is such an argument valid? There seems to be two fundamental problems with it, one relating to its premise and one relating to its consequence. First the consequence: if we accept the premise for the sake of argument, if we accept, that is, that Western societies are indeed fragmented as far as the values of different groups in those societies are concerned, does it follow from there that *eo ipso* the discussion of values in separate domains must also start from a pluralistic view? I think that conclusion does not follow at all. There are many domains of knowledge and expertise in Western societies where despite cultural pluralism unity still reigns. Do engineers start from pluralistic values when they discuss the characteristics of different materials when planning the construction of a bridge? Do judges have multitudes of ways to declare someone indicted guilty or not guilty? Are musicians no longer able to distinguish between technical mastery and lack of it in playing an instrument? If commonalities of value continue to exist in these professional groups, why would one have to exclude the evaluation of literary texts as a professional activity?

On the other hand, I am not impressed by the premise of the argument. Is it really the case that there are few common values in Western societies? I think this view is deeply flawed: societies that do not share strong commonalities in values could hardly survive for long, and Western societies would be no exception to this. Despite a broad spectrum of values held by individuals and groups, however, Western societies continue to function on the premises of liberal democracy: individual freedom, equality before the law, freedom of the press, separation of powers, monopolization of legitimate violence through a police force, controlled by parliament, the monopoly of tax collection by the state, freedom from governmental intervention in personal beliefs and individual conscience, freedom to travel and form associations, the right to actively and passively involve oneself in law-making through free elections, the right to self-protection through the law and its officers, the readiness to enter international agreements and controls, etc. It may be, of course, that not all individuals subscribe to such principles, and it may also be that these values do not always function perfectly or friction-free in such societies. That is not in itself, however, an argument against the observation that Western societies are bound by a great many values that must be shared by a large majority in order to be able to function properly. If the number of laws made and maintained in these societies is an indication of shared values, one may turn the argument on its head, and conclude rather the opposite, namely that Western societies have never been so unified in the observance of common norms. And thus the idea that pluralism in Western societies undermines or suppresses unitary canon formation is void.

Thus I believe the objections of power play, subjectivity, and pluralism are not arguments against the effort undertaken by the different essays in this volume, to work our way toward a better understanding of the relative weight of all factors – text, reader, context – in the evaluation of literary texts. The concentration on textual factors in this book is meant as a contribution toward the development of a more balanced and richer model than has hitherto been applied in literary studies. It is to be hoped that more work along this line will further inform us of that basic activity we become engaged in so spontaneously when confronting a literary text: evaluating it.

References

Berlyne, D. E. 1971. *Aesthetics and Psychobiology*. New York, NY: Appleton-Century-Crofts.

Culler, J. 1983. *The Pursuit of Signs. Semiotics, Literature. Deconstruction.* London: Routledge & Kegan Paul.

Darnton, R. 1996. *The Forbidden Best-Sellers of Pre-Revolutionary France.* New York, NY: W.W. Norton.

Eagleton, T. 1983. *Literary Theory: An Introduction.* Oxford: Basil Blackwell.

Elias, N. 1947[1969]. *The Civilizing Process.* Oxford: Basil Blackwell.

Fish, S. 1989. Canon-busting: The Basic Issues. *National Forum* 69: 13–15.

Guillory, J. 1993. *Cultural Capital: The Problem of Literary Canon Formation,* Chicago, IL: University of Chicago Press.

Hjort, M. 1994. *The Strategy of Letters.* Cambridge: Harvard University Press.

Smith, B. H. 1988. *Contingencies of Value. Alternative Perspectives for Critical Theory.* Cambridge, MA: Harvard University Press.

Stolnitz, J. 1991. On the Historical Triviality of Art. *British Journal of Aesthetics* 31: 195–202.

Taylor, C. 1993. Explanation and Practical Reason. In *The Quality of Life.* M. Nussbaum & A. Sen (eds), 208–231. Oxford: Clarendon Press.

van Peer, W. 1995. The Historical Non-Triviality of Art and Literature. A Rejoinder to Jerome Stolnitz. *The British Journal of Aesthetics* 35(2): 168–172.

Zyngier, S., van Peer, W. and Hakemulder, F. 2007. Love in Literature. Complexity, Foregrounding, and Evaluation. *Poetics Today* 28(4): 653–682.

PART I

Textual and generic comparisons

CHAPTER 1

Canon formation

Ideology or aesthetic quality?

Willie van Peer

This chapter examines the widespread claim that the literary canon is the product of political processes, involving the ideology of those in power. It carries out this examination by comparing two texts that are close in theme and historical emergence, but one of which is undeniably in the canon, the other mostly forgotten. The texts selected are Shakespeare's *Romeo and Juliet* and Arthur Brooke's *The Tragicall Historye of Romeus and Juliet*, published in London in 1562. As the analysis reveals, according to the 'political' claims, all the evidence points in the direction of Brooke's eligibility into the canon, Shakespeare's text towards its lack of chances of ending in the canon. That the actual situation is otherwise, is taken as empirical evidence that the political theory about the canon is false.

I

For the past decade, discussion concerning the literary canon has been going on in 'political' terms. Because the canon is a prestigious social institution, based on selection and evaluation, it is widely thought that these are the right terms. Selecting something for inclusion in the canon (and excluding others) would seem to be political action in the very sense of the words. Is not evaluation always relative to some aims or purposes, thus readily linked to political choices? Thus has the canon come to be seen by many as the result of politically motivated actions, taking place within specific social structures that entertain an intimate relationship with power, prestige and influence. The 'test of time' ultimately becomes a test of the success of the ruling classes. One finds a clear formulation of this position in Barbara Herrnstein Smith (1988), who writes about the dominant classes in society:

> since the texts that are selected and preserved by 'time' will always tend to be those which 'fit' (and indeed have often been designed to fit) their characteristic needs, interests, resources, and purposes, that testing mechanism has its own built-in partialities (p. 51).

Note the word 'always' in this quotation. For Smith and many partisans of so-called critical theory, political motives do not play a merely incidental role in the selection of canonical works, but a determinate one. The canon, in this perspective, is an instrument to stabilize the political balance in favor of those in power, and to reproduce social inequality:

> Since those with cultural power tend to be members of socially, economically, and politically established classes (or to serve them and identify their own interests with theirs), the texts that survive will tend to be those that appear to reflect and reinforce establishment ideologies. (p. 51)

The claim is clear enough, then, in the direct link it establishes between politics and canon formation. Based on arguments such as these, the discussion of canonization processes has been politicized over the past decades, at the expense of considerations of quality. While earlier generations might have believed the canon to be made up of those works which have the highest literary quality, such beliefs have now been condemned as theoretically naïve and politically suspect. What should be done instead – according to this view – is to investigate the political mechanisms and implications involved in canonization processes. On the more practical level, one should 'subvert' the canon, either by stigmatizing canonical authors for their politically 'wrong' views, or by promoting other authors into the canon (mostly on the basis of their belonging to 'oppressed' groups), and so redress the balance, or – better still – eradicate the dominant views and practices.

An interesting aspect of formulations like the one by Smith is that they can be submitted to some objective test. If, for instance, two works of literature deal with the same subject matter (and are also similar in other respects), the one that reflects and reinforces prevailing ideologies of dominant groups most closely will have more chances of ending up in the canon than the one that expresses criticism of such ideologies. This is the claim I wish to inspect in this article. By looking at two texts that are close enough in their production (time and place), in their theme and subject matter, but which differ dramatically in their ideological mechanisms and content, I will investigate the extent to which the politicized view of the canon can be sustained. What the analysis will reveal is that it cannot: the text closely mirroring the prevailing ideologies of the dominant groups of its time has not even had the faintest chances of becoming canonical, while the text that radically undermined such ideologies has enjoyed canonical prestige which – although attempts have been made to downgrade its status – can hardly be denied. The case I shall examine in testing these assertions is *Romeo and Juliet*.

II

Romeo and Juliet occupy a central place among the famous love couples that Western literature has created, next to Paris and Helen, Odysseus and Penelope, Tristan and Isolde, Abelard and Héloïse, Paolo and Francesca, Lotte and Werther, and perhaps also Bogart and Bacall. But Romeo and Juliet may be the most famous couple in this company. And of all of Shakespeare's plays, *Romeo and Juliet* is perhaps, after *Hamlet*, the most popular one. Since the time of Elisabeth I it has been performed time and again, and "has always enjoyed great popularity, both in the theatre and in print". (Levenson 1987:1) William Hazlitt, in his 'Prefatory Remarks' to Oxberry's edition of 1819 remarks that "[Of] all Shakespeare's plays, this is perhaps the one that is acted, if not the oftenest, with most pleasure to the spectator" (quoted in Levenson 1987:17). This is in itself somewhat strange, since traditional Shakespeare criticism has often characterized it as an "immature and imperfectly constructed work" (Ryan 1988) that "disappoints those critical expectations that the major tragedies arouse and satisfy" (Hamilton 1967:203). In what follows, I shall argue that such a judgement must be based on a careless reading, fed by a repressed emotionality, or a cynical disbelief in any utopian vision of the relationship between men and women. Such a reading also fails to explain the play's popularity. The platonic argument so often employed in situations like this, that the story appeals to base emotions, superficial sentiments, or vulgar taste, cannot really be taken seriously in this case. Thus the question arises how the popularity of the play should be explained.

Shakespeare wrote *Romeo and Juliet* around the years 1593/4, in a period of intense activity and stormy literary development, in which he "explored an astonishingly wide diversity of poetic and dramatic styles; he must have written with great rapidity" (Gibbons 1980:29). Its title refers to the main protagonists. But Shakespeare's is not the only treatment of the story of these lovers. It is almost certain that he took his lead from Arthur Brooke's rhymed novella *The Tragicall Historye of Romeus and Juliet* (1562), itself being one of the many Elizabethan imitations and adaptations of Luigi da Porto's *Historia novellamente ritrovata di due nobili amanti* (c. 1530). If Romeo and Juliet are prototypical lovers in Western culture, then it must be explained why it is Shakespeare's version of their fate, and not Brooke's (or indeed any other version antedating Shakespeare) that became canonical. A detailed comparison of both texts, the one by Shakespeare and the one by Brooke, will allow us to test Smith's assertion that the literary canon is political in nature. In doing so, concentrating on the differences between both texts will be instructive, because they will reveal characteristics which may explain their very different reception.

First, there is a difference in genre. Shakespeare's work is a play in blank verse (with occasional rhyming parts in it), Brooke's a novella in rhymed couplets. The choice for the theatre may have been motivated by the potential for creating more powerful psychological effects. An implication to be drawn from this view is that *Romeo and Juliet* would be considerably less popular nowadays had Shakespeare written a narrative poem about them. (Note that Shakespeare did write such poetry: *The Rape of Lucrece* is an example. Its status in the canon is far less uncontroversial than that of *Romeo and Juliet*.) In other words, there seems to be a relationship between a work's genre and its potentialities for ending up in the canon. In *Romeo and Juliet* the intimacy of the lovers is depicted, not in the symbolic privacy of one's own reading, but on the stage – in the presence of an audience. Drama regularly involves the transgression of such boundaries between private and public, or between the sacred and the profane, as Miner (1990:35) has convincingly argued: while in *Antigone*, for instance, an external conflict is interiorized, in *Romeo and Juliet* an internal utopia is externalized. Such encounters of separate experiential domains, acted out on the stage, confront individual spectators with their own affective world, and force them to reflect on it.

Secondly, Shakespeare's play is considerably more complex than Brooke's novella. It contains more characters (and more groups of characters) and its plot contains more story lines. There is also a marked tension between public and private scenes, between 'high' and 'low' characters (Snyder 1979), and between gravity and humour, another generic innovation of Shakespeare's (Levin 1976). Moreover, the story line has been significantly condensed in Shakespeare's text. While the story time takes up nine months in Brooke's version, this period has been reduced to a couple of days in Shakespeare's play. The combination of complex subject-matter and a short time interval may deepen and enhance the audience's emotional involvement.

Another important distinction between these texts is narrative perspective. In Brooke's novella the point of view rests with an external narrator who does not hide his motives for telling the story, as they are expounded quite explicitly in the preface 'To the Reader':

> To this good ende, serve all ill endes, of yll begynnynges. And to this ende (good Reader) is this tragicall matter written, to describe unto thee a coople of unfortunate lovers, thralling themselves to unhonest desire, neglecting the authoritie and advise of parents and frendes, conferring their principall counsels with dronken gossyppes, and superstitious friers (the naturally fitte instruments of unchastitie) attemptyng all adventures of peryll, for thattaynyng of their wished lust, usyng auriculer confession (the kay of whoredome, and treason) for furtheraunce of theyr purpose, abusyng the honorable name of lawefull mariage, the cloke the shame of stolne contractes, finallye, by all meanes of unhonest lyfe, hastyng to most unhappye deathe.
>
> (Gibbons 1980:239, all quotations are from the Arden Shakespeare edition)

The lovers here are not only 'unfortunate', but also 'unhonest' (twice), and 'unhappy'. Brooke's motive for publishing his work, as announced through the voice of the narrator, is unambiguous: he wants to moralize, to warn the reader against unconditional love of the type portrayed in his story. This perspective dominates all the concrete narrative instances of the text, and makes it into a rather boring piece of propaganda, anti-erotic and anti-utopian in style and spirit.

Although in a play one does not normally have a narrative point of view, we nevertheless find in *Romeo and Juliet* indications of a voice outside the action of the play that comments upon the events, thus providing perspective. What strikes home immediately is that in Shakespeare's work the moral lessons that drive Brooke's text are virtually absent. And certainly the lovers are not called 'unhonest'. The Prologue, spoken by the Chorus, which opens the play, is abundantly clear on this matter:

> [Enter Chorus]
> Chorus. Two households both alike in dignity
> > (In fair Verona, where we lay our scene)
> > From ancient grudge break to new mutiny,
> > Where civil blood makes civil hands unclean.
> > From forth the fatal loins of these two foes
> > A pair of star-cross'd lovers take their life,
> > Whose misadventure'd piteous overthrows
> > Doth with their death bury their parents' strife.
> > The fearful passage of their death-mark'd love
> > And the continuance of their parents' rage,
> > Which, but their children's end, nought could remove,
> > Is now the two hours' traffic of our stage;
> > The which, if you with patient ears attend,
> > What here shall miss, our toil shall strive to mend.

(p. 81)

These protagonists are far from immoral. In fact, the immorality here arises from the feud between the two families: 'civil blood makes civil hands unclean'. By means of the chorus, the audience is informed that the ruin of the 'star-cross'd lovers' may be 'fearful', but that it also puts an end to the blood feud: 'Which, but their children's end, nought could remove'. The conflict between the generations is described here in terms of a recognition of youth's positive contribution, and in terms of an inexorable critique of the elder generation's stubborn egoism and materialism. If this critique can be termed moralistic or didactic, then it is so only with reference to the adult world and its lack of tolerance. This is in sharp contrast to the unreservedly positive description of the young lovers and their aims, as voiced by the chorus. That this is no 'slip of the pen' may become clear when we look at the Prologue of Act II, which, by means of unusual live metaphors, depicts the dangerous predicament the lovers find themselves in, a situation in which Romeo is forced to complain about his fate to his arch enemy,

> And she steal love's sweet bait from fearful hooks.

(II, i, 8; p. 122)

But also here the Chorus is on their side:

> But passion lends them power, time means, to meet,
> Tempering extremities with extreme sweet.

(II, i, 13–14; p.122)

All this makes Shakespeare's work thematically the opposite of Brooke's; one could almost interpret it as a guide book for nonconformist love.

Such nonconformity also manifests itself in other things. One such crucial moment in the play is when the protagonists renounce their parentage. This is the famous scene in which Romeo, at Juliet's request, gives up his own name:

> Juliet.   What's in a name? That which we call a rose
>   By any other word would smell as sweet;
>   So Romeo would, were he not Romeo call'd,
>   Retain that dear perfection which he owes
>   Without that title. Romeo, doff thy name,
>   And for thy name, which is no part of thee,
>   Take all myself.
> Romeo.   I take thee at thy word.
>   Call me but love, and I'll be new baptis'd:
>   Henceforth I never will be Romeo.

(II, ii, 43–51; p. 129)

It is presumably no coincidence that 'what's in a name?' is such a famous quotation from *Romeo and Juliet*, in popularity perhaps even rivalling 'to be or not to be'. It is the very essence of the unconditional love which is epitomized here: all contingent qualities of the beloved are shaken off. What remains, and what counts, is the person *qua* person and his/her involvement. Compare this with a corresponding passage in Brooke's story, where Juliet also first learns about Romeus' kinship:

> The woord of Montegew, her joyes did overthrow,
> And straight in steade of happy hope, dyspayre began to growe.
> What hap have I quoth she, to love my fathers foe?
> What, am I wery of my wele? what, doe I wishe my woe?

(355–358; p. 248)

Here, after having heard the family name of her beloved, love itself is disqualified ('her joyes did overthrow'), and instead of happiness, another emotion is called forth: 'dispayre'.

Similarly, in Brooke's work the protagonists behave in a highly predictable way. They swear oaths of allegiance, as is the custom in sentimental stories:

> The love I owe to you, the thrall I languish in
> And how I dread to loose the gayne which I doe hope to win
> And how I wishe for lyfe, not for my propre ease,
> But that in it, you might I love, you honor, serve and please
> Tyll dedly pangs the sprite out of the corps shall send.
> And therupon he sware an othe, and so his tale had ende.
>
> (511–516; p. 250)

Initially, Romeo also wants to engage in this conventional love ritual, but Juliet cuts him short twice:

> Romeo.   Lady, by yonder blessed moon I vow,
>   That tips with silver all these fruit-tree-tops –
> Juliet.   O swear not by the moon, th'inconstant moon,
>   That monthly changes in her circled orb,
>   Lest that thy love prove likewise variable.
> Romeo.   What shall I swear by?
> Juliet.   Do not swear at all.
>   Or if thou wilt, swear by thy gracious self,
>   Which is the god of my idolatry,
>   And I'll believe thee.
> Romeo.   If my heart's dear love –
> Juliet.   Well, do not swear.
>
> (II, ii, 107–116; p. 132)

The ritual of swearing oaths has become redundant: its necessity has disappeared beyond the horizon of a love that knows no restrictions *vis-à-vis* the beloved person.

Especially instructive in this respect is also the end of both works. Brooke's story ends with harsh punishment: Juliet's nurse – in spite of her old age – is banished. And the apothecary, for selling Romeo the poison, is killed:

> Thapothecary, high is hanged by the throte,
> And for the paynes he tooke with him, the hangman had his cote.
>
> (2993–4; p. 279)

The addition that the executioner received the man's coat 'for the paynes he tooke with him', is a sinister inversion of human suffering. If we compare this to what is said about the apothecary in Shakespeare's text, then this again yields a shocking contrast:

> Romeo.   There is thy gold – worse poison to men's souls,
>> Doing more murder in this loathsome world
>> Than these poor compounds that thou mayst not sell.
>> I sell thee poison, thou hast sold me none.
>> Farewell, buy food, and get thyself in flesh.
>
> (V, ii, 80–84; p. 221)

Gold, probably the major cause of the feud between the two families, that is the *real* poison. The addition here is not a cynical one, but a vivifying one: 'buy food, and get thyself in flesh'.

All this means that in the two texts under consideration, love is depicted in a dramatically different way. In Shakespeare's, authenticity (of feelings, of will, of responsibility to the other), overrides conformity to transient social conventions. In Brooke's, contrarily, precisely such conventionalism is the central message: love is frightening and dangerous because it may undermine or disturb the social order. The text itself is a warning against such love. Consequently, the lovers are portrayed in Brooke's story as acting out of inner instincts. Thus the lover, through his eyes

> swalloweth downe loves sweete empoysonde baite.
>
> (219; p. 245)

Shakespeare's line from the Prologue to Act II, quoted before, closely echoes the one by Brooke:

> And she steal love's sweet bait from fearful hooks.
>
> (II, i, 8; p. 122)

However, the contrast can hardly be more significant. Apart from the fact that the line refers to different protagonists, which is irrelevant for the present purposes, the differences are the following:

(a) 'swalloweth downe' *vs.* 'steal';
(b) 'loves empoysonde baite' *vs.* 'love's sweet bait'.

In other words, while the 'bait' is 'empoysonde' in Brooke's, it is 'sweet' in Shakespeare's text. Moreover, the metaphor of the bait is further elaborated by Shakespeare: it is not swallowed, but stolen from the hooks (absent in Brooke), dramatized as cruel instruments that threaten to destroy the lovers continuously. These 'fearful hooks' are presumably nothing but symbols for the hatred of the two families.

Finally, in Shakespeare's play love is unconditional, mutual and truly egalitarian, without calculations of profit. In Brooke's novella, the lovers are uncertain about their cause, driving them into swearing oaths of allegiance, and into reminding each other not to break these oaths. In contrast, Shakespeare' play shows us a utopian outlook on sexual relations between women and men, without the stifling constraints of a rigid social order. Brooke is a moralist, demanding absolute adaptation of the individual to the prevailing social conditions, however arbitrary these may be, without critique, without reflection. I venture that it is precisely this utopian vision on love which has assured both the survival of Shakespeare's text and the obscurity of Brooke's. Only when literary texts show us values and ideas that transcend the historical situation in which they are embedded is there any guarantee against the erosion of time. How remarkably unusually this is done in Shakespeare (certainly against the background of standards enforced in Elizabethan England) emerges from the fact that a good deal of the action in the play is psychologically initiated by Juliet. We see this in her resistance to the oath ritual and her demand that Romeo give up his name, but we also witness it at another dramatic moment in the play.

Before we look at this final example of the emancipatory subject-matter of Shakespeare's play, however, it is relevant to comment briefly on yet another reason why Shakespeare's text is in the canon and Brooke's is not. It is simple enough in itself: the literary quality of the former is far superior to that of the latter. In spite of the difficulties one may experience in trying to define something as imprecise as 'literary quality', it is an undeniable factor which enters into the reading process. This means that, while it may be difficult to define literary quality in principle, it is not so difficult to demonstrate it in practice. In this respect, reading the two texts (Shakespeare's and Brooke's) several times consecutively is a highly instructive experience. If only for that reason, it would be well if we would also, from time to time, read badly written texts in literary classes. After (myself) having gone through the rather boring experience of reading Brooke's text several times, it occurred to me that those among us who deny that literary quality is related to properties of the text nevertheless themselves prefer to read first rate literature most of the time. Perhaps these nay-sayers should be obliged (if they really mean what they say) to read third and fourth rate texts exclusively.

It may be possible to get around the problem of literary quality by seeing statements bearing on it as 'holistic' pronouncements, resting ultimately on specific concrete measures, which *ceteris paribus* are higher in work A than in work B. It is not inconceivable that canonical works of literature score higher on many such separate quality measures, which individually are neither necessary nor sufficient for making the text a good piece of literature, but which, when added together, cumulatively create the effect we usually label as 'quality'. Especially when hundreds of such separate parameters add up, the effect can be quite powerful. Some of these parameters have already been mentioned. To these could be added the originality and boldness of Shakespeare's use of language. We have already seen this at work when we discussed the metaphors of poison, bait and hooks. Many such instances can be quoted to corroborate the general superiority of Shakespeare's text still further. Thus, for instance, the representation of Romeo's perception and feelings when he first sets eyes on Juliet:

> O, she doth teach the torches to burn bright.
> It seems she hangs upon the cheek of night
> As a rich jewel in an Ethiop's ear –
>
> (I, v, 43–45; p. 116)

This certainly is a remarkable string of metaphors to depict one's beloved. First, Juliet pictured as a teacher seen in front of a class of torches, instructing them how to burn brightly (herself being better at it than any of them), then Juliet is seen as a star, hanging on someone's – the night's – cheek, adorning the night as a precious gem adorns the earlobe of an Ethiopian. These are images of a force and vividness one will rarely – if ever – encounter in Brooke's text. Compare, for instance, the corresponding passage there:

> At length he saw a mayd, right fayre of perfect shape
> Which Theseus, or Paris would have chosen to their rape,
> Whom erst he never sawe, of all she pleasde him most.
>
> (197–199; p. 244)

To say nothing of the appallingly violent tone of the scene ('rape'), the description is painfully trite ('right fayre of perfect shape'), and particularly poor (and predictable) in rendering the emotionality of the experience involved ('she pleasde him most').

But the powerful expression of emotion in Shakespeare's text is not limited to the use of metaphors. Other, more global, compositional devices are at work. If one studies in somewhat more detail the prologues to acts I and II that we have already looked at, one will notice that they have been composed in the form of a (Shakespearean) sonnet. Compare in this respect also the marked effect found in Shakespeare's text of the change from blank verse into rhymed verse-lines when the lovers first address each other (it is perhaps also significant that there is no such change – nor anything comparable – in Brooke's work):

> Romeo.   If I profane with my unworthiest hand
>   This holy shrine, the gentle sin is this:
>   My lips, two blushing pilgrims, ready stand
>   To smooth that rough touch with a tender kiss.
> Juliet.   Good pilgrim, you do wrong your hand too much,
>   Which mannerly devotion shows in this;
>   For saints have hands that pilgrims' hands do touch,
>   And palm to palm is holy palmers' kiss.

Romeo.   Have not saints lips, and holy palmers too?

Juliet.   Ay, pilgrim, lips that they must use in prayer.

Romeo.   O then, dear saint, let lips do what hands do:

   They pray: grant thou, lest faith turn to despair.

Juliet.   Saints do not move, though grant for prayer's sake.

Romeo.   Then move not, while my prayer's effect I take.

                              [*He kisses her.*]

   Thus from my lips, by thine, my sin is purg'd.

Juliet.   Then have my lips the sin that they have took.

Romeo.   Sin from my lips? O trespass sweetly urg'd.

   Give me my sin again. [*He kisses her.*]

Juliet.   You kiss by th'book.

Nurse.   Madam, your mother craves a word with you.

                              (I, v, 92–110; p. 118-9)

Two genres merge here into a symbiotic whole: the dramatic dialogue is devised in such a way that the two protagonists together compose a sonnet: first a quatrain by Romeo (lines 92–95), then one by Juliet (96–99), subsequently each producing a verse-line in turn twice, together making up the third quatrain (100–103), and finally another line each, forming the couplet (104–105), immediately followed by the first kiss. *The* classical model for the poetic representation of courtly love – the sonnet – is subtly inserted here in a theatrical dialogue, which immediately afterwards takes another significant turn in verse 109, where we once more observe how Juliet takes the initiative, again reproaching Romeo for his conventionality and superficiality, as if he had learned how to kiss out of an instruction manual.

III

It is now time to retrace our steps and come back to our initial question. That question concerned the canonical position of *Romeo and Juliet* in Western culture. A comparison with the highly similar and almost contemporaneous work by Arthur Brooke revealed a number of significant insights. The story itself was popular in the sixteenth century, and Shakespeare certainly cannot be credited with having invented it. However, both formally as well as thematically some marked differences emerged between the ways in which both works shaped the history of the protagonists. Thematically, the fundamental equality of the lovers, the proportionally more prominent role given to Juliet in guiding the action, as well as the emphasis put on the authenticity of the protagonists' emotions, make Shakespeare's play considerably more attractive than Brooke's didactic moralism. Formally, the qual-

ity of Shakespeare's text is many times superior to that of Brooke: its originality
and perceptivity out-rank Brooke's specimen of doggerel verse.

But what about the critics? They have spared no effort to remove the sting
from the play, for instance by reading it as an admonition not to transgress beyond the existing conventions of love and sexuality. Kiernan Ryan (1988:108) has,
to my mind, convincingly demonstrated that literary critics of the twentieth century have tried hard to deny, minimize, or repress the play's central theme. The
protagonists die, after all.... To interpret this as a condemnation of their love is remarkable, to say the least, for in doing so, one reduces Shakespeare's work to that
of Brooke. That nevertheless actors continued to perform Shakespeare's work, and
readers continued to read Shakespeare (and not Brooke), shows how important
readers' judgements are in the process of canonization – and how little critics may
achieve in this respect. Hence the institutional factors in canon formation may be
less important than many would have them be. Even a relatively large-scale operation by literary critics to suppress the play's critical, egalitarian, and emancipatory
force could not stop (male and female) audiences and readers from being moved
by the model that Juliet and her husband present to us, i.e. a sexual relationship
which is unconditional, and in which men and women meet on the basis of true
tenderness, faith and fairness. So long as human nature and social structures im-
pede the realization of this utopian vision, so long will Romeo and Juliet enjoy
a high rank in the canon of famous lovers, maybe even against the teachings and
tastes of the critics. But then literary critics are often people who 'kiss by the book'.

The previous analysis establishes one thing rather clearly: it falsifies the claim
made by Smith and others, that the canon is made up of works that are in the interests of those in power. If indeed the dominant groups in society did select texts to
be included in the canon because of their upholding, legitimizing, and furthering
the ideology of these very same groups, then Brooke's work should have been in
the canon, not Shakespeare's. We have seen that the opposite is the case, and that
it was a work that radically undermined the values held by traditional patriarchal
society in Elizabethan times that was made canonical, while a work defending and
celebrating many of these values (materialism, revenge, unconditional adherence
to one's own clan, the exclusion of all otherness, etc.) has been virtually forgotten
except by the literary historian and the Shakespeare specialist. It may be, of course,
that one objects to Shakespeare's ideas, that one is not in favour of such a utopian
vision of love relationships. If that be the case, then it would be good to say so. To
quote Lerner (1992:353) on this matter: "If you are skeptical whether the power
relations between men and women can ever be suspended, I take it that you are
skeptical whether true love is ever possible".

What this analysis does show is that the claim that the canon is composed
of works chosen out of political motives, is simply wrong. As the case of *Romeo
and Juliet* amply demonstrates, the canon may contain works that are absolutely at

odds with the central values of the traditional society from which they emerged. I do not see how the Foucauldian approach can honestly deal with such a falsification of its claims without at the same time having to give up one of its most basic tenets, i.e. that texts are always imbued with the power of dominant groups in society. Even the most central literary texts of Western culture, those in the canon, may go directly against the grain of that culture's ideology. Any assertion to the contrary is simply false.

Acknowledgments

Several people have provided valuable comments on earlier versions of this article. Although its general argumentative structure has remained unaffected by their comments, I would nevertheless wish to thank Ulrich Broich, Jan Gorak, Hans Ulrich Gumbrecht, Laurence Lerner, Paisley Livingston, David Miall and Ron Rebholz for their critical remarks. I owe special thanks to Donald Freeman for his meticulous reading and his many perceptive comments. Needless to say, none of these colleagues can be held responsible for any shortcomings the article may have.

References

Gibbons, B. (Ed.) 1980. *Romeo and Juliet*. London: Methuen. (The Arden Shakespeare)

Hamilton, A. C. 1967. *The Early Shakespeare*. San Marino: Huntingdon Library.

Lerner, L. 1992. Subverting the Canon. *British Journal of Aesthetics* 32: 347-358.

Levenson, J. L. 1987. *Romeo and Juliet*. Manchester: Manchester University Press.

Levin, H. T. 1976. Form and Formality in *Romeo and Juliet*. In *Shakespeare and the Revolution of Times*, H. T. Levin (Ed.), 104–120. Oxford: Oxford University Press.

Miner, E. 1990. *Comparative Poetics. An intercultural essay on theories of literature*. Princeton, NJ: Princeton University Press.

Ryan, K. 1988. "Romeo and Juliet" – The language of tragedy. In *The Taming of the Text. Explorations in language, literature, and culture*, W. van Peer (Ed.), 106–122. London / New York: Routledge.

Smith, B. H. 1988 *Contingencies of Value. Alternative Perspectives for Critical Theory*. Cambridge, MA: Harvard University Press.

Snyder, S. 1979. *The Comic Matrix of Shakespeare's Tragedies*. Princeton, NJ: Princeton University Press.

CHAPTER 2

Why Hugh Maccoll is not, and will never be, part of any literary canon

Stein Haugom Olsen

The argument given in support of the view that literary value is socially con-structed and therefore radically unstable, is, in all its forms, internally incoherent and conceptually confused. Part of the reason for this is that the argument focuses on artistically successful works which attract attention for all sorts of reasons and invites a whole range of judgements that have nothing to do with their artistic function. To bring the question of artistic value into focus one needs examples that have not attracted attention and invited this wide range of judgements: only through a discussion artistic failure can one throw light on the question of value. This article provides such an example and thus attempts to refocus the discussion of literary quality.

I

There exists an argument concerning how literary value is constituted which gained currency in the late 1970s and which has become orthodoxy among those who consider themselves cultural radicals. The argument runs something like this:

(1)   Literary value is socially constituted (a 'socially chosen value'[1]).

---

1.   Richard Ohman, 'The Shaping of a Canon: U.S. Fiction, 1960–1975' in Robert von Hallberg (ed.) *Canons* (Chicago 1984) p. 382. The argument can be found in a number of books and articles of the 1980s, some of them collected in the von Hallberg volume. The theoretically most sophisticated version of the argument is to be found in Barbara Herrnstein Smith, *Contingencies of Value. Alternative Perspectives for Critical Theory* (Cambridge, Mass. 1988). The argument has continued popular in the 1990s, though much less so than it used to be, since it has been subjected to sustained criticism from various quarters over the last ten years. See e.g. Hazard Adams, 'Canons: Literary Criteria/Power Criteria', *Critical Inquiry* 14 (1988), pp. 748–64; Albert Cook, 'The Canon of Poetry and the Wisdom of Poetry', *Journal of Aesthetics and Art Criticism* 49 (1991), pp. 317–29; Laurence Lerner, 'Subverting the Canon', *British Journal of Aesthetics* 32 (1992), pp. 347–358; Paisley Livingston, 'Justifying the Canon', in J.J. Kloek, S. Levi, and Willie van Peer (eds.) *In Search of a New Alphabet: Comparative Studies in Literature, Dedicated to*

(2) Because it is socially constituted, literary value is contingent.

(3) Being contingent, 'literary value is radically relative and therefore "constantly variable"'.[2]

(4) Agreement on the value of a literary work between many different (groups, communities of) people over an extended period of time under different conditions, is only apparent. The value of a literary work of art is constituted differently for different (groups, communities of) people at different times, under different conditions.[3]

(5) Agreement on the value of a literary work between many different (groups, communities of) people over an extended period of time under different conditions must either be ascribed to the fact that the social variables of which literary value is a function, are 'limited and regular – that is, that they occur within ranges and that they exhibit patterns and principles'[4] or to social conditioning.[5]

(6) In so far as *standards* of literary value exist, they are underwritten by power to impose them and not supported by reasons for accepting them. Reasons for

---

Douwe W. Fokkema (Amsterdam 1996) pp. 145–50: Willie van Peer, 'Canon Formation: Ideology or Aesthetic Quality?', *British Journal of Aesthetics* 36 (1996), pp. 97–108.)

2. Herrnstein Smith, *op.cit.*, p. 11. Or see Richard Ohman *op.cit.* p. 382: 'Excellence is a constantly changing, socially chosen value'.

3. Herrnstein Smith, *op.cit.*, Chapter 1. Here Herrnstein Smith gives an anecdotal account of how she herself has valued individual Shakespeare sonnets for different reasons at different times and suggests that this anecdote can be generalised. The point that the value of a great literary work is constituted differently for different communities through time is much older. It can be found in e.g. René Wellek and Austin Warren, *Theory of Literature* (Harmondsworth 1953), Chapter 18; Stephen C. Pepper, *The Basis of Criticism in the Arts* (Cambridge, Mass. 1945); George Boas, *Wingless Pegasus* (Baltimore 1950), Chapter III. The view as expressed by these three is discussed in Anthony Savile, *The Test of Time. An Essay in Philosophical Aesthetics* (Oxford 1982) pp. 56–9. Savile also quotes from George Boas, 'The *Mona Lisa* in the History of Taste', *Journal of the History of Ideas* 1 (1940):

> a given work of art may in different periods have an essentially different content – and therefore be admired for different, if not incompatible reasons. If this instance [i.e. *Mona Lisa*] is typical it would appear that works of art which 'withstand the test of time' change their nature as the times change. The work of art becomes the locus of a new set of values determined by the preoccupations and the predominant interests of the new critics or observers.

4. Herrnstein Smith, *op.cit.*, pp. 11–12.

5. Ibid. p. 50.

accepting standards of literary value are merely rationalisations of a desire to bolster or retain cultural power.[6]

(7)   Any standard of literary value is a means for the dominant social order to perpetuate it own ideological values:

> Since those with cultural power tend to be members of socially, economically, and politically established classes (or to serve them and identify their own interests with theirs), the texts that survive will tend to be those that appear to reflect and reinforce establishment ideologies. However much canonical works may be seen to 'question' secular vanities such as wealth, social position, and political power, 'remind' their readers of more elevated values and virtues, and oblige them to 'confront' such hard truths and harsh realities as their own mortality and the hidden griefs of obscure people, they would not be found to please long and well if they were seen *radically* to undercut establishment interests or *effectively* to subvert the ideologies that support them.[7]

This argument is not coherent but consists of a number of logically independent statements some of which appear to contradict each other (i.e. (4) and (5)). Between statements that do not contradict each other, there is no inferential route from one statement to another except where one can give a definition of the terms used that will secure a tautological connection. Thus (2) is plausible only if one construes 'contingent' in the strict logical sense as 'not necessary' or as 'dependent for its occurrence or character on or upon some prior occurrence or condition',[8] rather than more loosely as 'accidental', 'fortuitous':[9] socially constituted values need not be either accidental or fortuitous. However, if 'contingent' is interpreted as 'not necessary' or as 'dependent for its occurrence or character on or upon some prior occurrence or condition', then (3) does not follow: from the fact that something is contingent, it follows neither that it is 'radically relative' nor that it is constantly subject to change. Even should one grant that 'literary value is radically relative', one cannot conclude that it is 'constantly variable'. It may be both, but to establish that would take further argument.

---

6.   Ibid. p. 40.

7.   Ibid. p. 51. Some express themselves more bluntly: 'Aesthetic value arises from class conflict', Ohman, *op.cit.* p. 397. '[The canon] is the institutionalization of those particular verbal artifacts that appear best to convey and sustain the dominant social order', Arnold Krupat, 'Native American Literature and the Canon' in Robert von Hallberg (ed.), *op.cit.*, p. 310.

8.   *Oxford English Dictionary* (2nd ed., Oxford 1992) entry 7.a, 7.b, 7.c and 8 under 'contingent'.

9.   Ibid., entry 2.a and 4 under 'contingent'.

If (3) had been obviously true then (4) and/or (5) would not have been needed. One plausible interpretation of the thesis that literary value is constantly variable (the interpretation formulated in (4)), is that a literary work of art is judged by different (groups, communities of) people, at different times, under different conditions to have different value. So interpreted the hypothesis seems to be false. If it was true, there would be no literary tradition. Literary history would then be a history of changing artistic tastes, much like the history of fashion. Since there is a literary tradition, the agreement that it embodies has to be explained away. This is what (4) and (5) tries but fails to do. (4) and (5) can be construed either as alternative or as partial explanations of the agreement embodied in literary tradition. However, as explanations they fail under both construals: They fail because there is no evaluation of competing hypotheses fitting the state of affairs that constitutes the *explanandum*. Consensus about the value of a literary work may be the result of reasoned argument, rather than being just apparent, or due to social variables exhibiting 'patterns and principles', or to social conditioning. The existence of a consensus embodied in a literary tradition is more plausibly explained if one could show that it is in fact based in reasoned argument. (4) and (5) deny the reality of what needs to be explained: they explain it by explaining it away.

So neither (4) and (5) separately, nor together (as partial explanations) offer any inferential basis for (6), which, in its turn, confuses two issues: the question whether standards of literary value can be supported by reasons is independent of the question whether these reasons are also underwritten by power to impose them and of the further question whether they function as rationalisations of a desire to retain or bolster cultural power. If it was found that agreement about literary value rested on reasoned argument rather than being conditioned by social factors, then (6) would have to be reformulated. Furthermore, even if (6) was true, it does not follow that (7) would be true. (7) is a new empirical hypothesis which is independent of (6), and independent also of the question of the validity of a standard of literary value.

II

The discussion of how literary value is constituted almost always takes the form of a discussion of artistic excellence rather than artistic failure, with examples taken from among highly valued works rather than from works considered to be failures. The reason for this is not far to seek: bad literary works are not available for discussion in the way that works of artistic excellence are available. They have simply dropped out of circulation: even their titles are no longer remembered. The focus on artistic excellence and highly valued works does, however, tend to steer the discussion in unfruitful directions. A highly valued work attracts notice in a way that an artistic failure does not. Though 'To pass time's test . . . a work of art has to hold our attention for reasons that bear on its critical estimation as the work it is',[10] survival over time as an esteemed object also ensures that such a work will attract attention for reasons that has no bearing on our critical estimation (reasons that have nothing to do with its artistic excellence). *Lady Chatterley's Lover* and *Ulysses* both attracted attention for what at the time was thought of as sexually explicit content. Most works by well-known authors have been used as source-material for their biographies. Jane Austen's novels can be read as escapist romances or used as source-material for a historical work on the situation of spinsters in the late eighteenth and early nineteenth centuries. Ibsen's *A Doll's House* has attracted attention because it can be enlisted in the feminist cause etc. etc. There is no limit to the kinds of reasons for which an esteemed literary work can attract attention simply because as an esteemed work it is visible. Some of this attention will necessarily be negative. Some people are offended by sexually explicit content. Some are offended by moral views that are different from their own. Some are simply baffled when they try to pay a literary work of art some attention. Many do not bother to pay attention to literary works of art and make a virtue of that ('It does nothing for me so why should I bother to read it'). The result is that any discussion of literary value will be faced with a whole range of judgements about highly valued literary works of art that are often contradictory and sometimes incommensurable. It is this situation which gives (3) some initial plausibility and which makes (4) and/or (5) seem reasonable moves.

What this suggests is that the discussion of literary value needs to be refocused. It is not enough to move the discussion away from works of recognised excellence to works where no such recognition exists. New works are published all the time and these will necessarily have received no recognition. However, in modern Western society they will attract reader and critical attention because they are new and they may thus be in the same position as works of established excellence, at least for a time. Being works *of our time* they are also likely to present what Peter Lamarque and I have elsewhere called 'topical themes', themes that are of more or less intense interest to a group, class or community of people at a certain time in its history, but which, when the external situation that gave rise to the interest changes, are simply forgotten.[11] Topical themes are controversial and thus such works will attract different evaluations. And, as Hume points out, there are 'all the caprices

---

10.   Anthony Savile, *op.cit.* p. 7.

11.   Peter Lamarque and Stein Haugom Olsen, *Truth, Fiction, and Literature. A Philosophical Perspective* (Oxford 1994) p. 426ff.

of mode and fashion, all the mistakes of ignorance and envy'[12] which will influence our judgements of taste until the passage of time has made them fade into insignificance.

The other category of works that has no recognised value is past works that have been forgotten. Such works will not deal with topical themes and since they are forgotten they will be beyond 'all the caprices of mode and fashion, all the mistakes of . . . envy', if not of ignorance. There will be no body of contradictory and incommensurable evaluative judgements that will have to be taken into consideration and explained. One may say that there is a silent consensus that these works are not valuable enough to merit continued attention, but this is to say no more than that they are forgotten. Forgotten works help to focus the discussion of literary value because the absence of a body of value-judgements leaves a socio-anthropological approach to literary value with no obvious material to work on. Literary works may be forgotten for different reasons, but the question can always be raised if a forgotten work *deserves* to remain forgotten or if there are reasons for paying the work critical attention after all. This question cannot be answered by adopting the socio-anthropological approach. It requires a discussion of reasons and thus focuses theoretical attention on reasoned argument as a basis for agreement on literary value.

One may sharpen the focus of the discussion of the possibility of agreement concerning literary value even further by distinguishing between two classes of forgotten works. There are those works which will, after all, 'hold our attention for reasons that bear on its critical estimation as the work it is',[13] and which we shall therefore judge to possess a sufficient measure of artistic excellence to merit continued reader/critical attention, though they have been forgotten up to the moment when they are 'rediscovered'. This process of what Leavis called 'revaluation' is a continuous and important aspect of literary criticism and of reading literature generally. In this century the reassessment of the metaphysical poets and rediscovery of Gerard Manley Hopkins are important landmarks in criticism. In the last twenty years there has been a particular effort to reassess literary works written by women, and this work has produced some notable successes. However, the majority of forgotten works continue to fail to reward reader attention. Such attention reveals no reasons for ascribing literary value to them. It is this latter class that is of particular theoretical interest in the discussion about the role of reasons in achieving agreement on literary value.

---

12. 'Of the Standard of Taste' in David Hume, *Selected Essays* (ed. Stephen Copley and Andrew Edgar; Oxford 1993) p. 139.

13. Anthony Savile, *op.cit.* p. 7.

It is unlikely that, for all members of the class of forgotten works, there is a set of social circumstances in which each and every one of these works have been forgotten, that are sufficiently similar to form the basis of a systematic explanation of why they should have been forgotten. Any explanation in social terms will therefore be *ad hoc.*[14] For the subclass of forgotten works that are found after all to possess a sufficient measure of artistic excellence to merit continued reader attention, the fact that they have been forgotten can *only* be explained *ad hoc.* It *must* be ascribed to social accident that can be assigned no theoretically interesting general features. However, in the case of forgotten works of the second subclass, there is available a systematic explanation: they do not repay aesthetic attention. There is no reason why anyone should have paid these works continued attention. And this is the *only* systematic explanation available why works of the second class have been forgotten. Aesthetic justification is the only explanation that is not *ad hoc.*

III

The force of the argument from artistic failure can only be felt if one tries to look in some detail at an artistic failure, not a grand failure, but an ordinary failure that simply does not repay attention. There is virtually no such discussion in the debate about literary value. And for obvious reasons: no one wants to waste one's time on such writing. It does not give pleasure or provide inspiration for reflection; nor does it promote careers. However, from time to time occasions arise where artistic failures become the focus of attention for other reasons. Thus at the moment an attempt is being made to reassess the contribution made by an unknown Scottish school teacher, Hugh MacColl (1837–1909), to the foundation of modern logic.[15] It so happens that MacColl also had literary ambitions and published two novels

---

14.   Though champions of various groups of authors which can be classified together on what is assumed to be social identity grounds (gender, race, and class) tend to see such groups as 'silenced' or 'marginalised' by the dominant culture. This is a systematic explanation of why these have been 'forgotten' but it applies only to a relatively limited number of all forgotten works of literature that have been 'rediscovered'. The weaknesses and incoherence in the argument that gender, race, and class 'determine' the (negative) evaluation of a literary work of art has been fully exposed by John Guillory in his *Cultural Capital. The Problem of Literary Canon Formation* (Chicago 1993), pp. 6–19.

15.   A conference on MacColl with leading historians of logic and mathematics was held at the University of Greifswald in March 1998 and a special issue on MacColl is being published by the *Nordic Journal of Philosophical Logic* in late 1999.

and a short story.[16] In addition he wrote three novels that were never published.[17] MacColl's novels never became part of the tradition of English literature and today they are forgotten and unread. While there may be good reasons for believing that renewed attention to MacColl's contributions to logic may give him a significant place in the history of logic, a study of his novels only confirms that they are best left unread and forgotten.

MacColl's novels were not forgotten because they dealt with marginal or esoteric subjects of no interest to the reading public of the time. Both novels deal with current topics that attracted serious interest from many quarters, among them authors of fiction. *Mr. Stranger's Sealed Packet* is the third novel in English to be published about Mars and one of fourteen novels about Mars published in the last two decades of the 19th century.[18] Mars in these years was a topic made popular by new discoveries about the Red Planet. In 1877, the American astronomer, Asaph Hall (1829–1907), had discovered the two moons of Mars, Deimos and Phobos, and calculated their orbits. More importantly for imaginative literature, in the same year the Italian astronomer and senator Giovanni Virginio Schiaparelli (1835–1910) reported to have observed groups of straight lines on Mars. Schiaparelli called the peculiar markings he observed *canali*. The word, erroneously translated into English as 'canals' instead of 'channels', led to widespread speculation whether the 'canals' were constructed by intelligent beings and thus touched off much controversy about the possible existence of life on that planet.

Ednor Whitlock deals with an equally current and also controversial theme. It is a novel of faith and doubt and as such joins a genre that includes novels like Samuel Butler's *The Way of All Flesh* (written 1873–84; published 1903); William Hale White's *The Autobiography of Mark Rutherford* (1881), Mrs Humphrey Ward's *Robert Elsmere* (1888); as well as Edmund Gosse's autobiographical *Father and Son (1907)*.

---

16. *Mr. Stranger's Sealed Packet* (London: Chatto & Windus, 1889); *Ednor Whitlock* (London: Chatto & Windus, 1891); 'Mrs. Higgins's Strange Lodger', *Murray's Magazine* X (1891), pp. 937–76.

17. According to Chatto & Windus Manuscript Entry Books MacColl submitted manuscripts in 1891 (*Was She his Wife?*), in 1893 (*Sister Joan*), and in 1896 (*The Search for Meerin*).

18. The frequency and number of novels about Mars increases further in the first decades of the 20th Century. A bibliography of novels about Mars is to be found on the BookBrowser site on the Internet at *http://www.bookbrowser.com/TitleTopic/mars.html*. This bibliography lists novels about Mars chronologically as well as by author. An even fuller bibliography comprising all fictional stories about Mars has been compiled by Gene Alloway, Senior Associate Librarian, University of Michigan (NSF/NASA/ARPA Digital Library Project), available on the Internet (*http://www-personal.engin.umich.edu/* ~ *cerebus/mars/index.html#bibs*).

Nor can it be argued that MacColl's novels were marginalised or silenced because they attempted to 'undercut establishment interests' or 'subvert the ideologies that support them'.[19] Both MacColl's novels present and endorse values entrenched among the majority of the reading public of the time.[20] His central women characters are docile, obedient to their fathers and (when they marry) husbands. They are definitely the weaker sex, impressionable, fearful, and emotional ('the heaving of her bosom betrayed her agitation', *Mr. Stranger's Sealed Packet*, p. 143.). But they also have that inner emotional strength and moral fibre that was central to the separate spheres view that became dominant in the last part of the century and was famously formulated by John Ruskin in *Sesame and Lilies*.[21]

As was the case with a large section of the educated public at the time, MacColl is enthusiastic about the progress and possibilities of science and technology. In *Mr. Stranger's Sealed Packet* the characters move in a world governed by scientific laws which man and the Martians utilise for their benefit. Stranger himself becomes an example of the modern, professional scientist who has to give up all humanistic studies to dedicate his life to science. When his father dies, Stranger withdraws from his public school, Classicton,[22] to carry out his father wish that he should dedicate himself exclusively to science. Though an enthusiast for science and technology, MacColl shows deep commitment in his two novels to the Christian faith and institutionally to the Church of England. The main story of *Ednor Whitlock* is how Ednor finds his way back to faith after it has been shaken by arguments, which he accidentally comes to read in the *Westminster Review*, against the tenability of the Christian belief in the resurrection of Christ. Ednor's religious mentor, the Reverend George Milford, is moreover a clergyman in the Church of

---

19.   Herrnstein Smith, *loc.cit.* p. 2.

20.   For a detailed discussion of MacColl's attitudes and beliefs as expressed in his two published novels see my 'Hugh MacColl – Victorian', *Nordic Journal of Philosophical Logic*, Special Issue on *Hugh MacColl and the Tradition of Logic* (forthcoming, autumn 1999).

21.   [Woman] must be enduringly, incorruptibly good; instinctively, infallibly wise – wise, not for self-development, but for self-renunciation: wise, not that she may set herself above her husband, but that she may never fail from his side: wise, not with the narrowness of insolent and loveless pride, but with the passionate gentleness of an infinitely, variable, because infinitely applicable, modesty of service – ... John Ruskin, *Sesame and Lilies* (1871) (*Worlds Classics*, London 1916) pp. 99–100

22.   The name of the school is an unsubtle reference to the domination of classical languages in the curricula of the Public Schools and their neglect of scientific subjects. One may perhaps also spot in MacColl that anti-intellectualism so well characterised by Walter E. Houghton in chapter five of *The Victorian Frame of Mind* (New Haven 1957): 'In bourgeois society the conception of utility became too narrow to include the great but intangible utility of the humanities' (p. 119).

England who reacts strongly when an attempt is made at the French school to which he sends his daughter, to convert her to the Roman faith (pp. 205–6). Furthermore, MacColl is not satisfied simply to present to the reader Ednor's journey back to a tested and therefore mature faith. *Ednor Whitlock* also addresses a running argument to the reader with the aim of convincing him too of the truth of 'all the essential doctrines of Christianity' (p. 35), a state that has been reached by the Reverend Milford after having considered all 'the religious difficulties of modern times'(p. 33). Again MacColl presents, endorses and reinforces views widely accepted among the educated general public.

The impression that MacColl did not challenge prevalent views but endorsed and defended them, is strengthened if one looks at his political and moral attitudes. Mr Stranger in *Mr. Stranger's Sealed Packet* goes to Mars to colonise:

> At last it was finished. How my pulse throbbed with the excitement of that supreme moment! What was Columbus's discovery of a new world in comparison with this? A new world, forsooth! A new portion merely of the same old world on which mankind had toiled monotonously for so many ages. His discovery opened up new fields, new outlets, new resources, for the already overcrowded inhabitants of Europe. Well, it was a great achievement, and a great boon both to his contemporaries and to us, their posterity; but what was this achievement, this boon, in comparison with *my* exploit, in comparison with the benefit which *I* was about to confer upon humanity? It is not Europe alone that is overcrowded now; the whole earth will soon be over-peopled; and to relieve the great and increasing pressure upon the available means of subsistence *we must send colonies to other planets.* (p. 28; italics in the text)

Stranger gives up his plan for colonising when he finds that Mars, though accidentally, has already been colonised by humans who have developed a culture in many ways superior to that of terrestrial man, but his imperialist attitude manifests itself in other ways. On Mars there are two societies, the Grensum and the Dergdunin. The former is an advanced civilisation which is essentially non-aggressive and peace-loving. The latter is a barbarian society against which the Grensum have constantly to defend themselves. To save civilised values the barbarians must be subdued by force and subjected to the benign discipline of the Grensum. Here MacColl employs a barbarian-civilised distinction which is typical of the imperialist attitude. And this distinction is absolute. There is no moral nuànce.

Finally, one cannot argue that MacColl's two novels were marginalised or silenced because they represented 'those deviant, unrepresentative experiences discoverable in much female, ethnic and working-class writing'.[23] MacColl was an

---

23.   Toril Moi, *Sexual/Textual Politics. Feminist Literary Theory*, (London 1985) p. 78.

educated man, though he did not have the benefit of the best education.[24] His brother was Malcolm MacColl, famous as a controversialist and a pamphleteer for Gladstone. Hugh himself was a schoolteacher with a passion for logic and mathematics that required considerable intelligence and intellectual investment. He had extensive correspondence with Bertrand Russell and with C. S. Peirce who intended to visit MacColl at Boulogne in May 1883.[25] MacColl might have been on the margins of British intellectual life at the time both geographically and in terms of position, but he was not excluded from it.

What is more, MacColl was deeply interested in literature. 'For . . . twelve or thirteen years', he says in a letter to Bertrand Russell, 'I devoted my leisure hours to general literature'.[26] From 1883 to 1896 there is no work from MacColl's hand on logic, but it is in this period that he produces his two published and three unpublished novels as well as the short story. *Mr. Stranger's Sealed Packet* and *Ednor Whitlock* display both an awareness of what were the current literary topics of the day as well as a certain level of technical skill. There is an interesting use of a frame-story in *Mr. Stranger's Sealed Packet* which points forward to Conrad's use of the same device, and the novel also draws on various sub-genres of the novel such as travel literature and utopian literature. *Ednor Whitlock* combines the traditional orphan motif with the religious quest motif as well as with the standard romantic comedy pattern of successful courtship and marriage for the deserving characters.[27]

---

24.   John MacColl died when his youngest son was only a year old. . . . This early loss had a far- reaching impact on Hugh MacColl's life. In particular his scholarly education did not respond adequately to the needs of his talents. He was almost 40 years old and living on private teaching in Northern France when he took his B.A. in mathematics. Michael Astroh, Ivor Grattan-Guinness, Stephen Read, 'A Biographical Note on Hugh MacColl', *Nordic Journal of Philosophical Logic*, Special Issue on *Hugh MacColl and the Tradition of Logic* (forthcoming, autumn 1999). All the information in this paragraph is abstracted from this biographical note. Mac-Coll took an external degree at the University of London in mathematics in 1876. His examiner was John Venn, famous for the Venn diagrams of class relationships.

25.   In 1865 MacColl moved to France. For the rest of his life he settled at Boulogne-sur-Mer. Little is known about the kind of life he was leading there.
    Michael Astroh, Ivor Grattan-Guinness, Stephen Read, 'A Biographical Note on Hugh MacColl'.

26.   Letter to Bertrand Russell, 17 May 1909.

27.   See my 'MacColl – Victorian', *Nordic Journal of Philosophical Logic*, (forthcoming).

IV

However, both *Mr. Stranger's Sealed Packet* and *Ednor Whitlock* fail artistically. They do not fail grandly trying to realise an ambitious artistic goal. They fail trivially in many respects. To detail such failures are boring and do not offer the usual rewards of critical appreciation to the reader: and enhanced experience of the work under discussion. However, the failures can be illustrated by looking in some detail at two or three aspects of these novels.

Like in other novels of faith and doubt the spiritual crisis in the hero's life is central also in *Ednor Whitlock*. Ednor is a young man whose faith is undermined by exposure to new scientific ideas and to the historical criticism of the *Bible*, and the novel chronicles his spiritual crisis and the journey towards a reaffirmed but modified Christian faith. As in other novels of faith and doubt the spiritual crisis is compounded by considerations of the effect of apostasy on those nearest and dearest to him, and on his career prospects. Ednor fears the devastating effect his apostasy will have on his parents and his sister, and he has to give up his projected career in the Church of England. However, MacColl's conception of Ednor's spiritual crisis is weak. It is almost exclusively described in clichés and from the outside. Below is MacColl's description of Ednor's reaction when the crisis first occurs. Ednor appears from the library in the little town of Wishport having just read the article in the *Westminster Review* that shakes his faith:

> Feeling like a person in a dream, and unable to fully realize what had happened to him, Ednor Whitlock paced his way slowly and almost unconsciously homewards. He seemed to have suddenly undergone a species of transmigration, to have virtually passed into a new existence. Only two hours before, he had been living in a world over which an all-powerful, all-seeing, and all-loving God held undisputed sway; he now found himself in a world presided over by a blind unfeeling deity called Nature, to whom the most virtuous deeds and the foulest crimes were alike indifferent. How was he, with his habits of thought and his training, to adapt himself to the necessities and requirements of these new and wholly unexpected conditions? What would his father say if he knew? What anguish would he not suffer? And his mother and his sister – he had one sister two years older than himself – how would their tender, loving hearts bear the shock of such a dire calamity, as most assuredly they would consider it? No, no, it must not be; the dread secret must be locked up in his own breast; he must bear his sorrow alone.
>
> When he reached home, Ednor avoided his parents and even his sister. He felt too troubled to meet their eyes with his customary frank and open look; so, on the excuse of having to work for his examination (he was going to try for a Cambridge entrance scholarship), he shut himself up in his room to think. But the questions that occupied his brain were not those discussed

in the mathematical book which lay open before him. They were questions which no cunningly-contrived figures, no ingenious combinations of symbols, could help him to answer. By a natural rebound his mind had sprung from an absolute faith in every dogma of the particular religion in which he had been brought up into an utter disbelief in all religion. The very existence of a God had become doubtful. Where were the proofs of it? He cast his glance through the open window. It was spring. The day was softly warm; the birds were chirping gaily; nature looked her loveliest.

'No, not that,' he said, with a shiver; 'at least, not yet. Atheism is an impossibility. A God there surely is, though he may not be the God of the Christian.'

Yielding to a sudden impulse, he threw himself upon this knees, clasped his hands, and in a voice of anguish exclaimed –

'Oh, God help me!'

Then he buried his face in his hands on the chair beside him, and burst out sobbing.

(Ednor Whitlock, pp. 3–5).

Ednor's crisis is presented in a series of questions concerning how he will adapt to the new situation and how his parents and sister will react to his apostasy. The questions are matter of fact, without any emotional charge. There is no focus on the inner emotional tumult that one might expect Ednor to feel. There is also the insertion of background-information in the middle of the presentation of the crisis that dissipates any concentration there might have been. The very change of perspective into which Ednor is forced, is formulated in a series of clichés: 'an all-powerful, all-seeing, and all-loving God', 'a blind unfeeling deity called Nature', 'held undisputed sway', 'in a world presided over by', 'the most virtuous deeds and the foulest crimes'. Clichés also dominate the descriptions of the way in which Ednor perceives both the natural environment ('It was spring. The day was *softly warm*; the birds were *chirping gaily*; nature *looked her loveliest*'; my italics) and his parents and sister ('how would their *tender, loving hearts* bear the shock of such *a dire calamity,* as *most assuredly* they would consider it?' my italics). The 'esemplastic power' as Coleridge calls the imagination, does not seem to be much in evidence here.[28]

---

28.   [The imagination] dissolves, diffuses, dissipates, in order to re-create; or where this process is rendered impossible, yet still at all events it struggles to idealize and to unify. It is essentially *vital*, even as all objects (*as* objects) are essentially fixed and dead.

Samuel Taylor Coleridge, *Biographia Literaria*, Chapter 13, 'On The Imagination, Or Esemplastic Power', (1817) (ed. J. Shawcross, London 1907) p. 202.

The best way to bring this out is to contrast it with a similar moment in *Robert Elsmere*:

But Elsmere did not trouble himself much with the critic, as at any rate he was reported by the author of the book before him. Long before the critical case was reached, he had flung the book heavily from him. The mind accomplished its further task without help from outside. In the stillness of the night there rose up weirdly before him a whole new mental picture – effacing, pushing out, innumerable older images of thought. It was the image of a purely human Christ – a purely human, explicable, yet always wonderful Christianity. It broke his heart, but the spell of it was like some dream-country wherein we see all the familiar objects of life in new relations and perspectives. He gazed upon it fascinated, the wailing underneath checked a while by the strange beauty and order of the emerging spectacle. Only a little while! Then with a groan Elsmere looked up, his eyes worn, his lips white and set.[29]

Elsmere, like Ednor, has been reading a book that applies to the biblical stories (though not in this case the Gospel Stories) the principle of the 'higher criticism' that emanated from the German universities. As for Ednor, this is for him the moment when these views really take hold. Like Ednor, Elsmere seems to enter a 'dream-country'. However, the whole situation is dramatically conceived in a way that Ednor's situation is not. There is the stillness of the night, the groan, the worn eyes, and the white set lips indicating the emotional upheaval: 'the wailing underneath' the new perspective which Elsmere can consider and find intellectually attractive. This new perspective is itself conceived concretely through the metaphor of a 'mental picture'. 'Familiar objects' change as they are seen in 'new relations and perspectives' and 'old images of thought' are driven out. It is a 'spectacle' with a 'strange beauty': thus is its intellectual attraction for Elsmere rendered. There is also the fact that, unlike the episode in *Ednor Whitlock*, this episode has been well prepared for: it occurs at the end of Book III, 'The Squire' which across 75 pages describes Elsmere's journey into crisis (the subsequent Book IV is simply called 'Crisis'). It is not the result of accidentally reading an article in the *Westminster Review*.

MacColl also fails to motivate the importance he assigns to Ednor's mental crisis both in words and in the role he gives it in the structural scheme of the book. The only indications of a mental crisis are in the last few lines when Ednor shivers and, 'yielding to a sudden impulse', throws himself on his knees and sobs. Again the very few clichés that MacColl spends on this, fail to bring before the reader the nature of the crisis. The anguish, the sense of loss, the utter despair is not realised for the reader in the writing, not here, nor later in the novel. Again it may

29. Mrs Humphrey Ward, *Robert Elsmere* (1888) (Oxford 1987), p. 314

be illuminating to juxtapose MacColl's rendering of Ednor's reaction with one of many passages in *Robert Elsmere* which presents Elsmere's mental agony:

> And there he sat for hours, vaguely watching the reflection of the clouds, the gambols and quarrels of the waterfowl, the ways of the birds, the alternations of sun and shadow on the softly-moving trees, – the real self of him passing all the while through an interminable inward drama, starting from the past, stretching to the future, steeped in passion, in pity, in regret. He thought of the feelings with which he had taken orders, of Oxford scenes and Oxford persons, of the efforts, the pains, the successes of his first year at Murewell. What a ghastly mistake is had all been! He felt a kind of sore contempt for himself, for his own lack of prescience, of self-knowledge. His life looked to him so shallow and worthless. How does a man ever retrieve such a false step? He groaned aloud as the thought of Catherine linked to one born to defeat her hopes, and all that natural pride that a woman feels in the strength and consistency of the man she loves. As he sat there by the water he touched the depths of self-humiliation. As to religious belief, everything was a chaos. What might be to him the ultimate forms and condition of thought, the tired mind was quite incapable of divining. To every stage in the process of destruction it was feverishly alive. But its formative energy was for the moment gone. The foundations were swept away, and everything must be built up afresh. Only the *habit* of faith held, the close instinctive clinging to a Power beyond sense – a Goodness, a Will, not man's.[30]

This passage is built around a notion which is wholly absent from MacColl's treatment of Ednor's crisis: the notion of an inner stage where the crisis is acted out, 'an interminable inward drama' from past to present which contrasts with the placid outward scene. The inner drama is presented through an interior monologue that is detailed and nuanced, focusing on the rejected attitudes and beliefs of the past; the anguish he will cause his wife; the chaos of his inner life and his lack of strength to build his faith on a new ground. The monologue captures the dynamic of the crisis in flexible but precise formulations; precise, that is, in relation to the goal of rendering Elsmere's mental crisis.

It is not only MacColl's treatment of 'the inner stage' that displays the absence of 'the esemplastic power' in the two novels. Many of the aspects of the social environment in which characters move and act are as thinly and poorly conceived. One central social phenomenon in the novels of faith and doubt is orthodox religion. Orthodox religion is the central social phenomenon to which the protagonists in these novels react. It is not the same orthodoxy that the reader meets in all novels of faith and doubt. In *The Way of All Flesh* and *Robert Elsmere* it is a particular

---

30. Ibid. pp. 336–7.

strand in the Church of England that provides the background; in *The Autobiography of Mark Rutherford* and *Father and Son* it is strict Calvinism. But all the authors spend considerable imaginative effort developing a picture of orthodox religion. In *Ednor Whitlock*, too, orthodox religion is important. Ednor from his childhood

> had breathed a religious atmosphere. His father was a clergyman of the strictest orthodoxy, as well as zealous, energetic, and sincerely pious; his mother shared her husband's views and feelings; and he himself, with the full approval of both parents, intended to take Holy Orders.
>
> (*Ednor Whitlock*, p. 2)

This orthodox religious background has formed his character and made him religious as well as given him a sound and unfailing moral sense. Ednor's moral superiority to the two villainous characters of the novel, Reginald Pulting and Fräulein Hartman, is ascribed to his religious upbringing (p. 112; p. 166). However, there is no description in the novel of what this orthodox religion is like. Ednor's parents die of typhus on page 9, and no portrait of them or the religious environment they provide is given. The novel never shows the reader how Christianity is practised nor is the reader shown the thoughts and attitudes that go with a certain kind of religious practice. It is therefore impossible to form a notion of what Ednor has been deprived of when he starts doubting, and what he is working his way towards when he tries to rebuild his faith. One can contrast this with the very specific kind of orthodoxy that is defined in *Robert Elsmere* by Catherine Leyburn who becomes Elsmere's wife, in *The Way of All Flesh* by Christina and Theobald Pontifex, in *Father and Son* by the religious attitudes and practices of Gosse's parents and the Plymouth Brethren to whom they belong, and in *The Autobiography of Mark Rutherford* by the community of Calvinistic Independents that is described in detail in the three first chapters of the novel.

One could continue aspect by aspect with MacColl's two novels and demonstrate this lack of imaginative realisation of events, situations, characters, and relationships, and how this is closely linked with an extensive use both of clichés in the language and of stock situations and characters. With this goes a constant tendency to conceive emotional, religious, moral, and political themes in the simplest possible terms. The two are connected together: a nuanced and rich conception of a theme cannot be expressed in clichés and through stock characters and situations. One could argue, though I shall not do it here, that MacColl's endorsement of what appears as crude social, moral, and political attitudes in his two novels is an *artistic* failure; a failure to create characters with, as Henry James says, 'the power to be finely aware and richly responsible'.[31]

---

31.   Henry James, *The Art of the Novel. Critical Prefaces* (New York 1934) p. 62. The argument that it is one of the major features of literary art that it shows this fine awareness, has been made

V

The above argument from artistic failure is aimed at establishing an alternative hypothesis to (4) and (5), i.e. that agreement on literary value is not a matter of consensus (arrived at no matter how) but of reasoned argument. The response to this from the supporters of the 'instability of value' view, will be to invoke (6): the status of reasons is just what is in question. Demonstrating that reasons can actually be produced in support of value-claims made about a literary work, whether it is forgotten or has retained attention, has no bearing on the question whether value is ultimately contingent, since reasoned agreement must itself be a result of social conditioning. The reasons one produces in response to the question whether a work deserves continued critical attention from readers, will be a product of the dominant interests and needs of the community to which one belongs. Consequently, different communities will give different answers. The forgotten work may not have attracted contradictory and incommensurable value-judgements, but this does not alter the fact that any such judgement, when made, will be contingent.

To see what is wrong with this argument and to bring out the full force of the argument from artistic failure one need to make a distinction that the 'instability of value argument' fails to make. The 'instability of value' argument rests squarely on the notion of 'consensus in a community'. The notion of a community is defined by reference to social identity (race, gender, class) but could also be defined through some other set of criteria delimiting a social group. To get a conceptual framework rich enough to deal with the problem of artistic standards of excellence, the notion of a community needs to be supplemented with the notion of a social practice or social institution which has currency among many communities and which is defined without reference to the criteria through which any social community is defined. Such social practice is defined through the concepts and conventions it makes available to anyone who is socialised into it. It is trivially true that the objects and actions of a practice can be recognised, acted on, and evaluated only by those who have been socialised into the practice. The question of the value of MacColl's novels arises only among those who are interested in literature and the standards they apply will have been internalised through their socialisation into the practice of reading with appreciation. The initiation into the practice is necessary for reasons to 'take' or have purchase. This socialisation is a necessary

repeatedly by Martha Nussbaum. See Martha Nussbaum, *Love's Knowledge. Essays on Philosophy and Literature* (Oxford 1990), in particular the essay '"Finely Aware and Richly Responsible": Literature and the Moral Imagination' as well as her other essays on James. Nussbaum makes the point with reference to *moral* themes. However, the same point can be made with reference to any 'perennial theme'. For the notion of 'perennial theme' see Lamarque and Olsen, *op.cit.* pp. 405–411.

precondition for *any* social practice to operate. It is a *general* point about social practices and institutions that they are defined by concepts and rules that one has to internalise to enter into the practice. To continue over time social practices or institutions must have *some* members at any one time. However, such social practices/institutions are not defined through their membership. They constitute their own membership: the *only* requirement to this membership is that it has to some extent internalised the concepts and conventions of the practice/institution and applies them. Social practices of this kind cannot therefore be identified through *other* criteria defining a community (e.g. criteria of social identity).

Aesthetic value is socially constituted and aesthetic justification can only be recognised after a process of socialisation. However, aesthetic value is not constituted through consensus in a community but in a social practice governed by rules and concepts cutting across many communities which can be defined in many different ways.[32] Consensus does not constitute value. The theoretical advantage of the argument from artistic failure is that it leaves no opening for community interests: no community has *a stake* in an artistic failure and thus *nothing to say* about it that can be related to its dominant interests *as a community*. It is consequently easier to recognise that the reasons produced for denying it further critical attention must have a basis different from that of the dominant interests of a community.

Once it is recognised that reasons for denying further critical attention to artistic failures can have their basis outside the dominant interests of a community, it is easy also to recognise how implausible is the assumption that a community defined by e.g. common social identity should be able to agree on a set of artistic standards of excellence that can be derived from, or that supports the dominant interests of that community. It is here that one sees a conceptual blurring in the 'instability of value argument' whereby members of a community are assumed to be participants in the same social practice. Or, conversely, there is a conceptual blurring in the definition of community: it is tacitly assumed that people who engage in the practice of reading literature appreciatively as works of art constitute a community that necessarily has a common social identity. However, there is no reason to believe that white, middle-class, middle-aged men who, as cultural radicals claim, possess cultural power, but who are *not* interested in literature or art, should share a set of standards of artistic excellence that can be seen as underpinning their main common interests. Those white, middle-class, middle-aged men who *are* interested in literature and art, *will* share such standards, but they will share them because they are participants in a social practice that may (though it need not) go beyond the community of white, middle-class, middle-aged men. This social practice is not

---

32. For a detailed argument that literature is this kind of social institution or practice, see Lamarque and Olsen, *op.cit.* pp. 255–67.

defined by reference to such criteria as defines the community, if any, to which all white, middle-class, middle-aged men belong.

It is here that the argument from artistic failure displays one further advantage. 'The instability of value argument' does not in good faith attempt to analyse how literary value is constituted. It is a political move aimed at changing, modifying, or abolishing what is thought of as a secular, literary canon[33] in order to give 'voice' to groups that have been silenced because of their gender, class, or race.[34] There are several ways in which these suppressed groups can be given a voice. One can insert them into the literary tradition as it exists today. One can construct alternative canons, or one can construct anti-canons, works that are supposed to embody values opposite to those embodied in the traditional canon. The values invoked in this struggle are asserted explicitly to be moral and political in nature. However, the argument from artistic failure can be used here to suggest that the rejection of aesthetic value by advocates of suppressed social groups, is only superficial. If the social identity of the author or the ideological content of the work were sufficient to secure a place for a work in an alternative canon or in a list of non-canonical

---

33.   I have argued elsewhere that the notion of canon may not be a very useful concept when discussing literary tradition and how it is constituted. There is no strong analogy between a closed body of writing defined by the Church through its authority and an open tradition of works defined through aesthetic criteria and constantly added to. Only societies without a tradition have the need for a canon in the scriptural sense. The theoretical disadvantage of the concept is that it invites political attack exactly for those reasons which makes the analogy between a scriptural canon and literary tradition a weak one. See 'The Concept of a Literary Canon', in *ΧΡΟΝΙΚΑ ΑΙΣΘΗΤΙΚΗΣ* (*Annals for Aesthetics*), 36 (1996), pp. 71–85. In *Cultural Capital* John Guillory makes a similar point:

> The word 'canon' displaces the expressly honorific term 'classic' precisely in order to isolate the 'classics' as the object of critique. The concept of the canon names the traditional curriculum of literary texts by analogy to that body of writing historically characterized by an inherent logic of *closure* – the scriptural canon. The scriptural analogy is continuously present, if usually tacit, whenever canonical revision is expressed as 'opening the canon'. We may begin to interrogate this first assumption by raising the question of whether the process by which a selection of texts functions to define a religious practice and doctrine is really similar *historically* to the process by which literary texts come to be preserved, reproduced, and taught in the schools.   (p. 6)

34.
> The literary canon of 'great literature' ensures that it is this 'representative experience' (one selected by male bourgeois critics) that is transmitted to future generations, rather than those deviant, unrepresentative experiences discoverable in much female, ethnic and working-class writing. Anglo-American feminist criticism has waged war on this self-sufficient canonization of middle-class male values.

> Toril Moi, *op.cit.*, p. 78.

works, then it would not matter whether works that figured in such alternative canons were artistic failures. I shall now suggest without arguing the point, that this is not the case. No one would want MacColl in *their* particular canon or non-canon, and for the reasons set out above. One could change his social identity, one could rewrite his novels slightly so as to change the ideological values they embody (and at the level of crudity that MacColl operates this could easily be done without much damage to the narrative fabric of the novels), but he would still not be a candidate for inclusion in any canon.

The thesis that inclusion in alternative canons or in non-canonical lists are also determined by the same aesthetic criteria as is inclusion in the traditional canon, is an empirical one. It seems intuitively plausible and there is some circumstantial evidence that can be cited, e.g. that proponents of the instability of value argument never analyse artistic failures and that relativists and their founding fathers tend to stick to discussion of classics.[35] However, nothing follows for the present argument even if the hypothesis cannot be confirmed. For one can, of course, stand outside a practice, or reject it altogether and suggest that one starts doing something else. If one stands outside the practice of producing and appreciating literature, one will simply have no way of, or interest in, evaluating the productions or actions made within the practice. If one rejects the practice of appreciating literature, one does this for a reason or reasons which can be political, moral, or social, but not aesthetic, since aesthetic reasons are only defined within the practice. Since the time of Plato there have been repeated attempts to banish the poets from the City and to forbid poetic practice because of its pernicious moral effects. And since Aristotle there have been defences of literature and of poetic practice. The argument that there are no aesthetic standards and therefore no aesthetic values, if it is consistent, can only bee seen as a form of neo-moralism[36] of the puritan type, uninterested in literature but eager to impose its moral standards on those who may happen to appreciate it. One is, perhaps unfairly, reminded of Edmund Gosse's portrait

35.
Derrida writes about Ponge rather than Béranger ... Hillis Miller writes about Mrs. Gaskell rather than about Mrs. Oliphant... Roland Barthes had the habit of dragging in James Bond for illustration, lest anyone get the idea that he was confined to the high cultural productions that, on the evidence, did in fact educe his most prolonged and painstaking attention.   Albert Cook, *op.cit.*, p. 318.

36.
The reversion to moralism is determined by the equation of text-selection with value-selection. For this reason much of what passes for political analysis of historically canonical works is nothing more than the passing of moral judgement on them. The critique of the canon moves quickly to reassert absolute notions of good and evil; ...
                                   John Guillory, *op.cit.*, p. 25.

of his mother, an extreme puritan and a member of the Plymouth Brethren: 'She had a remarkable, I confess to me still somewhat unaccountable impression [this is Gosse, the man of letters, speaking] that to "tell a story", that is, to compose fictitious narrative of any kind, was a sin'.[37] As a result

> Not a single fiction was read or told to me during my infancy. The rapture of the child who delays the process of going to bed by cajoling 'a story' out of his mother or his nurse, as he sits upon her knee, well tucked up, at the corner of the nursery fire – this was unknown to me. Never in all my early childhood, did anyone address to me the affecting preamble, 'Once upon a time!' I was told about missionaries, but never about pirates; I was familiar with humming-birds, but I had never heard of fairies. Jack the Giant-Killer, Rumplestiltskin, and Robin Hood were not of my acquaintance, and though I understood about wolves, Little Red Ridinghood was a stranger even by name.[38]

Different values, but much of the same attitude?

---

37. Edmund Gosse, *Father and Son* (1907) (Gloucester 1984), p. 13.

38. Ibid. p. 14.

CHAPTER 3

Popular / Canonical

The case of *The Secret Agent*

Jan Gorak

Largely through "the soft consensus of lowered expectations," contemporary theorists like Barbara Herrnstein-Smith and Paul Lauter have promoted the idea of a tight connection between high literary reputation and ideological conformity. Using Joseph Conrad's *The Secret Agent* as my test-case, but with broad reference to a range of contemporary spy fiction, this essay explores the troubled relationship between that novel and ideas of family, state, and public order.

1. Introduction

In 1907, during the middle of May, Joseph Conrad received the proofs of *The Secret Agent*. Their condition did not delight him, and "he almost cried" when he thought how few of the necessary corrections he could afford to make. Yet the manuscript as a whole "did not strike me as bad at all" he told his literary agent James Pinker. The reasons for this assessment are intriguing, and audaciously calculated even for Conrad:

> There is an element of popularity in it. By this I don't mean to say that the thing is popular. I merely think that it shows traces of capacity for that sort of treatment which may make a novel popular. As I've told you my mind runs very much on popularity just now. I would try to reach it not by sensationalism but by means of taking a widely discussed subject for the *text* of my novel. Apart from religious problems the public mind runs on questions of war and peace and labor. I mean war, peace, and labor in general not in any particular way or in any particular form of labor trouble.   (Karl & Davies 1988, Vol. 3:3 439–40)

In the light of the typically traumatic financial relationship Conrad enjoyed with Pinker, he did well to emphasize the popular potential of his latest volume. But does "popular" indicate anything more than Conrad's eagerness to impress his publisher that his novel was "likely to sell well"?

We can begin by noting that Conrad thinks of "popular" in two distinct ways. In the first place, he refers to a popular "sort of treatment"; in the second, to "a widely discussed subject", subsequently elaborated as congruent with what "the public mind runs on". The first kind of popularity leads an author to the status of the bestseller; the second to an alliance with the literary journalistic typically seen as harmful to the artist; and both lead to the composition of texts as an accumulation of *doxa*. This does not seem the stuff a canonical work as we understand it is made of.

Conrad's letter to Pinker does not share our prejudices, however. It begins by drawing a distinction between the decision to cast his novel in a popular mode – the spy story – and the commitment to follow that mode slavishly. He assures his correspondent that the first choice does not necessarily entail the second. Conrad will avail himself of the form of the spy story, but will divest it of its "sensationalism". Spy fiction, the Edwardian successor to the invasion narratives of the mid-Victorian England inaugurated with Sir George Chesney's *The Battle of Dorking* (1871), enjoyed significant popular esteem in the British mass circulation press. Like its predecessor, spy fiction combined social forecasting, patriotic exhortation, and xenophobic ritual in a conventional literary vehicle. I. F. Clarke (1970) has linked the genre to the swelling anti-German feeling fanned by the Northcliffe press and the drive toward rearmament.

Ian Watt (1979: 42–3, 55, 128–29, 359) has reminded us that Conrad is unique among canonical moderns in his unwillingness to jettison traces of popular narrative from even from his most ambitious masterpieces. Yet for many critics Conrad's indecision about whether to enter the school of Henry James or the gymnasium of G. A. Henty marks the line that separates the canonical from the apocryphal Conrad. The influential pages devoted to the author in Q. D. Leavis's *Fiction and the Reading Public* (1932) equate the popular Conrad with the escapist Conrad of transparent lagoons, tropical virgins, and strong, silent heroes. Mrs. Leavis's study presents Conrad as a central figure in the republic of modern letters, a territory catastrophically divided between popular trash and difficult masterpieces. As a dual citizen in both republics, Conrad calls for special vigilance from his critics:

> Conrad... became popular as "the Kipling of the South Seas" (when his first novel appeared he was so hailed in *The Times*), and the dust-jacket of the cheap edition of *Lord Jim* used to describe the contents as the story of a young man who after various failures finally made good. Conrad's best work – *The Secret Agent, Heart of Darkness*, and some others is not popular: it allows no such romantic interpretation, the irony is too apparent and destructive.   (Leavis 1979: 210)

From this perspective a "popular" novelist has vacated the public space to erect a crowd-pleasing exotic substitute.

The dedication of *The Secret Agent* to H. G. Wells hints at a Conrad very different from the complex ironist canonized by Mrs. Leavis. Wells's busy journalistic pose has proved deeply repellent to twentieth-century intellectuals like Virginia

Woolf and Johan Huizinga, who saw it as a means of suburbanizing history and consciousness. This is popularity, but one derived from making modernity more manageable than it is, a fraudulent popularity that the course of twentieth-century history will expose as a complacent lie. "The chronicler of Mr. Lewisham's love, the biographer of Kipps, and the historian of the ages to come," praised in Conrad's dedication viewed "the ages to come" from the comic perspective of a suburban reading public seduced by the belligerence and cosiness of the yellow press. At the very least, this is a popularity too insulated from the larger course of European history, too narrowly British in an imperialist world. In Huizinga's judgment, "an anachronistic strain" runs through Wells's view of history, together with a perpetually humorous perspective that "kills all historical understanding" (Huizinga 1968: 192). This was the escapism of comic Englishness that matched the exotic escapism deplored by Mrs. Leavis.

Mrs. Leavis sees Conrad as a hostage to the popular sensibility; the Wellsian Conrad confines himself to insular Englishness in a global world. In each instance, Conrad becomes a deeply representative case: representative of the schismatic state of modern letters, the limitations of the English ideology, of the tacit but irrefragable threads that bind literary culture to national culture. The peculiar ambition of being a "popular" author makes Conrad somehow a lesser author. In each case the alien artist overcompensates by adapting all too well to the local prejudices and practices of his adoptive country.

In this essay, I want to dispute this assessment by arguing that Conrad's aspirations to popularity are the very essence of his continued canonicity. A Conrad confined to the aesthete's cork-lined room would have been a Conrad less attentive to the points of fracture and conflict in early twentieth-century Europe. I shall therefore explore *The Secret Agent* as Conrad's bid to utilize a popular instrument (the spy novel) to prosecute a serious public inquiry into the major shift in definition of nationality, civil society and public order that sweeps through England and Europe during the early twentieth century. In this novel, the *doxa*, the ideology and the conventional narrative forms of early twentieth-century Europe all find their way into Conrad's pages. To that extent, Conrad could hardly have written his novel without a firm commitment to the popular. At every turn, however, Conrad avails himself of the canonical work's prerogative of taking the accepted symbol and changing its value, of transvaluing accepted notions into bizarre combinations. (For some very interesting work on this aspect of the canonical work see J. H. Hexter's introduction to the Yale edition of Sir Thomas More's *Utopia*.) In Conrad, canonicity and popularity are interdependent; the novelist makes his lasting claim on our notice by exploiting familiar symbols and situations in order to expand, or reverse their meaning. Consequently, Conrad's work is not valuable only for its complex refashioning of a simple narrative vehicle. It is an indispensable instrument for cultural analysis as well, able to take conventional national symbols and institutions and explore hidden conflicts and tensions behind them.

The London of *The Secret Agent* contains such imposing and acceptably popular monuments to public order as the Houses of Parliament and the Greenwich Park Observatory. Its streets also conceal the latent structures of violence and dissidence (Mr. Verloc's sex shop, the Silenus tavern) ostensibly dedicated to eroding that order. Few of Conrad's readers would have sprung away in horror from the proposition that the national capital houses order and anarchy. As the novel continues, however, the gap between these two rival systems, officially so great according to every organ of British culture, proves actually to be non-existent. The perpetual traffic between the institutions responsible for the maintenance of public order and their anarchic antagonists increases throughout the book. The stability of imperial Britain depends on the continued inertia of the anarchists; the security of the dissident counterculture depends on the continued inertia of imperial Britain. The only losers in this benign conspiracy between order and anarchy are the innocent victims like Stevie and Winnie. The "atrocious" and "monstrous" character of their loss, as Conrad repeatedly terms it, serves to annihilate popular expectations about the predictable relationship between order and stability the novel initially appeared to support. Conrad's genius lies in his ability to force separate items from the public sphere into confrontation with each other. His canonicity rests not from some blissful immunity from popular assumptions and conventions but in his talent for pursuing their implications and associations to unpopular conclusions.

By October of 1907, the reception of *The Secret Agent* in the British press dashed Conrad's hopes of a rendez-vous with the popular once again. As he complained to Edward Garnett: "I've been so cried up of late as a sort of freak, an amazing bloody foreigner writing in English (every blessed review of *The Secret Agent* had it so – even yours)." (Conrad, *Letters*, Vol. 3, p. 488) The aspiring "popular" author had still not lost his status as the nation's Slavic resident outsider.

2.   A tale of two Europes

Conrad's novel appeared at a time when the identity of Europe had reached a point of crisis. Was the European inheritance a progressive, commercial, peaceful formation of independent states? Or was its destiny to realize a future utopia after ordeal by blood and iron? Could England retain exemption from continental developments by remaining in splendid isolation, or was the nation drifting down the same troubled stream as the continent as a whole? The Europe described in W. E. H. Lecky's *History of the Rise and Influence of the Spirit of Rationalism in Europe* (1861) and Thomas Buckle's *History of Civilization in England* (1878), balanced the competing claims of science, force, orthodox belief, and sceptical tolerance in a complex equilibrium. This Europe historians imagined as the privileged terminal point visible at the end of progress's long forward march. It is this slowly accumulating rational space Buckle praises as harbouring "everything worthy of the name of civilization". Europe stands or falls as an ideal of civil society, Buckle suggests, since

> [i]n Europe alone has society been organized into a scheme, not indeed sufficiently large, but still wide enough to include all the different classes of which it is composed, and thus by leaving room for the progress of such, to secure the permanence and balance of the whole. (Vol. I, p. 82)

Such a deep, seamless continuity serves as a mythic legitimation of existing civil society and its institutions. By the end of the century, however, a set of much darker mythologies about Europe were moving slowly into focus. Their reference point is not the Europe visible in any metropolitan city, but a Europe not yet realized, a Europe at present discernible only in the symbolic fragments of the past. Where Buckle's reasonable social mythology aims to tranquilize the subject, this more violent alternative works toward inciting the group. The promoters of this vision share little of Buckle's Whiggish confidence in current social institutions. J. A. Cramb's popular volume *The Origins and Destiny of Imperial Britain and Nineteenth-Century Europe* rewrites the national history not as a commemoration of autonomous institutions and civic habits but in terms of a larger continental quest for a latent order realizable in an unspecified future. To be sure, Cramb pays handsome tribute to Britain's contribution to European culture. At the same time, every page of his book betrays impatience with the present and distaste for the cowardly compromises of politics as usual. Cramb substitutes for Buckle's Europe of revered public memories a subterranean Europe decipherable not through the presiding monuments of civil society but glimpsed through "the half-effaced image on a coin, the illuminated margin of a medieval vision". The prophetic historian inspects these "to discover their connecting bond, the ties that unite them to each other and the One" (p. 2–3). Where Buckle sees Europe as the legatee of a rational history, as a living monument to deep regularities and controlled change in human affairs, Cramb mines history in search of revelation, commandeering it in a crusade for the soul of a future visionary order.

In his closing pages, Europe has metamorphosed from rational legacy to revelatory future. Cramb describes how "the last sun of the dying century goes down upon a world brooding over an unresolved enigma, pursuing an ideal it but darkly discerns". (p. 275) Britain's role in this mystic process must be to seize its leadership opportunities, to reawaken its visionary potential for the good of the globe. Cramb's history aims implicitly to supplant Buckle's. For the massive, quasi-scientific homage to continuity of his predecessor, Cramb substitutes a history written to incite youthful energies on behalf of a barely defined mission.

From the conflicting but representative testimony of Buckle and Cramb, it is clear that European history and European civilization constitute no unified conceptual field for Conrad's generation. Rather, Europe represents a social space contested by rationalizing Whigs like Buckle and messianic visionaries like Cramb. Naturally, in an age where, as Conrad's senior embassy official Mr. Vladimir tells us, science calls the shots, each party claims scientific status. These shared scientific claims, however, mask deep structural and ideological conflicts about the inheritance and ultimate direction of history. "Science" can sponsor violently opposite views about the nature of civil society. "Science" can find itself attached to both the general laws that serve as the unconscious framework for current cultural practices and the enigmatic future that lies just beyond them.

J. A. Hobson's *Imperialism: A Study* (1902) reports on imperial England's territorial addition of 4,754,000 square miles and its increase in population of about 88 million over one generation. This expanded England is a Janus-faced England, an England torn between its foreign mission and its domestic malaise. In such an England, city life no longer stands for Buckle's single unquestionable good. Instead, the domestic cities represent Paradise Lost, while the colonial cities feature as Paradise Regained. In *Oceana* (1885), J. A. Froude discerns in the expansion of English territory "the saving of our national soul... the saving of the souls of millions of Englishmen hereafter to be born" (p. 388). But what were they being saved from? From England itself, Froude answers unequivocally as he sketches a London that resembles "the monstrous city" of *The Secret Agent* in its habit of cannibalizing its inhabitants and destroying its children. In London Froude imagines an anonymous proletariat condemned to:

> miles upon miles of squalid lanes, each house like a duplicate of its neighbour: the dirty street in front, the dirty yard behind, the fetid smell from the ill-made sewers, the public house at the street corners. Here with no sight of a green field, with no knowledge of the flowers and forest... . with no entertainment but the music hall, no pleasure but in the drink shop, hundreds of thousands of English children are now growing up into men and women. (p. 8)

Buckle's metropolitan city actualizes principles of social organization that maximize the chances of individual mobility while simultaneously preserving the apparatus of public order. Froude interprets the city by the light of a political eschatology in which the metropolis is an island of lost souls and its colonial fragments so many vales of soul-making. The mission of regeneration preached by Cramb and Froude cannot be accommodated to Buckle's myth of Europe as a site of gradual, incremental progress, and slow deliberation conducted through established institutional channels.

From the beginning of Conrad's novel, it is clear that the myth of a civil society rooted in gradual change and regular habits will be subject to severe strain. The opening paragraphs of the book describe a world that simulates Buckle's orderly, industrious shifting social system. Yet Mr. Verloc's shop reverses the accepted national business procedures. Similarly the narrator's description of the Verloc household, where "his wife was in charge of his brother-in-law" (13) supplants the language of affection in favour of the language of control. In the process, it prepares its audience for the threatening impersonality of the England of orphanages, charity homes, and intelligence networks that the remainder of the novel will expose. In as yet unspecified ways, Conrad's first two paragraphs hint that although the physical traces of the national political mythology remain – shops, families, consumers – its institutional and ideological core is no longer intact. This is the slowly progressing commercial England of Buckle or Wells taken down several notches, reduced to a shadow of itself.

Conrad cuts across these long-established social habits when Mr. Verloc is called to his interview at the embassy. As Mr. Vladimir outlines his performance payment plan and the new idiom of violence and atrocity that will define his regime, Mr. Verloc glimpses "the broad back of a policeman watching idly the gorgeous perambulator of a wealthy baby being wheeled in state across the Square". A few seconds later, after an almost forlorn demonstration of his celebrated vocal powers does nothing to impress Mr. Vladimir, Mr. Verloc's façade of docility disappears. In the new world order, the orator's golden lungs and the mimic's mastery of "the social revolutionary jargon" count for little. Mr. Verloc, redundancy looming over him, responds to Mr. Vladimir's "You haven't ever studied Latin, have you?" with a seething resentment:

> "No," growled Mr. Verloc. "you did not expect me to know it. I belong to the million. Who knows Latin? Only a few hundred imbeciles who aren't fit to take care of themselves" (29).

As the novel continues, Conrad repeatedly exposes a culture pushed to its limits of patience and endurance by a new order where no job is secure, no residence permanent. "This ain't an easy world," as the night cabby who takes Winnie's mother to the "charitable institution" that will be her new home complains. The objective harshness of social conditions in the modern city, however, is not nearly as dangerous to civic tranquillity as the subjective anguish acknowledgment of such conditions triggers in those least able to support it. In this culture of spontaneous and unpredictable resentment Conrad dramatizes as spreading across Edwardian England, Stevie Verloc carries representative status because of his inability to control his inarticulate resentment:

> "Poor! Poor" stammered out Stevie, pushing his hands deeper into his pockets with compulsive sympathy. He could say nothing; for the tenderness to all pain

> and all misery, the desire to make the horse happy and the cabby happy, had reached the point of a bizarre longing to take them to bed with them. And that, he knew, was impossible. For Stevie was not mad. It was, as it were, a symbolic longing; and at the same time it was very distinct, because springing from experience, the mother of wisdom. (140)

The paradoxical violence of Stevie's "symbolic longing" for a kinder, gentler society threatens the stability of the social fabric in Conrad's London. Buckle's old social script written for automata yields to a new scenario performed by desperate hysterics. Conrad borrows Buckle's image of a vast, impersonal machine while fusing it to Cramb's vision of an enigmatic, violent future peopled by Froude's lost illiterates. The result is the beleaguered, resentful subject who wanders through the London of *The Secret Agent*: the night cabby, Stevie, the "Professor", Winnie after her murder of Mr. Verloc. By the end of the novel Mr. Vladimir's city of science has metamorphosed into Kafka's despairing monstrosity. As many critics have noted, *The Secret Agent* is Conrad's most Dickensian novel, exploring a tale of two Europes pledged to mutual destruction.

Early twentieth-century social critics recognized the dangerously volatile properties of "the Stevie problem" in modern Europe and the multiplying institutional means for fanning that problem. George Bernard Shaw warned the readers of his *Fabian Essays* (1908) about the incendiary properties of a popular press fanned by belligerent plutocrats like Lord Northcliffe. For Shaw, the modern newspaper offered the potential for "a new sort of crime – the incitement by newspapers of mobs to outrage and even murder – hitherto tried on religious impostors, is beginning to be applied to politics". (288) In modern newspapers J. A. Hobson found "a Roman arena, a Spanish bull-ring, and an English prize fight rolled into one. The popularization of the power to read has made the press the chief instrument of brutality".[1] Defenses of war and violence arrive from all sides of the political spectrum; Cecil Rhodes's spokesman C. de Thierry in *Imperialism* (1898) pronounces that "peace... is a pool that, without war at intervals becomes stagnant" (p. 94). Edward Demolins's *Boers or English: Who Are In The Right?* (1900) plots Rhodes's South African war as a war for civilization that sets "a superior race" against its inferior rivals. Demolins predictably adds that such a verdict is "not a judgment expressed on men and deeds... science holds itself aloof from the disputes of individuals". (p. 5)

On the Left Georges Sorel, whose *Reflections on Violence* appeared as articles in *Mouvement Socialiste* a year before *The Secret Agent*, projects a complementary mythology of violence from below. In Syndicalist violence Sorel finds an antidote

---

1.   J. A. Hobson (1901:3)

to the poison of cooptation masked as cooperation. For Sorel "proletarian acts of violence" must be viewed as the prologue to a new creation. Such violence

> carried on as a pure and simple manifestation of the class war, appears thus as a very fine and heroic thing; it is at the service of the immemorial interests of civilization; it is not perhaps the most appropriate method of obtaining immediate material advantages, but it may serve the world from barbarism. (p. 98)

The cult of a cleansing violence re-enters European culture as a legitimate political language. The same "science" that once legitimated slow steady progress now legitimates a violence that fulfils objective laws unconnected to personal conditions. Modern political thought and modern states have more important things than persons to concern themselves with. As Sorel submits, the historian's "business is to understand what is least important in the course of events; the questions which interest the chroniclers and excite novelists are these which he most willingly leaves on one side." (p. 59)

What Sorel discards to the ash heap of history, Conrad puts at the heart of his political vision. Stripping violence to the skin, he stripped of all mythologies but instead as "the fact of a man blown to bits for nothing even most resembling an idea" (9). Before he reaches this climactic discovery, however, Conrad shows violence as political theatre. In an embassy anteroom, Mr. Vladimir spells out the conditions of Mr. Verloc's continued employment, a violent attack on the chief symbol of public order, the Greenwich Observatory. Too many settled interests depend on each other, however, to make such an act possible for any existing performer on Mr. Verloc's script. Only Stevie lacks the "interest" in the status quo necessary for carrying out Mr. Vladimir's instructions; only Stevie's heightened but entirely non-ideological fury at social injustice will be willing to unleash the necessary violence that will fulfil Mr. Vladimir's commands. Stevie's senseless death incites Winnie to a countering violence, rooted in her legitimate sense of deep personal betrayal. Winnie's revenge, into which "Mrs. Verloc had put all the inheritance of her immemorial and obscure descent, the simple ferocity of the age of caverns, and the unbalanced fury of the age of bar-rooms" (212) draws from the same fund of symbolic longing that incited Stevie's response to the night cabman. Winnie and Stevie are for Conrad representative citizens of modern civilization.

At the end of the novel, no larger cleansing violence has arrived; the great day awaited by so many of his contemporaries, the day of invasion, revolution, once-and-for-all liberation does not arrive in this novel. Unlike Cramb or Sorel, Conrad does not hook violence to some great idea of the future, but personifies it in "the incorruptible Professor" who:

> had no future. He disdained it. He was a force. His thoughts caressed the images of ruin and destruction. He walked frail, insignificant, shabby, miserable – and terrible in the simplicity of his idea calling madness and despair to the regeneration

of the world. Nobody looked at him. He passed on unsuspected and deadly, like a
pest in the street full of men (249).

What does this exploration of "the public mind" tell us about Conrad's methods
in composing *The Secret Agent*? Incitements to violence through the promulga-
tion of messianic or scientific ideologies, so significant in the incitement culture
of early twentieth-century Europe and Edwardian England, feature in *The Secret
Agent* as well. In his own pages, however, Conrad habitually dislodges violence
from the larger ideological and scientific structures typically used to legitimate
it for the popular mind. He captures the religious intensity of the culture of incitement that gripped both Left and Right in these years, but its mouthpieces are
marginal madmen, not policy scientists like Thierry or Demolins. He acknowledges Science and Religion as two seams of dominant discourse, but he forces
them together in the violent and meaningless collision of Stevie's death. He does
not integrate them within any larger intellectual synthesis like Cramb's. His proletariat functions not as Sorel's agency of redemptive delivery, nor even Froude's
lost underclass found again, like Mr. Micawber, on a fatal shore. Conrad's pro-
letarians are as exploitative as the petty-bourgeois anarchist Mr. Verloc himself,
and the target of their exploitation is identical to his own. Both Mrs. Neale, the
grumbling, tipsy domestic help of the Verlocs, and the maimed night cabby tap
Stevie's deep reserves of manic sympathy, reserves that will subsequently fund Mr.
Verloc's subsequent murderous plan. The politics of *The Secret Agent*, epitomized
in Winnie's revenge on Mr. Verloc, Stevie's outrage at the fate of the poor, "the
Professor's" frustration at his lack of worldly recognition, or even Mr. Verloc's own
revulsion from Mr. Vladimir's Hyperborean manners, however, remain stubbornly
personal. The overall effect of Conrad's narrative is to expose a subculture incited
into ever more hysterical resentment. Conrad retains the threatening atmosphere
of this culture and the corresponding threat of imminent violence in the public
sphere. Yet he lops off any larger grounds that might cushion these outbreaks. He
privatizes the violence that does arrive, so that it destroys a "family" and leaves systems and public officials inviolate. In a world of indestructible impersonal systems
and post-individual histories, Conrad's is a political imagination enmeshed in the
authenticity of the personal.

3. Spy fiction as modern chivalry

In the mounting uncertainties and hostilities of early-twentieth century Europe,
invasion narratives and spy stories play a crucial role in maintaining confidence
and morale inside the national culture. With their call to renewal of the nation
in decline, their almost loving simulation of the material details of the nation's

political institutions and cultural apparatuses, spy novels in Edwardian Britain are deeply conservative vehicles. For the impersonal violence of early twentieth-century societies, they substitute a ritualized conflict that pits barbarous German against chivalrous British gentleman. The social psychology of modern culture, the compound of rage and disappointment so central in *The Secret Agent* and in the larger, public sphere does not surface in these novels. A key figure in absorbing this rage and deflecting conflict is the central protagonist, upper-class but disenchanted, and frequently forced into secrecy and disguise that in the end subserves the reconstruction and reconfirmation of his identity as national savior – a surviving Sidney Carton.

Johan Huizinga's description of the Burgundian chroniclers, for whom "the conception of chivalry constituted ... a sort of magic key, by the aid of which they explained to themselves the motives of politics and history" (1965:66) can be applied to these authors as well. As Huizinga observes, the terrors and puzzles of history melt away when tamed by style and form, by which violence is channelled into a sublimated ritual, and fear of the unknown expelled by immersion in the rules of a predictable game. Where the earliest invasion narrative, Sir George Chesney's *The Invasion of Dorking* (1871), centres on the experience of Britain's defeat at the hands of the Germans, his successors pull back from contemplating such a loss. The nation's reformation, achieved through the exemplary reformation of a representative gentleman, not the experience of defeat, is the centrepiece of the genre.

If popular Edwardian spy stories sublimate violence by translating it to a chivalric idiom, then they also saturate their audience in simulated replicas of everyday reality. William Le Queux's *The Invasion of 1910* (1906) presents a pseudo-history of the modern state through assembling mock Government proclamations, Cabinet minutes, state maps, and simulated briefs. He adds to these the dummy headlines, pseudo-editorials, and expert reports that belong to the larger cultural apparatus of contemporary England. The "fact gathering" method behind his own narrative is matched by the fact-finding operations of the enemy. As Le Queux tours the country to expose facts the Government wants to keep hidden for the readers of the *Daily Mail*, German agents trawl the country for similar facts to relay to their national government. "To each agent – known as a "fixed post" – is allotted the task of discovering some secret, or of noting in a certain district every detail which may be of advantage to the invader when he lands." (p. x) This is a fiction that reconciles a comforting positivist faith in fact while inciting its audience by relaying the recurrent national fantasy of foreign invasion. By combining these two opposing aims Le Queux offers his audience the properties of a world as regular and predictable as clockwork but plummeting toward the brink of disaster.

In *Riddle of the Sands* (1903) Erskine Childers introduces his hero Carruthers to us as an edgy, restless clubman. We then follow him from a well signposted world of privilege to a solitary testing ground of rivers, maps, secret signals – *facts* comprehensible only to those expert enough to master them and shrewd enough to conceal their mastery. As the novel reaches its climax, however, class privilege momentarily resurfaces when the hero orders "the perfect bed in a perfect hostelry hard by the Amstel river". Such retirement is no longer the symbol of class distinction, but rather the means of national salvation. The hotel that welcomes Carruthers is not a hotel as the blessed hospice offered Sir Gawain or Sir Lancelot as history modulates from facts to romance before our eyes. Following this idyllic interlude, Carruthers re-emerges fortified "with a vast excess of strength", and a new disguise. "In a third-class carriage bound for Germany, dressed as a young seaman, in a pea-jacket, peaked cap, and comforter", he begins the last phase of his ordeal. By temporarily relinquishing his identity in crossing class and national lines, the knight errant can preserve the continued stability of England and the elaborately stratified social system the nation supports. Carruthers's principal adversary, also incognito, proves to be a renegade Englishman now pledged to the German cause. The facts, as collated so industriously by Le Queux, will no longer suffice to reveal to the British what they must do to restore their identities. Myths of gentleness in humble disguise, cross-class alliances, ordeals by water, all plot the course of England transformed, ready to recapture its international hegemony in the interests of global stability. Narrative lends imaginative authority to the nation's favoured image of itself as privileged, honourable, and not to be messed with.

The authors of spy fiction submerge their audience in the social realities of contemporary England all the better to emancipate them through studiedly obsolescent fantasies. In their pages, violence is as graceful and skilful as a minuet. Edgar Wallace's *The Four Just Men* (1905) appears to offer a much more drastic version of the national crisis, since it presents the survival of the nation as securable only through foreign intervention and terrorist violence. This apparently drastic solution, however, actually only confirms the benignly fantasizing nature of the genre. For Wallace's turns out to be a fantasy of release from the national crisis through art, a reversion to De Quincey and Wilde rather than Malory or Spenser.

At the start of the novel, Wallace presents an England about to relinquish a valuable item from nineteenth-century civilization. Through the Alien Political Offences Bill Foreign Secretary Sir Philip Ramon hopes to secure the deportation of foreign agitators. The Just Men are quick to realise that Sir Philip's proposal threatens the very heart of British civilization, which uniquely guarantees free speech and unrestricted movement in a harshening European political climate. So the alien Just Men must shadow Great Britain, lest Great Britain fade into an alien shadow of itself. In the course of the novel, one of the group impersonates a long-serving Member of Parliament (one of Chesney's good county families), the detective responsible for Sir Philip's security, and even the jury foreman at his inquest. The group as a whole float a company on the London Stock Exchange, and merge imperceptibly if expensively into the city's most famous public spaces throughout the novel. Because Wallace's world is one where objects like cars, telephones, and official publications can be reproduced easily and endlessly, then the Just Men can function as a lesser Britain inside the greater.

Are we to take this as a nightmare variation on the preoccupations of the spy story? Does Wallace present a fantasy of the national identity dispersed and lost to foreign infiltrators rather than reclaimed by its aristocracy? This would make *The Four Just Men* at once a massively popular and a deeply subversive vehicle, an extremely desirable commodity for today's postmodern academy. As the story unfolds, however, it becomes clear that this Wallace will not offer his audience this novelty. Instead, he pits three just men from abroad against the inflexible ardour of a fourth just man at home, the Foreign Secretary. In Sir Philip Ramon, Wallace displays the national virtues calcified; through his three alien antagonists the national exceptionalism confirmed. The retributive action of the Just Men guarantees that Great Britain alone of European states will maintain its legacy of liberty. What appears to be Cramb's intimations of a new order of blood and iron turns out to be Buckle's vision of deep national and European continuities. The three just men, with Sir Philip as their necessary fourth tragic sacrificial victim, save the idea of justice for an authoritarian Europe and fix it permanently on British shores. Like their foe and fellow Classicist Sir Philip, they stand aloof from all sordid consideration of gain or trade, sharing ties of education and idealism unavailable to any other character in the novel. (Significantly Wallace characterizes the criminal who fails the just men, Thery, as a simple career criminal, a pro whose motives are drably sexual rather than imaginatively ethical.)

By the end of the novel, Wallace's deeply conservative rationale has become clear. In a world of endlessly reproducible entities and political realities of mounting coercion, justice uniquely cannot be reproduced or bartered and Britain uniquely still harbours justice. Justice cannot be left to politicians, who all ultimately share Sir Philip's lack of imagination and compassion. The preservation of the national legacy, so important a matter in this type of fiction and at this time for the nation as a whole, Wallace daringly entrusts to foreigners, but foreigners who are *artists*. Through glancing allusion (to Thomas De Quincey, to Nero, to popular dramatic forms like melodrama) and conversational aside, Wallace's novel repeatedly emphasizes the artistry of the ostensibly criminal acts performed by the Four Just Men. On one instance, detective Falmouth tells Sir Philip:

> men who are capable of making such disguise are really outside the ordinary run of criminals.... One of them is evidently an artist at that sort of thing, and he's the man I'm afraid of. (p. 55)

On another, the Prime Minister corrects his colonial secretary for describing the plan of the four just men as "monstrous", preferring instead to characterize their plan as "a poetic idea". The premier views their arrest as inevitable but regrettable, and laments: "If we catch them they will end their lives unpicturesquely, in a matter of fact, commonplace manner in a little shed in Pentonville Gaol, and the world will never realize how great are the artists who perish." (p. 66)

This allusion to Nero's dying words suggests that *The Four Just Men*'s solution to the problem of the nation's salvation might be as much an authoritarian fantasy of domination as a tribute to the politics of the aesthetic imagination. Wallace confronts the same question as other spy novelists: how will English identity be saved, and who will save it? Art, or more accurately, *imagination* can preserve British identity and the integrity of British institutions in *The Four Just Men*. In the long run, the nation can preserve itself by a judicious blood transfusion and the sacrifice of one of its finest gentlemen. Wallace maintains the sublimating, upperclass habits of a genre his novel initially promised to subvert.

Where Wallace, illegitimate child and sometime newspaper hawker, viewed British society from below, Conrad saw it as an outsider. Thus Wallace's paean to the conservative imagination in *The Four Just Men* dips sharply into the conservatism "with nothing to conserve" that Daphna Erdinast-Vulcan (1992) detects in *The Secret Agent*. For Wallace, the uniqueness of England remains the one nonnegotiable item and the gifted individual the agent responsible for preserving that uniqueness. In Conrad's novel national identities and individuals are swept into the larger apparatus for fragmentation and depersonalization that is modernity. Winnie has a foreign appearance; her husband a foreign name; the Assistant Commissioner looks foreign to Winnie; Chief Inspector Heat, indomitable in his English virtues of slow patient procrastination, reminds the Assistant Commissioner of a tribal chief encountered in an unspecified colony; in sum, deracination is for Conrad a general condition of modern experience.

By the same token, Conrad makes none of the distinctions between professional and amateur, gentleman and player, or artist and tradesman that are so central to Wallace's novel. As Chief Inspector Heat recognizes, modern corporate organizations are systems in which functions are far more important than classes or talents: "Assistant Commissioners come and go, but a valuable Chief Inspector is not an ephemeral office phenomenon" (107). In *The Secret Agent* individuals are the necessary stooges for an age of ideology, dispensable enough at any level. What triggers the final tragedy of the novel is the interchangeability of persons not their integrity. Mr. Verloc's belief that Stevie can perform his anarchist outrage all the better because of his slow wits is a baleful commentary on the scientific, bureaucratic tendencies of a modernizing urban society already sketched out by Mr. Vladimir. In fact, Mr. Vladimir only crystallizes for Mr. Verloc what he knew already: "Anarchists or diplomats were all one to him. Mr. Verloc was temperamentally no respecter of persons. His scorn was equally distributed over the entire field of operations" (199). Conrad adds to Weber's sense of modern bureaucracy as essentially impersonal his own conviction of its moral neutrality as well.

Conrad's most drastic change to spy fiction comes in his intuition of a coming age where individuals are not the apex of society but its detritus. The long and grotesquely comic effort to trace a Stevie now fragmented enough to be scraped up on a shovel epitomizes a new post-individualism. In such an epoch, chivalry has no place and Conrad transforms completely the figure of his secret agent. For Le Queux, Childers, and Wallace, the secret agent embodies the values of individuality, good breeding, and cool courage. The secret agent of the spy novel answers the fears of the invasion narratives that the national virtues have entered decline. Le Queux's Ray Browne, Childers's Carruthers, and Wallace's martyred Sir Philip all give the lie to this verdict, playing to the nation's complacent belief that in difficult times God will call on his Englishmen, even if He has to put them into disguises. In the character of Mr. Verloc Conrad explores directly opposite possibilities for the nation, as he glimpses at an impending and inglorious disaster:

> There is no occupation that fails a man more completely than that of a secret agent of police. It's like your horse falling dead under you in the midst of an uninhabited and thirsty plain. The comparison occurred to Mr. Verloc because he had sat astride various army horses in his time, and had now the sensation of an incipient fall (54).

The ideology of chivalry, like the mythologies of violence and European apocalypse, suffers a deflationary bump in *The Secret Agent*. Conrad deploys a popular form in order to trace a nation and a continent on a *rendez-vous* with disaster. It is interesting that Verloc's "rival" for Winnie's hand was the son of a butcher. This unobtrusively presented fact is possibly Conrad's last *dédoublement* and emphasizes for him that butchery, not chivalry, is at the centre of the social order.

4. Nasty greatness

By choosing to cast his fiction in the popular form of espionage fiction, Conrad signals his willingness to meet his readership halfway. At the same time, however, he imprints a series of deviations and inflections on this popular pattern that leave his audience groping in the dark. In *The Secret Agent* the dominant ideology and popular form can be recognized only as the "grisly skeleton" described in a subsequent Author's Note. Conrad's representation of what troubled the public mind swerves sharply away from that public's assumptions. His attempt to negotiate with the popular mind through the medium of popular narrative one could describe very accurately as a case study in failure. But Conrad's exemplary failure can fund much larger research about the relationship between the literary imagination, canonical art, dominant ideologies, and popular culture at the start of the twentieth century. Conrad takes issues of popular concern and public discourse on board only to dissolve them in the kind of savage farce T. S. Eliot detected in Marlowe's *The Jew of Malta*. In *The Secret Agent* Conrad entertains the ideas that rivet the public mind just as Marlowe hosts many of the issues that troubled Reformation Europe in *The Jew of Malta*. But like Marlowe, he entertains such issues only to discredit them. Sometimes he does this by ridiculing those who espouse them, so that the Professor's insane career pollutes the goals of a society officially sanctioned by merit and science just as surely as the avarice and prejudice of Marlowe's Governor Ferneze pollutes the goals of a society officially bonded by Charity and Love. Sometimes he exposes the deep structures of victimage beneath the machinery of a civilized society. Like Marlowe's Abigail, Conrad's Stevie functions as innocent scapegoat in societies of systemic aggression. Throughout their works, both Conrad and Marlowe scatter allusions to reigning ideologies in travestied situations. Where Marlowe's Barabas quotes Scripture as he steals treasure from convents, Conrad's revolutionaries parrot scraps of radical thought from the back room of a sex shop. Conrad and Marlowe both honour the concerns of the popular as much in the breach as the observance. In the course of his narration Conrad subjects popular forms and timely concerns to the uncompromising severity that Lillian Furst has seen as characteristic of canonical writing, or what she wittily calls the "'Nasty' Great Books".[2]

References

Buckle, T. 1878. *History of Civilization in England*. 3 Vols. London: Longmans Green.

Clarke, I. F. 1970. *Voices Prophesying War 1763–1984*. London: Panther Books.

Childers, E. 1995. *Riddle of the Sands*. Oxford: OUP. [Orig. ed. 1903].

Cramb, J. A. 1913. *Origins and Destiny of Imperial Britain and Nineteenth-Century Europe*. New York NY: E.P. Dutton.

Demolins, E. 1990. *Boers or English: Who Are In The Right?* London: Leadenhall Press.

Erdinast-Vulcan, D. 1992. Sudden Holes in Space and Time: Conrad's Anarchist Aesthetics in *The Secret Agent*. In *Conrad's Critics: Essays for Hans van Marle*, D. Erdinast-Vulcan (ed.), 207–21. Amsterdam: Rodopi.

Froude, J. A. 1904. *Oceana: On England and her Colonies*. New York NY: Charles Scribner's.

Furst, L. 1972. Reading the 'Nasty' Great Books. In *Through the Lens of the Reader: Explorations of European Narrative*, L. Furst (Ed.), 139–51. Albany, NY: SUNY Press.

Hobson, J. A. 1901. *The Psychology of Jingoism*. London: Grant Richards.

Hobson, J. A. 1902. *Imperialism* London: Allen and Unwin.

---

2. Lillian Furst (1972).

Huizinga, J. 1965. *The Waning of the Middle Ages.* Harmondsworth: Penguin Books.

Huizinga, J. 1968. Two Wrestlers with the Angel. In *Dutch Civilization in the Seventeenth Century,* P. Geyl & F. W. N. Hugenholtz (eds), 158–218. New York, NY: Frederick Ungar.

Karl, F. & L. Davies 1988. *The Collected Letters of Joseph Conrad.* New York, NY: CUP.

Leavis, Q. D. 1978. *Fiction and the Reading Public.* Harmondsworth: Penguin Books.

Le Queux, W. 1906. *The Invasion of 1910.* London: Everleigh Nash.

Melchiori, B. A. 1985. *Terrorism in the Late Victorian Novel.* London: Croom Helm.

More, T. 1964. *Utopia,* ed. J.H. Hexter. New Haven, CT: Yale University Press.

Shaw, G. B. 1962. Preface to the 1908 Reprint of *Fabian Essays,* 282–92. London: George Allen and Unwin.

Sorel, G. 1961. *Reflections on Violence.* New York, NY: Collier Books.

De Thierry, C. 1908. *Imperialism.* London: Duckworth.

Wallace, E. 1995. *The Four Just Men.* Oxford: OUP.

Watt, I. 1979. *Conrad in the Nineteenth Century.* Berkeley, CA: University of California Press.

CHAPTER 4

Literary evaluation and poetic form

Poetic form and creative tension

Tom Barney

In this paper I argue that poetic form – a poem's rhyme and stanzaic structure – can and should be used as a means of evaluating a poem. Form is a constraint within which a poet must achieve verbal virtuosity, and it is clearly more difficult to achieve this when the words one may use are partly dictated by the need to compose to a set pattern of lines and rhymes as well as by what one wishes to say. There is a danger that verbal subtlety and the rhetoric of poetry will suffer because of the need to satisfy the dictates of the form. The best poetry both conforms to and transcends its formal constraints. I illustrate this with an examination of the villanelle – an especially tight form and therefore an especially severe test of a poet's technical ability. I make a close formal, syntactic and semantic analysis of two villanelles, Ernest Dowson's *Villanelle of Marguerites* and William Empson's *Reflection from Anita Loos*, and by this means show how Dowson does not and Empson does achieve a subtle use of words and a coherent argument within the form.

For the purposes of this paper I define poetic *form* as the fixed pattern of rhyme and stanzaic structure. It is, that is to say, an aspect of poetic structure which is distinct from metre but like metre provides a regular pattern with which the variable pattern of the words used provides a creative tension.

To compose a poem to a set form is to accept a constraint on the way words may be used. The composer Judith Bingham, speaking of the influence Bram Stoker's *Dracula* had on her piece *Beyond Redemption*, observed in the programme note for the work's premiere that 'When I started to think about this piece, I knew I wanted the Carpathians, visited by me only in my imagination, to be the gameboard on which this orchestral fantasy is played out.' (Programme for BBC Philharmonic Orchestra concert, Free Trade Hall, Manchester, 9 February 1996.) For a poet the form chosen is the 'gameboard', on which its verbal composition must be played out. The need to find rhymes and to confine the argument to a fixed, and perhaps strictly limited, number of lines grouped in a particular way affects what that verbal composition may be.

This paper is intended to make the case for the use of form as one criterion for the evaluation of poetry. How well does the poet exploit a form's possibilities? How well does he or she transcend or overcome the limitations and constraints imposed by the chosen form, while preserving that form intact by strictly observing those constraints? How far does the poet widen by example the bounds of what may be done within the constraints of a form? I explore these questions by examining two poems, by different poets, which are composed in the same form, the villanelle. By keeping form constant we are comparing cases where both poets were subject to similar constraints, ensuring that we have comparability. We can then examine how successfully each poet handles the form, how successfully they each create original and profound content despite the need to observe the formal constraints, how successfully they maintain coherence while observing those constraints and how well their authors resist the severe constraints of the form to achieve a satisfying poem.

Tension between breaking free from and remaining within the bounds of a pattern is a phenomenon which exists at other levels in poetry, for example the tension between metre and speech rhythm, and in other arts as well; the successful handling of these tensions can be shown to be a criterion of evaluation. Christmas card verse, for example, is rarely incompetent in the sense of failing to scan; on the contrary it scans all too well. Its undoubted badness in the matter of prosody consists in the fact that there is no significant tension between metre and rhythm, so that the result sounds like a mere jingle. There is none of the subtlety that allows a regular beat and the suggestion of everyday speech to exist simultaneously. To go to the other extreme of aesthetic quality, Debussy (whose early works were decidedly Wagnerian) surely paid Wagner a compliment when he called Wagner's music 'a beautiful sunset which was mistaken for a dawn' (Griffiths 1978: 25). Debussy's suggestion was that Wagner's harmonic innovations represented not an absolutely new sound-world, but conventional tonality stretched to its utmost limits, its constraints observed but transcended. As Attridge (1995: 12) observes, one of the functions of poetic rhythm is to give a poem unity; but to the extent that one of the functions of art is the reconciliation of disparate elements, when this is successfully done diversity will exist within that unity.

The villanelle

In this paper I choose to examine the villanelle, a form which imposes especially severe constraints on the use of words. A tight form such as this foregrounds sharply the degree of success with which its constraints are transcended; it is thus particularly well suited to an examination of that very question.

The villanelle consists of a series of tercets, usually five, rhyming *aba*, and a final quatrain rhyming *abaa*, making nineteen lines in all. The first and third lines of the first stanza are repeated alternately at the end of the remaining tercets as refrains, so that the second and fourth stanzas end with a repetition of the poem's first line, and the third and fifth stanzas with a repetition of the poem's third line; in the final quatrain both these lines are repeated. This degree of repetition severely limits the amount of new material that can be introduced, because 42% of the lines are occupied by the repeated material, because the repeated lines inevitably constrain what may be said in the remainder, and because the same rhyme-sounds are used throughout. Stillman (1966:95) observes that the villanelle 'lends itself very well to the creation of mood' because of the use of the refrains. Variation, new topics and the advancement of any kind of argument, then, are mainly confined to the first two lines of each stanza. There is also scope for what may be called syntactic punning in the refrains, where the same words in the same order may vary their grammatical status with each occurrence. For example in one of the most famous of all villanelles, Dylan Thomas's *Do not go Gentle into that Good Night*, the verb *Do* in the first refrain, which gives the poem its title, is an imperative verb in its first occurrence at the beginning of the poem, but an active verb in the third person plural when it occurs in the second stanza:

> Though wise men at their end know dark is right,
> Because their words have forked no lightning they
> Do not go gentle into that good night.

The two villanelles I have chosen to examine are Ernest Dowson's (1905) *Villanelle of Marguerites* and William Empson's (1955) *Reflection from Anita Loos*. Empson is described by Gardner and Gardner (1978:90) as 'more associated with the villanelle ... than is any other twentieth-century poet'. They continue:

> As is made clear by comparison with nineteenth century practitioners of the villanelle, Austin Dobson, Wilde and Dowson, Empson's specimen is very much his own. With the exception of Dowson in 'Villanelle of Marguerites', his predecessors employ lighter, three- or four-stress lines, and their villanelles, graceful, nostalgic or bitter-sweet, lack the plangent fullness given by Empson's pentameters and heavy monosyllables.

We may assume from these remarks that our use of *Villanelle of Marguerites* brings us as near to comparability between Empson's villanelles and a *fin de siècle* example as we can be.

Ernest Dowson: *Villanelle of Marguerites*.

'A little, passionately, not at all?'
She casts the snowy petals on the air:
And what care we how many petals fall!

> Nay, wherefore seek the seasons to forestall?
> It is but playing, and she will not care,
> A little, passionately, not at all!
>
> She would not answer us if we should call
> Across the years: her visions are too fair;
> And what care we how many petals fall!
>
> She knows us not, nor recks if she enthrall
> With voice and eyes and fashion of her hair,
> A little, passionately, not at all!
>
> Knee-deep she goes in meadow grasses tall,
> Kissed by the daisies that her fingers tear:
> And what care we how many petals fall!
>
> We pass and go: but she shall not recall
> What men we were, nor all she made us bear:
> '*A little, passionately, not at all!*'
> And what care we how many petals fall!

George Orwell regarded Dowson as one of the better poets of the end of the nineteenth century but, because he believed that this was a poor period for poetry, realised that this was not saying very much. Of Dowson's most famous poem, *Cynara*, he observed:

> I know it is a bad poem, but it is bad in a good way, or good in a bad way, and I do not wish to pretend that I never admired it... Surely those lines possess, if not actual merit, at least the same kind of charm as belongs to a pink geranium or a soft-centre chocolate.
>
> (Orwell 1970: 350)

I too must confess to some enjoyment of Dowson's poetry; it does not deserve to be altogether forgotten. Nonetheless 'charming but at best second-rate' is the judgement I would want to make about it in general, and about *Villanelle of Marguerites* in particular. The poem conveys little more than the vague 'mood' which Stillman suggested villanelles lend themselves to conveying. In other words, Dowson has not broken away from this form's prototypical function.

Except in the first two stanzas, the first line of each stanza begins with a present-tense statement about a person who is referred to simply as 'she'; and the first two stanzas contain such a statement beginning in the second line (which in the first stanza is after all the only line which is not a refrain). Each such statement shifts the poem's topic slightly, but there is no real 'argument': merely a series of loosely connected images. The stanzas can be divided into two groups, those that deal with the woman referred to in some kind of proximity to nature, and those that deal with the woman's attitudes to the body of (presumably) men referred to as 'we', who are in thrall to her. In the first group are the first and fifth stanzas, which refer to the woman's touching wild flowers, and possibly also the second stanza, although it is not clear whether 'wherefore seek the seasons to forestall?' refers literally to the seasons of the year or is some kind of metaphor referring to the possibility of going against human nature. In the second group are the third, fourth and sixth stanzas, and again possibly the second. The stanzas do not, however, occur in any clear planned order, and the statements contained in them consequently give a sense of being somewhat haphazard and self-contained, as if the refrains served mainly to divide the statements in the initial couplets of each stanza from each other.

There is some run-on between the first and second line of most stanzas. In *call/ Across, enthrall/ With* and *recall/ What* the run-on is between a verb and its adverbial or object; in *tall/ Kissed* between two adverbials (*in meadow grasses tall* and *Kissed by the daisies that her fingers tear*) belonging to the same clause. In the third, fourth and sixth stanzas there is a pattern of a long statement followed by a short one or vice versa, the clauses containing the statements being separated by a colon (stanza 3) *nor* (stanza 4) or colon + *but* (stanza 6). The division between long and short or short and long clauses either precedes or follows a run-on; the caesuras formed by the clause divisions facilitate the run-ons since a clause begun mid-line is more likely to overflow the line end than one which begins at the beginning of a line. There is, then, some variation against the set structure of the form, achieved by the way the damming and release of the flow of words is handled, and the consequent variation of what Golomb (1977:95) has called *syntactic length*: 'the actual number of segmental surface-structure elements (e.g. syllables, morphemes, words, phrases, etc.) that make up any given syntactically significant segment (e.g. phrase, clause, sentence... etc.)'. This variation, however, occurs only within the initial couplets of stanzas – the place in a villanelle where variation can most easily occur; the variation carries no resonance into the refrains or across stanzas such as would provide the poem as a whole with greater coherence or extend the possibilities of the form.

The refrains too resist the formal constraints but little. The first refrain, *A little, passionately, not at all!*, constitutes, except in the initial and final stanzas, the adverbial (postmodifying *care* and *enthrall*) to the main clause that precedes it in each stanza it occurs in; in these stanzas there is a very slight degree of run-on between the main clause and the refrain. In the initial and final stanzas this refrain simply abuts the material that follows or precedes it, and quite what the refrain means in these stanzas is unclear. Since the refrain is here printed in italics and enclosed in inverted commas it *may* be speech presentation, but this is not certain. And if it is speech presentation it is not clear who utters it, what its significance is or what relationship it has with the rest of the stanza. This refrain in these cases does nothing but contribute to the creation of a mood; it also contributes some incoherence.

The second refrain, *And what care we how many petals fall!*, occurs logically enough in the first and fifth stanzas, where there are references to wild flowers, and to the woman's tearing off of their petals, in the line that precedes the refrain in each case. In the other two stanzas in which this refrain occurs, however, the lines progress less logically. The refrains divide topically in the same way as the stanzas do, the first refrain belonging more to the 'thraldom' theme and the second to the 'nature' theme. But in the third stanza the second refrain occurs in a stanza whose first two lines are concerned more with the 'thraldom' theme; and it is not clear what petals have to do with calling across the years or with visions. The form dictates that the second refrain has to occur in the third stanza: Dowson seems merely to have used it without having been able to fit it properly into this stanza, which does not deal with its topic. Similarly, in the last stanza the form dictates that both refrains must occur, but the first two lines of the stanza give no *semantic* reason for the second refrain to do so. This, and the obscurity of the first refrain in this stanza, mean that the two refrains, now juxtaposed, do not hang together; there is no neat semantic closure of the poem to match the formal closure; the formal closure indeed operates only by repeating the words of the refrains.

The second refrain also closes off one possibility for variation within the form. This refrain is a main clause, co-ordinated with the main clause(s) which precede it in each stanza, and linked to them by *And*. The use of an unstressed syllable such as *And* is in fact essential to the iambic metre here; but the use of *And* does mean that the syntactic relationship between the refrain and what precedes it cannot be anything but co-ordination. This in turn means that there is no possibility of syntactic punning with this refrain, and so no possibility of any sense of formal tension.

In short, the formal constraints appear to defeat the poet: they trap him into doing without coherent meaning in several aspects, and render him unable to make full use of such scope for variation within the form as does exist. But even a tight form such as the villanelle does not have to do this.

William Empson: *Reflection from Anita Loos.*

No man is sure he does not need to climb.
It is not human to feel safely placed.
'A girl can't go on laughing all the time.'

Wrecked by their games and jeering at their prime
There are who can, but who can praise their taste?
No man is sure he does not need to climb.

Love rules the world but is it rude, or slime?
All nasty things are sure to be disgraced.
A girl can't go on laughing all the time.

Christ stinks of torture who was caught in lime.
No star he aimed at is entirely waste.
No man is sure he does not need to climb.

It is too weak to speak of right and crime.
Gentlemen prefer bound feet and the wasp waist.
A girl can't go on laughing all the time.

It gives a million gambits for a mime
On which a social system can be based:
No man is sure he does not need to climb,
A girl can't go on laughing all the time.

The title of this poem, and its second refrain, are derived, as Empson's own note on the matter in his *Collected Poems* tells us, from the following passage in Anita Loos's *Gentlemen Prefer Blondes*:

> So Dorothy said we might as well go out to Fountainblo with Louie and Robber if Louie would take off his yellow spats that were made out of yellow shammy skin with pink pearl buttons. Because Dorothy said, 'Fun is fun but no girl wants to laugh all of the time.' So Louie is really always anxious to please, so he took off his spats but when he took off his spats, we saw his socks and when we saw his socks we saw that they were Scotch plaid with small size rainbows running through them. So Dorothy looked at them a little while and she really became quite discouraged and she said, 'Well Louie, I think you had better put your spats back on.'

The poem is in Empson's typically dense, allusive style. Gardner and Gardner (1978) summarise it as follows:

> Empson elaborates a view of civilisation (the 'social system' of stanza 6) as a peculiar mixture of good and bad impulses, not amenable to the categoric simplifications of 'right and crime' (right and wrong). (p. 198)

and:

> [The refrains'] common denominator being the human wish for seriousness and improvement. The forms this wish takes – gold-digging, 'social climbing', love, worship – involve a vast range of 'gambits': opening moves which make a sacrifice in the hope of getting something valuable later. These create a 'mime' which either is, or is the basis for, life's 'social system'. (pp. 200–201)

The Gardners do not find this an entirely satisfactory poem. They comment:

> ...although a certain range of nuance is perceptible in its refrains as they recur, this is the least resonant and emotionally involving of Empson's three vil-

lanelles, moving briskly from one laconic end-stopped statement to the next with just enough coherence to maintain a mild intellectual interest. (p. 198)

One implication of this seems to be that Empson has not adequately exploited the villanelle form.

It is true that the great majority of the lines are heavily end-stopped; most line ends are also sentence ends. This poem does not in general share Dowson's use of run-on in the stanzas' initial couplets. There are just two exceptions to this: *prime/ There* in the second stanza, where an initial adverbial leads into a main clause, and *mime/ On* in the last stanza, where a head noun is followed by a prepositional phrase which post-modifies it. These, however, are not strong run-ons, since the line boundaries occur at places which, though the grammatical construction is not complete, are not unnatural places for momentary pauses.

Yet Empson uses end-stopping in such a way that he is not a prisoner of the villanelle form; on the contrary. The progression from one sentence to the next within the confined space of the stanzas – the confined space indeed of the initial couplets of the stanzas – allows the easy movement from one topic to the next, and the building up of the sustained structure of an argument. Within the stanzas the semantic content of the sentences follows logically. For example in the third stanza we infer that *All nasty things are sure to be disgraced* is an answer to, or a comment on, the question in the previous line, *Love rules the world but is it rude or slime?* Again, in the fifth stanza, *Gentlemen prefer bound feet and the wasp waste* illustrates the principle stated in the previous line, *It is too weak to speak of right and crime*: these examples of the subjection of women have in the past been built into the structures of civilisations and were so often accepted as inevitable parts of them – not as the wrong ('crime') they really were.

The array of different topics – love, religion, morality, oppressive social conventions and so on – does not merely contribute to the creation of a mood, but forms a constellation of propositions which add up to a whole, and which are encompassed in the 'social system' of the last stanza. The use of end-stopping also allows shifts of sub-topic within the stanzas as we move from one sentence to the next, for example in the fourth stanza where Christ's passion is referred to in the first line and His ministry in the second. This use of multiple statements on a single general topic increases the quantity of ground which can be covered in the space of the short poem.

Although the topic shifts are effected in the initial couplets of the stanzas, the argument does extend to the refrains; it is not penned in by the non-repeating material. For example in the first stanza the second line, *It is not human to feel safely placed* is a commentary on the first refrain, *No man is sure he does not need to climb*: it gives a reason for the sentiment expressed in the refrain. This use of a refrain in the poem's argument is perhaps more likely to occur in the first stanza, where a refrain is used at the beginning. But something similar happens in the fifth stanza where the refrain *A girl can't go on laughing all the time* comments on the preceding line: as the Gardners observe, the tight-lacing of the wasp waste would literally make laughing difficult.

The refrains do not use syntactic punning but do shift semantically in a way that causes a similar sort of shimmer. For example 'climb' refers in the first two stanzas to what the Gardners (1978: 199) call 'amatory/economic manoeuvres', but in the fourth stanza to heavenly aspirations; while the implications of not laughing all the time vary from the simple idea of momentary relief from frivolity (which is what Anita Loos was expressing) to the more serious point made in the fifth stanza, discussed above. These semantic shifts are effected against the background of the exact repetition of the words of the refrains. It is indeed the cohesion and progression of the argument throughout the poem which constitutes the variation – a remarkably wide variation – against the static form.

Conclusion

Amongst the pleasures we take in well-wrought poetry is the excitement aroused by the accomplished technician and executant. In this poets may be compared with virtuoso musicians, who thrill us by producing sounds whose production demands physical feats which to us, the listeners, are impossible, but which must be performed 'straight off'. Stephen Spender (1946: 64) remarked that 'genius, unlike virtuosity, is judged by greatness of results, not by brilliance of performance.' A creative artist's finest works, that is to say, may have been laboriously produced, whereas a performing artist's finest performances must show virtuosity *as they are produced*. This is true, but in Yeats's famous lines:

> A line will take us hours maybe;
> Yet if it does not seem a moment's thought,
> Our stitching and unstitching has been naught.
> (*Adam's Curse*)

The experience of reading a poem, however difficult it was to write, should be an experience of something that *appears* to be a brilliant spontaneous performance.

If we apply this criterion to the two poems we have examined we find that Dowson sacrifices coherence in order to live within the form – to succeed in writing a villanelle at all. There is little verbal virtuosity. Empson, however, is not intimidated by the strait path of the villanelle form: he overcomes the verbal tight-lacing which in a less skilled poet might have trapped him like the real tight-lacing referred to in the poem. His virtuosity consists in the amount he manages to fit, and fit elegantly, and despite the obligatory repetitions, into the constricted space at his disposal.

What is illustrated in our examination of these two villanelles applies, if less starkly, to all verse forms. This is so even of free verse, the writer of which imposes formal constraints, in the form of line breaks, of his own invention. The mark of the virtuoso writer of free verse is the ability to devise such constraints which have an auditory elegance and rightness, and which can achieve powerful foregrounding effects.

It is possible for a poet to be defeated by a form. 'Defeat' in this sense occurs when the requirement of observing the form allows the form to dictate the content too much; when the need for rhymes and verbal repetitions leads the poet too far astray from coherence and profundity; when in observing the dictates of the form the content comes too close to being the mere use of words. Obviously this is a matter of degree, but Dowson in *Villanelle of Marguerites* borders on defeat of this kind. The criterion by which we should evaluate the successful handling of a form is the extent to which the poet holds sway over the form while still obeying its rules. Success demands both mastery of the form and submission to it.

There is an affinity between this principle and the two conditions which Widdowson (1992:61–62) believes that a satisfactory poem should observe. The first of these, the *divergent condition* is that the poem 'disperses meanings and disrupts established ideas'. This alone, however, would lead to obscurity. The poem should also observe the *convergent condition*: 'the incongruity of the poem and the disruption it causes have to be made congruous, the disorder reassembled into a different order. Its lines have to bring about realignment, so that the divergence of response is made coherent within their limits.' Observing only this condition, however, leads to dullness. In the context of our present discussion it is the satisfactory handling of a poem's content which satisfies the divergent condition, when the poet manages to say a great deal, with depth: profundity implies originality and the disruption of established meanings. The observance of the form, on the other hand, satisfies the convergent condition: it is an established order within which the content unfolds, is interpreted and given context. Widdowson believes that, in the satisfaction of the convergent condition, 'the more patterning that one can discern within a poem, and the more integrated the patterns, the greater its aesthetic potential' (p. 62). A formal scheme such as the villanelle is one of the patterns within which coherence can be established: form provides a reference point which, even in forms that are new to us, is relatively quickly grasped. The very existence of a formal scheme, with its predictable recurrences, gives a settling effect which exerts a contrary pull to the disconcerting effect of the disruption. But these two extremes do not neutralise each other. It is the simultaneous existence of both at full strength which stirs us as readers; when they manage both to conflict *and* peacefully coexist this is one of the things that lead us to give a poem high marks.

More generally, amongst the qualities we admire in an author are successful risk-taking and an intelligence which sees into the depths of a theme; the successful transcendence of a poetic form is simply a special case of these qualities. Without formal constraints which might have defeated the poet no risk is taken; a risk is successfully taken when, within the formal constraints, a theme is explored in a way which provides endless reverberations through repeated re-readings and for successive generations of readers.

References

Attridge, D. 1995. *Poetic Rhythm: An Introduction*. Cambridge: CUP.

Dowson, E. 1905. Villanelle of Marguerites. In *The Poems of Ernest Dowson*, 17. London: The Bodley Head.

Empson, W. 1955. Reflection from Anita Loos. In *Collected Poetms*, 66. London: Chatto & Windus.

Gardner, P. & A. Gardner. 1978. *The God Approached: A Commentary on the Poems of William Empson*. London: Chatto and Windus.

Golomb, H. 1977. Interrelations Between Syntax and Line-division in Poetry: Towards a Syntactic-intonational Theory of Enjambment. PhD dissertation, Tel-Aviv University.

Griffiths, P. 1978. *A Concise History of Modern Music*. London: Thames and Hudson.

Orwell, G. 1970. As I please. In *The Collected Essays, Journalism and Letters of George Orwell*, Volume 4, S. Orwell & I. Angus (eds.), 348–350. Harmondsworth: Penguin.

Spender, S. 1970. The making of a poem In *Creativity*, P. E. Vernon (ed.), 61–76. Harmondsworth: Penguin.

Stillman, F. 1966. *The Poet's Manual and Rhyming Dictionary*. London: Thames and Hudson.

Widdowson, H. 1992. *Practical Stylistics*. Oxford: OUP.

CHAPTER 5

Poetic value

Political value

Laurence Lerner

Critics have tended to rely on tradition to inform us about the quality of literary texts. However, this is not enough, as the test of time does not help explain why quality is attributed. In many cases, it is precisely those works that resist history which are valued. Quality, then, does not depend on tradition but on the elements that make a text verbal art. To illustrate this point, two poems markedly political are contrasted, followed by the comparison of three non-political sonnets. The argument held here is that difference in quality is not a matter of politics or of tradition. It depends on the poet's skill to make art a memorable experience.

I

The traditional way to support value judgements in literature was by an appeal to consensus: standing the test of time, achieving immortality, acceptance by the judgement of the common reader, outlasting marble and the gilded monuments, speaking to us across the centuries. The essentially unhistorical nature of this appeal does not worry the believer in eternal values: it is precisely through its resistance to history that literary and artistic value is manifested.

Of course we have grown sceptical, in the late 20th century, about the unchanging nature of values. 'Immortality' now means simply 'lasting a long time'; and we now know that the test of time does not offer an unaltered and unalterable list of successful candidates. But all the same, the list does not change very much. Who are the great Romantic poets? For over a century the list was stable: Wordsworth, Coleridge, Byron, Shelley and Keats. In our century, Blake has been added, Shelley was questioned by the New Critics, Clare has been proposed, especially by those sympathetic to the idea of a poet sprung from the common people, but the list, though frayed at the edges, is still very similar to the one Matthew Arnold would have given.

The invocation of tradition, then, is valuable in telling us (more or less) what poems have been continually admired; but it cannot tell us why. Critics appeal to the test of time instead of identifying what elements in a poem are responsible for its success.

This essay is an attempt to do just that: to ask how far a difference in quality that is generally agreed on can be explained and defended.

II

Two poets sat down in the 1790s to write a political poem, fiercely critical of the existing social order. Here is what they produced:

The Birth-Day

Here bounds the gaudy, gilded chair,
    Bedecked with fringe and tassels gay;
The melancholy mourner there
    Pursues her sad and painful way.

Here, guarded by a motley train,
    The pampered Countess glares along;
There, wrung by poverty and pain,
    Pale misery mingles with the throng.

Here, as the blazoned chariot rolls,
    And prancing horses scare the crowd,
Great names, adorning little souls,
    Announce the empty, vain and proud.

Here four tall lacqueys slow precede
    A painted dame in rich array;
There, the sad, shivering child of need
    Steals barefoot o'er the flinty way.

'Room, room! Stand back!', they loudly cry,
    The wretched poor are driven around;
On every side they scattered fly,
    And shrink before the threatening sound.

Here, amidst jewels, feathers, flowers,
    The senseless Duchess sits demure,
Heedless of all the anguished hours
    The sons of modest worth endure.

All silvered and embroidered o'er,
    She neither knows nor pities pain;
The beggar freezing at her door
    She overlooks with nice disdain.

The wretch whom poverty subdues
    Scarce dares to raise his tearful eye;
Or if by chance the throng he views,
    His loudest murmur is a sigh!

The poor wan mother, at whose breast
    The pining infant craves relief,
In one thin tattered garment dressed,
    Creeps forth to pour the plaint of grief.

But ah! how little heeded here
    The faltering tongue reveals its woe;
For high-born fools, with frown austere,
    Condemn the pangs they never know.

'Take physic, Pomp!' let Reason say;
    'What can avail thy trappings rare?
The tomb shall close thy glittering day,
    The beggar prove thy equal there!'

           Mary Robinson, 'The Birth-Day' in *Poetical Works* (1806)

London

I wander thro' each charter'd street,
Near where the charter'd Thames does flow,
And mark in every face I meet
Marks of weakness, marks of woe.

In every cry of every Man,
In every Infant's cry of fear,
In every voice, in every ban,
The mind-forg'd manacles I hear:
How the Chimney-sweeper's cry
Every blackning Church appalls,
And the hapless Soldier's sigh
Runs in blood down Palace walls.
But most thro' midnight streets I hear

> How the youthful Harlot's curse
> Blasts the new-born Infant's tear,
> And blights with plagues the Marriage hearse.
>
> William Blake, 'London' from *Songs of Experience* (1794)

If human history is the story of exploiters and exploited, it should not be difficult to construct a radical poem. It will set rich and poor against each other in a series of contrasts, and if in (for instance) quatrains, it can follow two lines about the privileged with two lines about the wretched, clinching each contrast by the rhyme. If the aim is to excite indignation, the poor will regard the rich with envy and longing, and the rich will regard the poor with indifference and disdain: 'disdain', in fact, makes a good rhyme-word; so does 'sigh' ('tearful eye') and 'grief' ('craving relief'). If a series of stanzas built on this simple contrast begins to sound monotonous, one can observe that monotony is the flip side of cumulative insistence: if social injustice is universal and apparently irremovable, then calling attention to it ought to sound monotonous. As the poem nears its end, the pace can be slowed so that the poor are brought more into the centre: they can be allowed a whole stanza, perhaps even two, and the rich be relegated to the function of not noticing.

And how should such a poem end? With a reversal, surely, in which the rich are in some way unseated, so that the poor either become their equals, or replace them. If the poem were by Auden's Utopian it might look up at the lit windows of the Citadel, where the police are busy beating up political prisoners all night, and reflect 'One fine night our boys will be working up there'.[1] Such confidence is rare among poets nowadays; and one would like to think that such grim purposefulness is rare among everyone – but that is no doubt to reveal one's own political leanings. Traditionally, it has been commoner to hand the revolutionary function over to the one leveller who can be totally relied on:

> Death lays his icy hand on kings.
> > Sceptre and crown
> > Must tumble down
> And in the dust be equal laid
> With the poor crooked scythe and spade.[2]

The blueprint of a radical poem which I have been constructing is, the reader will have noticed, more or less the poem that Robinson wrote. The contrast between rich and poor on which it is based is clear and explicit: five stanzas begin 'Here',

---

1. W. H. Auden, 'Horae Canonicae: Vespers', from *The Shield of Achilles* (1955).

2. James Shirley, 'The glories of our blood and state' from *Ajax & Ulysses* (1659).

referring to the rich and three of them balance it with 'there' in line 3. The third stanza introduces no contrasting 'there', but does offer a contrast within the description of the rich ('great names adorning little souls'). Sometimes the verbal device for introducing the contrast will vary: instead of 'here ... there' we can have 'here ... heedless of', or a simple contrast in action, as the lacqueys shout 'stand back' and the poor scatter. The variant in Stanza 7 is, in terms of the presentation of the contrast, the most interesting. The first two lines deal with the Duchess, silvered and indifferent, and line 3 begins 'the beggar freezing at her door'. If the poem was in an inflected language, it would not be possible for us to assume, as we here do for a moment, that we are now to be shifted to the beggar's consciousness, so that the stanza will probably end 'Knows only hunger, cold and rain', or to his actions ('Holds out his pleading hand in vain'). In fact, the poem imitates the Duchess, denying any autonomy to the beggar, reducing him from 'der Bettler' to 'den Bettler'.

This is not a revolutionary poem: Death-the-Leveller poems never are. The glories of our blood and state may be shadows not substantial things, but if regarding them as shadows is the price of continuing to enjoy them, the rich and the powerful will be quite willing to pay it. If Death will make us all equal in the end, then the egalitarian job can be left to him: this will save us having to do it while we're still alive. Sceptre and crown will be equal to the poor crooked scythe in death – but not till then.

What a well-behaved poem Mary Robinson has written. It is metrically well-behaved, structurally well-behaved, and politically well-behaved. Its generous indignation is subversive neither of the norms of poetic discourse nor of the social structure. Is that what inevitably happens in a poem of social protest?

That it is not becomes clear as soon as we turn to 'London'. The first and most obvious contrast offered by Blake's poem is the use of the first person – an insistent, repetitive use, telling us that this is an individual's vision of London society, not an objective account. It might be thought that this would weaken the radical impact, and it is not easy to say why it does not: I can only suggest that if the speaker establishes himself as both fiercely indignant and perceptive, then our awareness of him as the speaker could actually strengthen the impact of what he notices.

The homology between social attitude and poetic strategy that was so striking in 'The Birth-Day' has disappeared in this poem. Now directness of passion is combined with verbal subtlety in a way one would hardly have thought possible. Look, to begin with, at 'charter'd'. The repetition insists that we read in anger, yet at the same time draws attention to the shift in meaning. There is, first of all, the ambiguity between a charter as a stuffy old document that grants privileges and restrictions, and a charter as offering freedom, so that in the very first line the poem seems to invite contrasting readings: London is a place where everything is regulated, even the river; or, London is liberated by a charter which was granted to every street – even the river, and therefore means nothing. Both indignant.

The simplest stanza is the second, where the indignation mounts with each repetition; and the subtlest, almost beyond analysis, is the third. 'Appalls' can mean 'shocks' or 'casts a pall over', 'church' is both institution and building; 'blackning' can be active or passive. As an institution the church blackens the moral scene; as a building it grows blacker, from the soot shed by the chimney-sweeper. Soldier is also an ambiguous figure: is he a deserter being shot, or, (a subtler reading, surely) a reluctant trooper crushing a riot – in both cases, the charter'd streets are the scene of oppression.

As for the final stanza, the crucial ambiguity resides in 'curse'. The fact that the poet hears it in the street suggests that the harlot, oppressed by society and perhaps even abandoned by the groom, shouts at the bridal carriage and makes it feel like a hearse to the pair riding in it; but if the harlot's curse is venereal disease, then what the poet is hearing is the lamentation of the parents, and the hearse is literally a hearse.

It should be clear by now that Blake's poem is radical in two senses. It is filled with indignation against the social order; at the same time it subverts our demand for clarity, since the meaning it offers constantly shifts into something else. If we describe both these effects as radical, are we indulging in the same kind of verbal shifting as the poem? Is the political impact of the poem strengthened or weakened by this verbal subversion?

There are two possible answers to this. What we might call the commonsense answer says that it is obviously weakened: the more we are thrown into linguistic confusion (or into the pleasure of sorting out what looked at first like confusion) the more we are distracted from the political message: does the poet want us to enjoy his skill, or does he want us to rally to his cause? But the politics of representation – the view that the form of representation chosen always has a political dimension – will reply that the really radical act is to undermine our confidence in the clear statements which enable established society to function. The most extreme form of this is perhaps the claim of Roland Barthes, that clear statements of the obvious, of the 'va-sans-dire', are a form of totalitarianism, that 'that which is paradoxical, that which cannot be brought within good sense', will always be liberating.[3]

---

3.   This view is frequently found in Barthes' critical writings: a particularly forceful and explicit statement of it is found in *Roland barthes par roland barthes*, in the series *Ecrivains de toujours* (Paris, Editions du Seuil, 1975): 'Il ne sortait pas de cette idée sombre, que la vraie violence, c'est celle du *cela-va-de-soi*: ce qui est évident est violent, même si cette évidence est représentée doucement, libéralement, démocratiquentent; ce qui est paradoxal, ce qui ne tombe pas sous le sens, l'est moins, même si c'est imposé arbitrairement; un tyran qui promulguerait des lois

It is doubtful if this issue can be settled by argument. I can simply declare my allegiance to what I have called the commonsense view, since the function of political radicalism is to replace oppressive elements in society by an improved version: the programme of the constructive radical needs clarity just as much as the conservative programme does. It is quite arguable that the kind of linguistic subversion Blake is indulging in has a conservative function, since it inhibits rational exploration of alternatives to oppression. But I want to argue that it is non-political. The conservative reader of 'London' can delight in the poetry and regard the radicalism with a tolerant smile; the radical reader can delight in the poetry and forget, for a while, the task of translating radical indignation into a programme the poetry-loving reader will become a kind of provisional radical, by willing suspension of disbelief, and how this relates to his actual political beliefs is suspended.

I conclude that the superiority of Blake's poem to Robinson's (which I hope is obvious) is not a matter of politics.

III

What is now required to balance the discussion is a comparison between two conservative poems: but this is not quite as easy to provide as one might expect. It is, arguably, part of the nature of conservatism that it does not see things as politically as do radicals: defending the present order against proposed changes, or preferring the past to changes that have already happened, it tends to see the order it is defending as natural, and the interference of meddling do-gooders as an unnecessary dragging in of politics. The disputes between conservative and radical often take the form of disagreement on whether we should see things in political terms at all: the radical may regard an institution, or an opinion, as designed to protect existing power-relations which the conservative may see as part of the normal functioning of society. Nostalgia, love of ceremony, even the simple celebration of the beauty of order, are emotions that can be seen in this double way.[4]

---

saugrenues serait à tout prendre moins violent qu'une masse qui se contenterait d'énoncer *ce qui va de soi*: le 'naturel' est en somme *le dernier des outrages*' (p. 88).

4. The cultural materialists are of course the critics who have most forcefully tried to politicise issues that had previously (naively in their view) been seen as non-political. The position is well formulated by Alan Sinfield in his Introduction to *Society & Literature 1945-1970* (Methuen 1983): 'Literature ... is involved in the process of self-understanding in the past and present ... by developing, through the refractive lenses of literary conventions, constructions of conceivable lives... And these constructions are not just responses, they are interventions ... helping society ... to interpret and constitute itself.' I regard this as a valuable but limited truth: I shall make

That is my apology – if one is needed – for choosing three poems that may not immediately strike the reader as political. All are sonnets, and all are by the same author:

Rural Ceremony

Closing the sacred Book which long has fed
Our meditations, give we to a day
Of annual joy, one tributary lay;
This day, when, forth by rustic music led,
The village Children, while the sky is red
With evening lights, advance in long array
Through the still churchyard, each with garland gay,
That, carried scepter-like, o'ertops the head
Of the proud Bearer. To the wide church-door,
Charged with these offerings which their fathers bore
For decoration in the Papal time,
The innocent Procession softly moves: _
The spirit of Laud is pleased in Heaven's pure clime,
And Hooker's voice the spectacle approves.

> Wordsworth, 'Rural Ceremony' is no XXXII of the
> *Ecclesiastical Sonnets* Part III (1822)

Few readers are likely to reel much enthusiasm for this rather humdrum sonnet, with its laboured opening, its commonplace epithets and its inversion ('garland gay') for the sake merely of rhyme. The poem has no glaring blemishes, and no obvious reason for being a poem. That it has a political dimension, however, is suggested by the title of the series, *Ecclesiastical Sonnets*: most of the poems are, in one way or another, about ecclesiastical politics.

No doubt Wordsworth thought of this sonnet as non-political, a celebration of a rustic custom that gave to the church a social function which the villagers enjoyed. It is a celebration of ordinariness, and that in itself is politically ambivalent: if ordinary folk are contrasted with great ones (as they often are in Wordsworth) then the implications are – surely – democratic; but if they are contrasted with meddling intellectuals (as they also are in Wordsworth!) or with malcontents, then the implication is conservative. In this sonnet there is no explicit contrast, but ceremony is placed in a wider context by the mention of Laud and Hooker, both of whom are placed on a higher plane: Laud is in Heaven, and Hooker 'approves' – the very last word of the poem turns us from simply enjoying the procession to reflecting on what it stands for. No-one could regard these two great ecclesias-

---

use of this approach in discussing Wordsworth's sonnets, while at the same time abandoning it when I think it ceases to be helpful.

tical statesmen as non-political figures: the poem concludes by telling us that this seemingly innocent local ceremony belongs in the great tradition of the established Church. What seemed to begin as the pleased observation of a villager, perhaps a parent, watching the children troop past turns at the end into a public statement: placing this rustic event in a larger context shows that we are good Anglicans and good subjects.

Something of the way this poem operates can be seen by comparing two of its adjectives: 'proud' and 'innocent'. The word 'proud' is rendered innocent by the way it is used: the only pride is that of the children given the chance to show off, and this seems to say that there is no great significance to this childlike event. But with 'innocent' something like the opposite occurs: its obvious meaning is to confirm the non-political nature of the procession – we all know that children are innocent – but it is so immediately followed by the last two lines with their invoking of Laud and Hooker, that it seems to enlist the children in making a political claim. Their innocence is betrayed, by the word 'innocent'.

Written in London, September 1802

0 Friend! I know not which way I must look
For comfort, being, as I am, opprest,
To think that now our life is only drest
For show; mean handy-work of craftsmen, cook
Or groom! – we must run glittering like a brook
In the open sunshine, or we are unblest;
The wealthiest man among us is the best:
No grandeur now in nature or in book
Delights us. Rapine, avarice, expense,
This is idolatry; and these we adore:
Plain living and high thinking are no more:
The homely beauty of the good old cause
Is gone; our peace, our fearful innocence,
And pure religion breathing household laws.

'Written in London, September 1802': no. XIII of the
Poems Dedicated to National Independence and Liberty

All the *Sonnets Dedicated to National Independence and Liberty* are imbued with similar emotion: patriotic defiance, nostalgia, and denunciation of the 'fen Of stagnant waters' which England is now becoming. The above is one of the less celebrated of them – deservedly so, I believe.

The subject of this poem is easily stated: *laus temporis acti*, the praise of past time, lamenting the decline in values of the present; and it suffers from most of the defects that lurk to threaten such poems – or indeed all such laments, whether in prose or verse. The assertions about the decadence of the present lean unquestioningly on their abstract nouns ('rapine, avarice, expense'), or make statements for whose truth it is hard to think what evidence could be brought forward ('The wealthiest man among us is the best'). Positive evaluation is attached so completely to the past, negative so exclusively to the present, that the poem soon becomes predictable.

Is this a poetic or a political criticism? Both for the poet, and for the politician denouncing the world around him, abstractions are too easy, and lists of abstractions easier still: there is no need to look carefully at contemporary society if all you are finding there is 'rapine, avarice, expense'. This poem does, however, contain some truly Wordsworthian language, the language of holy awe and natural piety which constitutes his poetic fingerprint,[5] here represented above all by 'plain living and high thinking' – a phrase that has passed into the language[6] – and by the last line. We could, surely, imagine a poem in which this reverential language was attached to the present, and the crude dismissive abstractions ('mean handywork', 'only drest for show') were attached to the past. Such a poem would be free of the ideological objections I have suggested, but clearly no better as poetry.

Or could we? Is there not something inherently nostalgic about 'pure religion breathing household laws'? It is not the way we talk about our own world when we are being merely descriptive; it seems to imply a contrast, in this case between the idealized past and a corrupt present, perhaps also between a present seen as under threat and the brutal invasion which threatens it. It is necessary to mention this alternative since so many of the sonnets in this series are better described as patriotic than as conservative, and deal with the situation of a society threatened by 'slaves, vile as ever were befooled by words' (*Poems Dedicated to National Independence*, Part I, no. XXIV*), a society whose very frailty lends a magic to the 'breathing of the common wind' ('To Toussaint L'Ouverture', *ibid.* no. VIII) that permeates them at their best.

---

5.   Critics of Wordsworth vary a great deal in the terms they use to describe his characteristic poetic effects, but I believe these often very different vocabularies show considerable agreement in substance. Here is a short scattering of critical extracts, which seem to me, when put together, to converge as a description of what I refer to as the Wordsworthian natural piety, the hushed awe before his own sentience of natural processes: 'He laid us as we lay at birth /On the cool flowery lap of earth;/Smiles broke from us and we had ease./ The hills were round us, and the breeze...' (Matthew Arnold 1850). 'Wordsworth's inmost intuition of *what it means to be alive*, to be a mind receiving the universe.' (Lascelles Abercrombie 1952). 'The pulse of the heart and englobulation of the blood, which were inseparable from the life-process itself.' (John Beer 1978). 'The permanence of the physical universe seems to anchor the divine beauty of the human mind.' (Kenneth Johnston 1984).

6.   Bartlett's *Familiar Quotations* includes the last four lines of the sonnet.

The conflict between Wordsworth's language of the love of ordinary things and the stridency of political insistence is very clear in lines 5–6. How very Wordsworthian is that brook glittering in the open sunshine; and how very un-Wordsworthian is the idea that you can tell anyone to run like a brook or else he will be unblest. The utter naturalness of the imagery is destroyed by its being harnessed as a moral imperative. This, surely, is what offended Keats when he complained that Wordsworth 'bullies us into a certain Philosophy engendered in the whims of an egoist', and declared his impatience with poetry 'that has a palpable design on the reader, and if we do not agree seems to put its hand in its breeches pocket.' (Keats, Letter to J. H. Reynolds, 3 February 1818).

I conclude – hesitantly – from this discussion that there is more than a merely verbal felicity in the expression of natural piety in Wordsworth's political sonnets: that the reverence which finds its way into the inimitable Wordsworthian phrasing (language that differs so little from ordinary prose, and yet becomes so memorable that it is immediately recognisable as Wordsworth) somehow depends on a contrast with what threatens to destroy it.

And now, finally, we need a poem of high quality that seems based on the same ideological position.

Mutability

From low to high doth dissolution climb,
And sink from high to low, along a scale
Of awful notes, whose concord shall not fail;
A musical but melancholy chime,
Which they can hear who meddle not with crime,
Nor avarice, nor over-anxious care.
Truth fails not; but her outward forms that bear
The longest date do melt like frosty rime,
That in the morning whitened hill and plain
And is no more; drop like the tower sublime
Of yesterday, which royally did wear
His crown of weeds, but could not even sustain
Some casual shout that broke the silent air,
Or the unimaginable touch of time.

No. XXXIV of *Ecclesiastical Sonnets* Part III

It may seem inconsistent, after castigating the too glib use of abstract nouns in the previous sonnets, to prefer a poem which is not about a particular person, building or event – not about *anything* in particular – and whose very subject is an abstract noun. Indeed, to begin with the negative case, the first few lines of the poem are not very different from the usual style of the *Ecclesiastical Sonnets*, insisting that to 'hear' the music of dissolution we must not meddle 'with crime, nor avarice, nor over-anxious care': easily the most moralising moment in the poem. And then 'Truth fails not': at first glance, the same sort of dogmatic assertion, governed by an abstract noun, as permeates the National Independence sonnets – 'the anarchy of terror', or 'Advance, dear Liberty' (*Poems Dedicated to National Independence*, Part I no. XXIV; and Part II no. X), but in this case, I suggest, wholly successful poetically, and moving. Followed by a series of haunting images for mutability, this simple statement in three monosyllables (no bolstering adverbs, no lists of abstractions) takes on an air of desperation, even of longing, and does not try to bluster its way out of the haunted melancholy that envelops the latter part of the poem.

Some of the verbal devices can be noted. There is the sequence by which we are first told that truth melts like frosty rime, then given a vivid picture of the presence of the frost, followed finally by the sadly simple 'And is no more.' Or the perfect placing of the monosyllable 'drop' at the beginning of its sentence, mimetic of the suddenness of the tower collapsing (we notice the collapse before we notice the tower), and the arbitrariness of 'some casual shout'. But much of the effect of these lines is too mysterious for its precise verbal cause to be identified: hence the wonderful appropriateness of 'unimaginable' in the last line. The touch of time works on the tower with the same elusiveness that the verbal quality of the poem works on its argument: we cannot predict the moment of collapse, nor explain how the poetry works on us. Beauty, like mutability, is both vividly imagined, and unimaginable.

What we learn from this poem is that some forms of abstraction can be very concrete indeed. Poetry requires not the avoidance of generalised or abstract subjects, but the ability to turn them, by means of its verbal art, into experience.

Two brief concluding points. Once again, the difference in quality is not a matter of politics. If we are to extract political implications from the poem – if we are to regard it as an 'intervention' into the social situation – we shall find nothing but the generalised conservatism we have already detected in so many undistinguished sonnets.

Finally: if any reader finds another sonnet, by Wordsworth which no-one has ever bothered to praise or put into an anthology, and can show that it uses much the same verbal devices as 'Mutability', and that all the verbal effects I have singled out for praise can be found there too, I would of course begin by reading it to discover if it was a neglected masterpiece; and if, as is probable, the answer to this was No, I would not conclude that my praise of 'Mutability' was misguided, but rather that my attempt to explain the reasons for its superiority as a poem had not, after all, succeeded.

CHAPTER 6

"Too soon transplanted"
Coleridge and the forms of dislocation

David S. Miall

In 1797 and 1798 Coleridge wrote two poems with rather similar topics, "To the Rev. George Coleridge" and "Frost at Midnight." The first is largely unread while the second is frequently and repeatedly anthologized, and is generally considered a significant part of the canon of English poetry. As a "Conversation Poem" the second seems to invite the participation of the reader; in the first, in contrast, the reader remains an observer. An analysis of the sound patterns and structure of the poems is undertaken, which shows how the poems differ at the formal level in a number of ways. Unlike the first poem, the feelings evoked in the reader by "Frost" invite self-referential exploration. It is argued that this process typifies literary works that become canonical.

To the Rev. George Coleridge
of Ottery St. Mary, Devon With some Poems

Notus in fratres animi paterni.
Hor. *Carm*. lib. II. 2.

A blessèd lot hath he, who having passed
His youth and early manhood in the stir
And turmoil of the world, retreats at length,
With cares that move, not agitate the heart,
To the same dwelling where his father dwelt;
And haply views his tottering little ones
Embrace those agèd knees and climb that lap,
On which first kneeling his own infancy
Lisp'd its brief prayer. Such, O my earliest Friend!
10 Thy lot, and such thy brothers too enjoy.
At distance did ye climb Life's upland road,
Yet cheer'd and cheering: now fraternal love
Hath drawn you to one centre. Be your days
Holy, and blest and blessing may ye live!

To me the Eternal Wisdom hath dispens'd
A different fortune and more different mind –
Me from the spot where first I sprang to light
Too soon transplanted, ere my soul had fix'd
Its first domestic loves; and hence through life
20 Chasing chance-started friendships. A brief while
Some have preserv'd me from life's pelting ills;

Frost at Midnight

The Frost performs its secret ministry,
Unhelped by any wind. The owlet's cry
Came loud – and hark, again! loud as before.
The inmates of my cottage, all at rest,
Have left me to that solitude, which suits
Abstruser musings: save that at my side
My cradled infant slumbers peacefully.
'Tis calm indeed! so calm, that it disturbs
And vexes meditation with its strange
10 And extreme silentness. Sea, hill, and wood,
This populous village! Sea, and hill, and wood,
With all the numberless goings-on of life,
Inaudible as dreams! the thin blue flame
Lies on my low-burnt fire, and quivers not;
Only that film, which fluttered on the grate,
Still flutters there, the sole unquiet thing.
Methinks, its motion in this hush of nature
Gives it dim sympathies with me who live,
Making it a companionable form,
20 Whose puny flaps and freaks the idling Spirit
By its own moods interprets, every where
Echo or mirror seeking of itself,
And makes a toy of Thought.

But, like a tree with leaves of feeble stem,
If the clouds lasted, and a sudden breeze
Ruffled the boughs, they on my head at once
Dropped the collected shower; and some most false,
False and fair-foliag'd as the Manchineel,
Have tempted me to slumber in their shade
E'en mid the storm; then breathing subtlest damps,
Mix'd their own venom with the rain from Heaven,
30 That I woke poison'd! But, all praise to Him
Who gives us all things, more have yielded me
Permanent shelter; and beside one Friend,
Beneath the impervious covert of one oak,
I've rais'd a lowly shed, and know the names
Of Husband and of Father; not unhearing
Of that divine and nightly-whispering Voice,
Which from my childhood to maturer years
Spake to me of predestinated wreaths,
Bright with no fading colours!

                    Yet at times
40 My soul is sad, that I have roam'd through life
Still most a stranger, most with naked heart
At mine own home and birth-place: chiefly then,
When I remember thee, my earliest Friend!
Thee, who didst watch my boyhood and my youth;
Didst trace my wanderings with a father's eye;
And boding evil yet still hoping good,
Rebuk'd each fault, and over all my woes
Sorrow'd in silence! He who counts alone
The beatings of the solitary heart,
50 That Being knows, how I have lov'd thee ever,
Lov'd as a brother, as a son rever'd thee!
Oh! 'tis to me an ever new delight,
To talk of thee and thine: or when the blast
Of the shrill winter, rattling our rude sash,
Endears the cleanly hearth and social bowl;
Or when, as now, on some delicious eve,
We in our sweet sequester'd orchard-plot
Sit on the tree crook'd earth-ward; whose old boughs,
That hang above us in an arborous roof,
60 Stirr'd by the faint gale of departing May,
Send their loose blossoms slanting o'er our heads!

    Nor dost not thou sometimes recall those hours,
When with the joy of hope thou gavest thine ear
To my wild firstling-lays. Since then my song
Hath sounded deeper notes, such as beseem
Or that sad wisdom folly leaves behind,
Or such as, tuned to these tumultuous times,
Cope with the tempest's swell!

                    These various strains,
Which I have fram'd in many a various mood,
70 Accept, my Brother! and (for some perchance
Will strike discordant on thy milder mind)
If aught of error or intemperate truth
Should meet thine ear, think thou that riper Age
Will calm it down, and let thy love forgive it!

                    But O! how oft,
How oft, at school, with most believing mind,
Presageful, have I gazed upon the bars,
To watch that fluttering *stranger*! and as oft
With unclosed lids, already had I dreamt
Of my sweet birth-place, and the old church-tower,
Whose bells, the poor man's only music, rang
30 From morn to evening, all the hot Fair-day,
So sweetly, that they stirred and haunted me
With a wild pleasure, falling on mine ear
Most like articulate sounds of things to come!
So gazed I, till the soothing things, I dreamt,
Lulled me to sleep, and sleep prolonged my dreams!
And so I brooded all the following morn,
Awed by the stern preceptor's face, mine eye
Fixed with mock study on my swimming book:
Save if the door half opened, and I snatched
40 A hasty glance, and still my heart leaped up,
For still I hoped to see the *stranger's* face,
Townsman, or aunt, or sister more beloved,
My play-mate when we both were clothed alike!

  Dear Babe, that sleepest cradled by my side,
Whose gentle breathings, heard in this deep calm,
Fill up the intersperséd vacancies
And momentary pauses of the thought!
My babe so beautiful! it thrills my heart
With tender gladness, thus to look at thee,
50 And think that thou shalt learn far other lore,
And in far other scenes! For I was reared
In the great city, pent 'mid cloisters dim,
And saw nought lovely but the sky and stars.
But *thou*, my babe! shalt wander like a breeze
By lakes and sandy shores, beneath the crags
Of ancient mountain, and beneath the clouds,
Which image in their bulk both lakes and shores
And mountain crags: so shalt thou see and hear
The lovely shapes and sounds intelligible
60 Of that eternal language, which thy God
Utters, who from eternity doth teach
Himself in all, and all things in himself.
Great universal Teacher! he shall mould
Thy spirit, and by giving make it ask.

  Therefore all seasons shall be sweet to thee,
Whether the summer clothe the general earth
With greenness, or the redbreast sit and sing
Betwixt the tufts of snow on the bare branch
Of mossy apple-tree, while the nigh thatch
70 Smokes in the sun-thaw; whether the eave-drops fall
Heard only in the trances of the blast,
Or if the secret ministry of frost
Shall hang them up in silent icicles,
Quietly shining to the quiet Moon.

1. Introduction

During 1797 and most of 1798 Samuel Taylor Coleridge (1772–1834) was living in a cottage on the edge of Nether Stowey, a small town in rural Somerset on the edge of the Quantock Hills. He celebrated his domestic situation in several poems. Two of these, of similar style and length, compare his current situation with his unhappy childhood: "To the Rev. George Coleridge," written in May 1797, and "Frost at Midnight," dated February 1798. Both poems are effective in providing a vivid sense of Coleridge's feelings, both in the present and in the past, and both enable us to share Coleridge's perspective on who he was in the past and how he comes to be who he is in the present. Yet the first poem is now read by almost no-one except the Coleridge scholar, whereas the second is frequently and repeatedly read, not only by scholars, but by numerous students and ordinary readers, since it has for many years been reprinted in every major anthology of English poetry.[1] Its prominence is also evident in the considerable secondary literature on the poem: especially over the last thirty years, "Frost at Midnight" has been the focus of numerous critical articles and chapters in books (e.g., Everest, Wheeler, Eldridge, Miall 1989; Fulford, Plug, Magnuson).

Why has the fate of the poems been so different? In this essay I assess some of the differences between the poems in their language, structure, and rhetoric. I will argue that at each of these levels the poems create an implied reader, but despite the similarities in the topics of the poems, one reader remains an observer whereas the other becomes a participant. I will conclude with some suggestions about how far this distinction might underlie the question of literary evaluation.

2. Rhetoric and figurative structures

The rhetoric of these two poems is characteristic of Coleridge. For most of the twentieth century a small group of Coleridge's poems, termed Conversation Poems, has held a central place in the canon of British Romantic writing. Of these, four are frequently anthologized: "The Eolian Harp" (first written in 1795), "This Lime-Tree Bower My Prison" (1797), "Frost at Midnight" (1798), and "Dejection: An Ode" (1802). The term Conversation Poem originates with Coleridge: a poem first printed in *Lyrical Ballads* (1798) is entitled by him "The Nightingale; a Conversational Poem, written in April, 1798." It was the early twentieth century critic George McLean Harper who in an essay of 1925 (reprinted in Abrams) first iden-

---

1. Usually reprinted from the text of Coleridge's final version, published in 1829. However, the first version of 1798 has been printed in some recent anthologies, e.g., Wu (1994). In this paper my discussion is based on the 1829 text.

tified eight of Coleridge's poems as sharing the conversational mode: his term "Conversation Poem" has been employed to identify the poems ever since (as a contrast to Coleridge's "supernatural poems": "Kubla Khan," "The Rime of the Ancient Mariner," and "Christabel"). Although "To the Rev. George Coleridge" shares most of the major stylistic and formal characteristics of this group, Harper did not include it in his list, a decision that implicitly excludes the poem from canonical status.

Each of the Conversation Poems in Harper's canon engages with Coleridge's immediate perceptions, following them as if in "real time" as the poem itself unfolds. Each also appears to be addressed to a named person, such as his wife Sara Coleridge ("The Eolian Harp"), his sleeping infant Hartley Coleridge ("Frost at Midnight"), or William and Dorothy Wordsworth ("The Nightingale"), although each poem is a kind of dramatic monologue in which the addressee is given no voice. In most of the poems, however, Coleridge appears to invite the addressee to notice his perceptions and to empathise with and benefit from them. In this way they appear to require a response from the reader, even though the reader's situation might be quite different from that of the poet. I will suggest that this apparent accessibility of the poems underlies the high valuation placed upon them over the last seventy years. "To the Rev. George Coleridge," in contrast, while addressed to Coleridge's eldest brother (which would appear to qualify it as a Conversation Poem), forestalls the participatory response that is called for in the more successful Conversation Poems.[2] Leaving the reader with nothing to do other than witness the progress of Coleridge's feelings and his accompanying claims, may be responsible for the obscurity in which this poem has remained.

As a child, Coleridge spent his early years in a small town in rural Devonshire, where his father was minister of the church. But he was removed to school in London at the age of nine, following the death of his father. Coleridge's resulting homesickness and fear of the headmaster, The Rev. James Bowyer, formed a key memory for the remainder of his life. This memory is a critical reference point for both poems. In "To the Rev. George Coleridge" we read: "Me from the spot where first I sprang to light / [was] Too soon transplanted" (17–18). In "Frost at Midnight," having referred to his "sweet birth-place" (28) Coleridge remarks that "I was reared / In the great city, pent 'mid cloisters dim" (51–52). In the first poem

---

2.   Kelvin Everest (one of the few critics to notice it) remarks that the poem "is in many respects a conversation poem, but it fails because Coleridge is too nervous about his audience to get talking" (p. 151). This is not quite correct, I think: Coleridge fills the poem with too many abstractions (especially the generalizations of the opening), and it lacks that sense of immediacy, of thought unfolding in the present, that is notable in the Conversation Poems. Humphry House, in one of the best early accounts of "Frost at Midnight," remarks that "the poem as a whole leaves us with a quite extraordinary sense of the mind's *very being*." (p. 81).

Coleridge frames his experience as a case history; the second poem on the other hand models a process to which we have all have been liable. The first attempts, but largely fails, to elicit a general truth from Coleridge's specific experience; the second makes the specific experience an occasion for the resonance of some parallel experience of the reader. In the first, some information about Coleridge's background seems obligatory to understand the poem; in the second, such information is incidental – helpful but inessential. How does Coleridge manage to engage his readers in the second poem but exclude them from the first? I will argue that the formal qualities of the later poem are what chiefly distinguish it and constitute the basis for the high valuation now placed upon it.

In the first poem, the addressee, George Coleridge, is explicitly invited to sympathize with Coleridge's position. George has fared well in life, but to Coleridge "Eternal Wisdom hath dispens'd / A different fortune and more different mind" (15–16). George, in other words, has not experienced the suffering that Coleridge has: George has returned to the parental home, where "fraternal love / Hath drawn you to one centre" (12–13). One of the unsatisfying features of the poem is this: that an inadequate and equivocal account is given for the states of mind that Coleridge reports; moreover, Coleridge's account is not quite consistent with what we know of his actual history. First, the poem begins with a general view of what makes for domestic happiness:

> A bléssèd lot hath he, who having passed
> His youth and early manhood in the stir
> And turmoil of the world, retreats at length,
> With cares that move, not agitate the heart,
> To the same dwelling where his father dwelt. (1–5)

Although this evokes a pleasant scene, and echoes briefly the familiar Romantic topos of the errant journey to acquire wisdom, Coleridge's continuation is contradictory. The father that appears to be deceased in line 5 is alive greeting his grandchildren in the next lines, since the returner now

> haply views his tottering little ones
> Embrace those agéd knees and climb that lap,
> On which first kneeling his own infancy
> Lisp'd its brief prayer. (6–9)

While this seems a trivial oversight, the language of the opening lines includes words suggesting that the feelings of Coleridge are over-determined: the generic figure does not return but "retreats," implying a weakness; and the "tottering" of the infants connotes a vulnerability consistent with retreating. The speaker's slip, creating a father who is both absent and present, implies a wound for which this wish-fulfilling scenario acts as a consolation. This semantic contradiction is confirmed by a further mistake. He continues: "Such, O my earliest Friend! / Thy lot, and such thy brothers too enjoy" (9–10). Since their father died in 1781, seven years before the first of the brothers even married (James and Luke married in 1788; George in 1796), the "lot" that Coleridge claims to see is historically impossible. His brothers only returned home and only produced offspring many years after their father's death.

In beginning the poem with a general claim about human life (he, who retreats to his father's house), Coleridge creates observers of his readers, since few will readily share his interest in this particular scenario. Moreover, since the opening lines of the poem are internally inconsistent, marked by feelings for which inadequate cause is apparent, and historically at odds with the facts (although this last problem is evident only to those familiar with Coleridge's family history), the meaning of the scenario that Coleridge invites us to contemplate appears to lie elsewhere, outside the lines themselves. The most obtrusive feature unsettling the lines is the absent-present father, but this prefigures a larger problem later in the poem, as I will show.

The opening lines of "Frost at Midnight," in contrast, make no general claim. Like the other Conversation Poems, the poem starts with an observation on the present moment, thus immediately locating the reader within the speaker's perceptions:

> The Frost performs its secret ministry,
> Unhelped by any wind. The owlet's cry
> Came loud – and hark, again! loud as before. (1–3)

As the lines unfold, Coleridge provides sufficient information for us to locate his position and understand his perspective. "The inmates of my cottage," he says, are "all at rest" (4); he is alone, except for an infant sleeping in the same room. Just outside the cottage are "Sea, hill, and wood," and "populous village" (10–11); yet, he can hear nothing of them in the "extreme silentness" (10). The opening lines are not unproblematic, but they invite the reader first to share the perspective, then to consider what meaning lies beyond the experiences being reported. In this way the reader comes to participate in the unfolding of the poem's meaning, not merely witness it as I suggested is the case in "To the Rev. George Coleridge."

This participatory response is invited in at least the following ways. First, in the opening line "The Frost performs its secret ministry," the reader (once the location of this event on a cold winter's evening in a cottage is grasped) will find two perceptions created. The literal work of the frost is being "performed," perhaps in creating patterns on the window pane, or rime on the vegetation outside the cottage; yet, this is also a "secret ministry," being carried out on grounds that appear to be sacred or at least benign, but whose purposes are secret, hidden from us. Second, we are aware by the fifth or sixth line of the poem, that the function of the "owlet's cry" has been to disturb the speaker and bring him to self-awareness, interrupting his "Abstruser musings." But while we are put in possession of the event, it is left unclear what the moment means. Given the speaker's evident unease with the silence,

> 'Tis calm indeed! so calm, that it disturbs
> And vexes meditation with its strange
> And extreme silentness. (8–10)

it seems that the speaker is also unclear about what has caused his response to being interrupted. But, unlike the "retreat" that opens "To the Rev. George Coleridge," this experience is both simpler and more common: while preoccupied with our own thoughts at night, something disturbs us and makes us attend to our surroundings, but as we listen we cannot at first tell what it is that "vexes" us. Coleridge seems to attribute his unease to the inaudibility of "Sea, hill, and wood" and "populous village" (10–11), but this seems insufficient; it is a symptom, not the cause of the unease.

As readers, that unease has now become ours. We too are motivated to look further in search of some deeper point of origin. In the remainder of the poem we continue to follow the train of Coleridge's thoughts. His unease prompts a memory of his childhood experiences at school, and we infer that being confined in school, where he daydreamed of his home village, has some implications for his lack of ease with his surroundings now. But, he tells us (addressing his infant son), Hartley will enjoy a different experience: as he grows up he will be a wanderer amidst the scenes of nature. Thus, Coleridge tells Hartley, "all seasons shall be sweet to thee" (65), a conclusion that may contrast with the position of Coleridge himself, which appears to remain unresolved. However, the poem returns us to its original point of departure, with "the secret ministry of frost" now enhanced by the "silent icicles, / Quietly shining to the quiet Moon" (72–74).

Whether or not the reader has experienced alienation at school similar to that of Coleridge, the psychological processes traced by the poem illuminate a central issue faced by us all: how the childhood we remember relates to the adult identity of which we are aware in the present. This, at least, is one way of construing "Frost at Midnight"; the poem's critics have proposed various other readings of the poem, some of which are compatible neither with this reading nor with each other.[3] Yet the poem continues to attract new generations of readers who, while engaging

---

3.   There is another argument that could be made here. Although critical interpretations of a text sometimes appear to be mutually incompatible, it is also necessary for critics to take account of the same notable phrases or lines and underlying structural features of the text. Canonical texts are "strong" in this respect, compelling attention to a specific set of features (cf. Zöllner, Miall and Kuiken). This would be an example of a nomothetic law, based on the formal prop-

with Coleridge's experience, appear able to construe the poem in ways that reflect on or illuminate their own experience. That the poem appears to work in this way with little or no introduction is not predicted by its critics. Harper, for instance, thought we required knowledge of who was addressed in the Conversation Poems: "They cannot be even vaguely understood unless the reader knows what persons Coleridge has in mind" (Abrams 145). Kelvin Everest offers a different emphasis: referring to the years during which the poems were written, he suggests that "we do not properly understand the poetry without a knowledge of the full range of experience that it draws on" (p. 11). Useful though such informing contexts may be for enriching understanding of it, they appear not to be obligatory. The independence of "Frost at Midnight" from its contexts, as its frequent appearance in anthologies bears witness, points to a dimension of the poem's meaning that is, I believe, central to its high evaluation.

Having engaged the reader's participation in the experience that unfolds at the beginning of "Frost at Midnight," the remainder of the poem then offers a series of significant perspectives in which to locate that experience and begin to understand something of what it means. That experience, to repeat, is Coleridge's inability to connect with the life around him beyond the cottage room where he sits at midnight, a sense that breaks in upon him and appears to disrupt his "musings." Anxiety about isolation has probably been felt by every reader of the poem. But in the thought process that follows we are able to review such anxiety through a series of windows, each opening a view on basic questions of development. What makes the series coherent is that each, to put it abstractly, offers an underlying schema of reciprocation;[4] and, insofar as these offer resolutions to the problem of isolation, the schemata proceed in a series from the inauthentic to the wholly authentic.

First, turning to the fire burning in the grate, Coleridge sees a film of ash fluttering there. Since this is the only thing moving in the room, he projects onto it his sense of isolation; endowed with "dim sympathies with me who live" it becomes "a companionable form" (18–19). As a model of reciprocation, however, this is immediately found inadequate: it is "the idling Spirit" that

> By its own moods interprets, every where
> Echo or mirror seeking of itself,
> And makes a toy of Thought. (21–23)

In other words, the feeling for an animate world beyond himself, the feeling that is thwarted in the opening section of the poem, is here projected onto an unworthy

---

erties of the literary text: only texts possessing such determinative features survive the ruthless processes of pruning involved in canon formation (van Peer 1997).

4.   For some further helpful commentary on images of reciprocation in this and other Coleridge poems, see Lau 1983.

object. As an escape from his solipsistic prison, this will not do. An earlier version of the poem is more explicit about the source of such projections: Coleridge previously called them "wild reliques of our childish Thought," alluding to the syncretic tendency that Freud was later to term the "omnipotence of thought."[5] But as a source of superstition, Coleridge is reminded, as he remarks in a footnote, that such a fluttering film of ash is "supposed to portend the arrival of some absent friend"; and this in turn reminds him of similar occasions at school where he watched the fire in the schoolroom. This leads to his second image of reciprocity. Sitting at his desk at school he would recall life in the village from which he was removed so early. In particular, his memory seems to focus on the sound of the church bells. These "stirred and haunted me / With a wild pleasure" (31–32), apparently evoking in him a powerful sense of connectedness to some future fulfilment, since he describes their sound as "falling on mine ear / Most like articulate sounds of things to come!" (32–33). But this experience is now in the past, recoverable only in memory, so it too is inadequate as a model of reciprocity, although less fanciful than the first. It is when Coleridge's attention returns to the present that he develops the third schema. Turning to consider the baby sleeping in the room beside him, he proposes a different upbringing for his child, one in which he will be a wanderer amidst natural scenes, and will thus "learn far other lore" (50). This culminating view is reciprocal in several mutually supporting ways: nature itself offers a pattern of reciprocity in which clouds "image in their bulk both lakes and shores / And mountain crags" (57–58); the child will "see and hear" (58) (thus implicitly answering the isolation of the poem's opening) the natural scene which is the "language" of God (60); and God as "Teacher" enables and invites reciprocity: "he shall mould / Thy spirit, and by giving make it ask." (63–64).[6] The insight thus

---

5.   Freud (1955), p. 240. Childhood thought is further discussed in Miall 1989. Successive versions of the poem show extensive revision to lines 19–23 in particular: these are discussed by Jack Stillinger, who argues that the final version of these lines represents "a complete reversal. Every suggestion of interactive mental creativity has been removed, and the focus is entirely on the trivial and bizarre" (p. 59).

6.   Not all readers have been convinced by Coleridge's peroration here: Geoffrey Yarlott, for instance, finds that in this passage "the metaphysic ... obtrudes perhaps too openly" (p. 116). Frederick Kirchoff is not convinced by the figure of the child as wanderer: "the phrase fails to embed Hartley in the natural world ... The fate Coleridge promises his son is remarkably like his own"; that is, the figure of Hartley "is an idealized image of Coleridge himself, the son able to function without a human father" (p. 375). Tim Fulford, on the other hand, in a remark that anticipates my comments on phonetic symbolism below, suggests the following justification: "Poetry, as the discoverer of harmony between apparently unrelated words through sound-effects, could be seen as an approximation to the words of God, in which sound and sense, signifier and signified were one living whole, not arbitrarily related" (p. 25). As Coleridge puts it in an earlier poem:

achieved is then directed to rereading the world outside the cottage in the last ten lines of the poem, ending with the highly appropriate image of reciprocity, the "silent icicles, / Quietly shining to the quiet Moon" (73–74).

The progress of the poem from inauthentic to authentic models of reciprocity is perhaps the backbone on which the poem as a whole depends. As such, the poem's structure is progressive, modelling through this series of images a sequence of thought that begins in the poem's opening line and culminates in the last, and does so in ways that require no special knowledge of the reader. The predicament addressed by the poem appears to be a universal one, and while the putative solution may not be agreeable to every reader, the processes of thought through which the solution emerges involve modes of feeling, memory, and anticipation that are available to all readers as they consider the relation of the self to the wider world beyond.[7]

If we turn back to "To the Rev. George Coleridge," a comparison of the different sections of the poem reveals no such backbone sustaining the development of a single, complex process of thought. Instead, continuing the problem we saw in the opening lines of the poem, there are several inconsistencies across the poem as a whole. These suggest that the sentiment of the poem, which may be all that binds it together, is a fragile one, and that behind the impetus that creates its main sequence of images Coleridge is being pulled in contradictory directions.

Coleridge has opened the poem by celebrating the domestic happiness of his brothers. In the second paragraph of the poem (lines 14–39), Coleridge turns to his own case. As in "Frost at Midnight" he shows us that his difficulties in life have their origin in childhood: he was "Too soon transplanted" (18). This barely noticeable (i.e. dead) metaphor unfortunately awakens to life in the light of his next series of metaphors: within four lines Coleridge introduces an elaborate metaphor of his

---

> For all that meets the bodily sense I deem
> Symbolical, one mighty alphabet
> For infant minds.
>   (*Destiny of Nations*, ll. 18–20)

The view Coleridge offers here is elaborated by James McKusick (pp. 30–31).

7.   Eldridge, who sees in the poem a model of how one might live, suggests: "Coleridge's account of general subjunctive features of human experience is plausibly *not* a special one, *is* plausibly applicable to human beings in general, in so far as the experiences of desire, frustration, and recollective calm which he records occur *involuntarily*, despite his best efforts to plot his life in such a way as to prevent their recurrence" (pp. 224–5). Michael Holstein also finds in this and the other Conversation Poems a power to generalize to the reader: "Because these poems habitually move from tedium or desolation to joy – a ritual of thought – they provide an imitable structure that offers a means to the sacred to others" (p. 218).

friends as trees who sheltered him from storms, or failed to do so. The metaphors conflict by positioning Coleridge first as a plant, then as a human object beneath a plant. Thus, unlike the metaphors of "Frost at Midnight," the connotations of these metaphors fail to converge upon a sense of the larger issues at work in the poem.

The trees metaphor itself may appear effective at first sight: Rosemary Ashton has remarked that "The sustained metaphor of trees giving shelter is cleverly managed; it comes naturally to Coleridge to think of himself as needing protection" (p. 98). However, Coleridge himself criticized it in a letter shortly after the poem was published, noting that "the metaphor on the diverse sorts of friendship is *hunted down*" (*Letters* I.334). His comment suggests that a degree of mechanical effort went into forcing the metaphor to work: first, trees that have sheltered him; second, trees that feebly bent, dropping "the collected shower" upon him (25); third, the fearful Manchineel that dropped its poison on him while he slept; and, finally, the oak that signifies his present true friend (Tom Poole at Nether Stowey).[8] Poetic use of the Manchineel had been interdicted by his teacher, the Rev. Bowyer, according to Coleridge's account of his schooldays published in 1817, "as suiting equally well with too many subjects" (*Biographia*, I.10) but this failed to inhibit Coleridge from using it not only in this poem but in several other contexts over the years.[9] Yet the Manchineel image suggests a cause for Coleridge's difficulties that remains unexpressed and out of sight. It prompts us to ask either what friend treated Coleridge so poorly, or what grief caused him to place such an extreme interpretation on a friend's behaviour.[10] In either case the poem fails to answer; it provides nothing adequate to the weight of the metaphor. On the contrary, the Manchineel problem, whatever that is, remains like an ulcer in the poem,

---

8.   The contrast drawn by Ronald A. Sharp between Coleridge's earlier and mature poems is apposite here. In a poem such as "To the Rev. George Coleridge" (not discussed by Sharp), Coleridge compares human life with nature: "human affairs bear a certain resemblance to natural processes … man is in some ways curiously like nature. Thus one may trace in nature illuminating analogies with the human condition." The later poems incorporate nature through suggestive metaphors rather than similes; thus nature is an "eternal language" in "Frost at Midnight" (p. 29).

9.   See *Lectures 1795*, p. 296; *The Friend*, I.568; *Logic*, p. 190. That the word was on the lips of the Coleridge circle during the year that he used it in this poem is shown by its appearance in a letter by Charles Lamb to Coleridge, dated September 1797: *Letters* I.123.

10.   Coleridge's dependency on others (notably father figures) has also been found in "Frost at Midnight," where the "stranger" has been seen as the narcissistic missing love-object. Frederick Kirchoff's perceptive account of this, however, seems to apply more appropriately to the present context, with its overdetermined trees metaphor. Coleridge's psyche, he remarks, is "fixated on an archaic self-object, that is, in search of or dependent on external figures who can supply the goals and ideals it internally lacks and thus function not as objects *per se*, but as parts of the otherwise incomplete self" (p. 372).

unregarded and untreated, casting doubt on the validity of the rest of Coleridge's claims about his state. Moreover, as the poem continues, Coleridge prevaricates regarding his emotional condition, alternating claims to his destined fame as a poet with further, partly unexplained complaints about his alienation. The tree image, moreover, returns in a further guise, this time producing a double conflict with the friendship metaphor. As Coleridge turns to celebrate the present moment in his garden, he has apparently forgotten the metaphoric use of the tree dropping its showers or poisons, since he now praises the tree on which he sits,

> whose old boughs,
> That hang above us in an arborous roof,
> Stirr'd by the faint gale of departing May,
> Send their loose blossoms slanting o'er our heads! (58–61)

Not only does this present a literal tree, which sorts oddly with the earlier metaphor; it also repeats the image of the tree dropping something in the breeze (since the "loose" blossoms must be those that are flying off the tree like the earlier showers). This shift in the ground of the metaphor, which here is not a metaphor, could perhaps be reconciled with the earlier part of the poem by an act of rationalization, but this would, in Coleridge's words, have to be "hunted down" deliberately. Although the lines are effective in themselves, the conflict they cause damages the thematic coherence of the poem.

Other minor conflicts also weaken the poem. While Coleridge celebrates his birthplace and the domestic happiness of his brothers, especially the fatherly goodwill of his eldest brother George, he inexplicably disrupts this image halfway through the poem by asserting that he is sad and "most a stranger... / At mine own home and birth-place" (41–42) where his brother resides. Near the end of the poem he claims to write "deeper" poems, which "tuned to these tumultuous times, / Cope with the tempest's swell!" (67–68) The metaphoric meaning of tempest here (presumably political unrest and war) once again quarrels with the storm, expressed as "life's pelting ills" (21), of the earlier tree metaphor. Finally, although Coleridge claims that folly has left wisdom behind (66), his poems are still liable to "error or intemperate truth" (72), for which George is invited to forgive him.

In sum, interesting and effective though "To the Rev. George Coleridge" often is in its parts, it fails to convince as a whole on two primary grounds, both of which tend to exclude the reader. First, the connotational implications of its main metaphors are inconsistent, unlike those of "Frost at Midnight"; and, second, it suggests deeper causes for the problems sketched in the poem than anything the poem itself explains. Whereas the problem of isolation in "Frost at Midnight" is amenable to being recognized by every reader of that poem, it is not clear to the reader of "To the Rev. George Coleridge" what problem Coleridge is addressing, except that of being "Too soon transplanted." The poem, in other words, requires special knowledge of Coleridge for a more than superficial understanding to emerge. Even then, interpretive activity that relies on evidence outside the poem is unstable (since historical evidence is usually amenable to a variety of interpretations) and inherently indeterminable (since there is no limit in principle to what we could bring to bear on the poem). More importantly, external information can never remedy deficiencies in the poetic structure of the poem itself. The poem thus fails to propose itself to readers as an effective agent for reflecting on their own concerns, which may be a central qualification of those texts that we value most highly.

3. Structures of sound

So far I have discussed the poems in terms of their rhetorical and figurative structures. The poems can also be compared at the level of sound. Effects of phonetic patterning and meter also make a significant contribution to the meaning of the poems. But here, too, I will suggest that in "Frost at Midnight" Coleridge manages this aspect of the poem more effectively. To a greater degree than in "To the Rev. George Coleridge," the aural textures of "Frost at Midnight" tend to mirror and strengthen its semantic implications. Coleridge himself was particularly interested in metrical effects; to those who praised the metre of a poem he would lecture at length on its principles (McKim 1992). Although unfortunately no record of his comments has survived, various scattered remarks in his published writings show his concern (e.g., *Biographia*, II.66–67, 71–72). His poem "Kubla Khan" has often been singled out as perhaps the most remarkable poem in English for the power of its aural effectiveness.[11] Thus it is no surprise to find that "Frost at Midnight" contains a range of subtle and appropriate features at the phonetic and metrical levels. I will point to a few of these, and then show how "Frost at Midnight" can be discriminated from "To the Rev. George Coleridge" on empirical grounds.

Metrically, both poems employ the typical blank verse five-stress line of iambic feet. This sets a pattern against which significant departures are perceptible, producing a metre that may underscore aspects of a line's meaning. For example, a notable deviation occurs early in "Frost at Midnight":

---

11. Illuminating accounts are provided by Purves (1962) and Tsur (1987). See also valuable discussions of individual poems by Austen (1989). For a wide-ranging but more theoretical account see Marks (1981).

> Sea, and hill, and wood,
> With all the numberless goings-on of life,
> Inaudible as dreams! (11–13)

The second line cited here is pronounced most appropriately with only four stresses, shown underlined as follows: "With all the numberless goings-on of life" (a stress is possible on "goings," but seems infelicitous in the context). The sequence of four unstressed syllables that occurs in the centre of the line strikingly points up the remoteness and inaccessibility of the life outside the cottage, of which Coleridge is complaining. This effect is intensified further by the next line, with its sequence of three unstressed syllables ("Inaudible as dreams!"). A similar example occurs later in the poem. In the two adjacent lines (shown here with the stresses marked),

> Fill up the interspersèd vacancies
> And momentary pauses of the thought! (46–47)

Coleridge again deviates metrically to produce sequences of unstressed syllables, reflecting that pause or space in which the breathing of the baby comes to his awareness. A contrasting effect is created in this line (stresses marked): "And saw nought lovely but the sky and stars" (53), where the sense of blockage (amidst the large buildings of London) is confirmed by three adjacent stresses. "Frost at Midnight" contains a number of remarkable and appropriate effects of this kind.

"To the Rev. George Coleridge," on the other hand, appears more regular in its successive five-stress lines. Indeed, in the letter mentioning the poem quoted above, Coleridge seems concerned about this, remarking that "the versification ever & anon has too much of the rhyme or couplet cadence" (*Letters*, I.334). To examine the lines of the poem for metrical deviations is to find that few occur, and these generally appear to be without significance. Among those that seem motivated, this line (stresses added) seems one of the most effective in the poem: "Send their loose blossoms slanting o'er our heads!" (61), with its onomatopoeic sequence of unstressed syllables suggesting the light movement of the flowers in the wind. Its effectiveness is dampened, however, by a slight awkwardness in the previous line, "Stirr'd by the faint gale of departing May" (60), where it seems most natural to place a stress on "faint," although the resulting adjacent strong stresses distract from the incipient sense of movement created by both lines. The poem contains several lines that cause doubt about the appropriate stress pattern, since each alternative seems slightly unsatisfactory. In the Miltonic "Nor dost not thou sometimes recall those hours" (62), for example, it is difficult to decide whether to stress "not"; the meter of the line seems to require it, yet it unduly emphases the negative, threatening to destabilize the line's meaning. Another metrically successful effect near the end of the poem is "Or such as, tuned to these tumultuous times, / Cope with the tempest's swell!" (67–68), indicating restlessness by the de-layed major stresses on tum<u>u</u>ltuous and t<u>e</u>mpest. Overall, however, this poem is undistinguished metrically. Coleridge was soon to write much more effectively in this respect, including "Kubla Khan," "The Mariner," "Christabel," and – as I have briefly suggested – "Frost at Midnight."

In the aural texture of poetry, not only stress patterns augment and support meaning; the choice of phonetic patterns is also of critical importance, serv-ing to distinguish the texture of poetry from the largely random distribution of phonemes in non-literary prose. Poetic effects at this level are commonly identi-fied in such features as assonance, alliteration, consonance, and the like, and many striking effects are due to this type of diction in "Frost at Midnight." An equally pervasive, but less commonly studied phonetic feature, however, is the distribu-tion of phonemes. In speaking, the various vowel sounds are located at different places along the oral tract, which also opens or closes to some degree according to the sound. For example, the vowel /i/ in *bead*[12] is pronounced at the front of the mouth with the tongue high, constricting the oral cavity; the /u/ in *food*, in contrast, is pronounced near the throat with the tongue depressed. The relative position of the vowels creates its own patterns which may make a distinctive con-tribution to the lines of a poem. This will be shown first at the local level, then examined for its relation to the overall tone of a poem.

In "Frost at Midnight," to take a local example, in the line "Which image in their bulk both lakes and shores" (57) the three vowel sounds that occur at the end of each half-line, "in their bulk" and "lakes and shores," mirror one another, since each makes a falling pattern, each vowel lower than the preceding one. This supports the semantic implication of mirroring described in the line. A falling pattern is, in fact, common to a number of figures of speech known as "linguis-tic freezes";[13] however, these usually occur singly, not in the close combination of forms apparent in Coleridge's line. Special effects can also be created by re-versing the pattern. In this line, "In the great city, pent 'mid cloisters dim" (52), Coleridge creates a rising pattern in the second half-line, with upward leaps across two vowels at "pent 'mid," then across three vowels at "cloisters dim." This serves to reinforce the effect of imprisonment, the vowel pattern mirroring the implied vertical pillars of the cloisters. The consonants also participate in the effect. Conso-nants contribute to linguistic freezes in a similar way, soft sounds (liquids, nasals)

---

12.   In the following discussion I employ the IPA (International Phonetic Association) symbols for phonemes, except in one or two places when this might confuse readers unfamiliar with this notation.

13.   See Landsberg (1995). Examples of freezes determined by initial consonant are: *here* and *there*; *now* and *then*; determined by vowel: *dribs* and *drabs*; *flip flop*. For one of several empirical studies see Pinker and Birdsong (1979).

at the beginning of word pairs typically preceding hard sounds (fricatives, plosives). Thus the reversal in the present line is also rather striking, occurring twice, at "great city" and "pent 'mid"; "cloisters dim" also suggests a rising pattern by opening with a plosive /k/ and concluding with a nasal /m/.

In "To the Rev. George Coleridge," on the other hand, some of the more perceptible effects at the phonetic level appear either to have no relation to the semantic meaning of the lines in which they occur or are inconsistent with them. For example, in the line "Some have preserv'd me from life's pelting ills" (21), referring to the help of friends, the rising vowel pattern at the end of the line in "from life's pelting ills" might appear to connote safety being found in a relatively high place. As the next line makes clear, however, safety (when it occurred) was found below, beneath the branches of a tree. Similarly, the vowel profile in "climb Life's upland road" (11) is actually a falling one, contrary to the meaning of the phrase. Where a striking pattern of rising vowels does occur, in "the Manchineel, / Have tempted me" (26–27) (with its supporting internal rhymes on /æ/ and /i/), there seems no good reason to relate the pattern to the semantic context.

The contrast of vowel or consonant positions, whether front-back, or soft-hard, can take on a figurative role in the context of a particular poem. In *Paradise Lost*, for example, I have found that narrow, front vowels tend to predominate in the description of the enclosed spaces of Hell in Book II; in contrast, in the passage on Eden in Book IV open vowels are more frequent. In "Frost at Midnight" there is a contrast between the enclosed spaces of the cottage, the schoolroom, or the city, with their negative implications, and the positive implications of the natural world through which the child will wander. Dividing the poem according to these contrasting sections (treating the following lines as negative: 1–6, 8–12, 23–26, 37–41, and 52–53), the distribution of consonants and vowels can be analysed.[14] A greater frequency of hard consonants can be expected in the negative lines compared with the positive lines. This is what occurs: the difference is highly significant on a statistical test, $t(72) = 3.41$, p < .01. In "To the Rev. George Coleridge," whose negative preoccupations concern Coleridge's false friendships, his estrangement, and his errors as a poet (negative lines: 18–30, 40-42, 46–48, 65–68, 71–74), the

---

14.   For the following study, the 24 consonants and 20 vowels are ordered following standard accounts of phonetic distributions: e.g., second formant order for high to low frequency; the vowel-space diagram for high-low and back-front; the least to most obstruent consonants (see, for example, Pinker and Birdsong; O'Grady and Dobrovolsky, pp. 28–34; Clark and Yallop, 66–69). Ranks are then assigned to each phoneme, enabling the mean ranks of vowels and consonants to be scored for each line of the two poems. This enabled, for example, statistical comparison (t-test) of vowel and consonant distributions in 55 positive and 22 negative lines in "Frost at Midnight." Rank scores approximated a normal distribution in each of the variables studied, hence the use of parametric statistics.

same test is also significant, but less markedly: $t(72) = 1.95$, p < .05. On an analysis of vowels, the positive lines in "Frost at Midnight" contain a higher proportion of high, front vowels, perhaps connoting a degree of intimacy, as Reuven Tsur has suggested (1992:61), although this difference is less significant, $t(72) = 1.44$, p < .10. "To the Rev. George Coleridge" contains no significant differences in its vowel distribution.

It might also be expected that the more systematically phonemes are deployed in a poem, the more likely it is that characteristic clusters of vowels and consonants will occur, distinctive to the purposes of that poem. This argument follows from the work of Jakobson (1987:41–46), who proposed the theory of the "dominant," and Mukarovský, who suggested that foregrounding in literary texts occurs in a systematic and hierarchical manner (1964:20). One way of assessing the evidence is to group phonemes by type, such as the liquids and nasals, or the plosives, then look for systematic relationships between the groups. In the following analysis the frequency per line of four groups of vowels and four groups of consonants was obtained; the eight sets of frequencies were then intercorrelated. In this and previous analyses I have found patterns of negative correlations that appear typical of English poetry: for example, front and back vowels rather consistently tend not to co-occur in the same line. "To the Rev. George Coleridge" shows these typical negative correlations, but no other significant feature. In "Frost at Midnight," on the other hand, there is a significant positive correlation of front vowels with the unvoiced fricatives and aspirates, $r(72) = .259$, p < .05. In the opening line of the poem, for example, there are six occurrences from each vowel and consonant group (vowels, underlined: "The Frost performs its secret ministry"; consonants: "The Frost performs its secret ministry"). This provides a tonal resonance that is threaded through the rest of the poem, the front vowels suggesting perhaps that missing sense of intimacy that will be troubling to the speaker, and the unvoiced consonants a sense of absence or elusiveness that, later in the poem, is transformed into the unseen but felt dimension of God's presence in Nature. Other lines notable for a high frequency of both types of phonemes are "Methinks, its motion in this hush of nature" (17) (part of a transitional and unsatisfactory resolution), and "Himself in all, and all things in himself" 62) (the climactic affirmation of Coleridge's renewed sense of participation). There is also a significant correlation between the back vowels and the voiced fricatives and aspirates, $r(72) = .266$, p < .01 – the following line contains 5 and 7 examples, respectively: "Whether the summer clothe the general earth" (66).

In these ways "Frost at Midnight" appears to be a poem with a demonstrably consistent phonetic palette, one that underlies and supports the evolving moods of the poem. While readers are unlikely to be aware as they read of the subtle contributions of such phonetic patterns and contrasts (their consistent presence is only revealed by detailed analysis), yet the compatibility of the phonetic tone with the poem's meaning is undoubtedly one of the central virtues of the poem, serving to attract generations of readers. The infrequency or contradictory nature of such effects in "To the Rev. George Coleridge" may be an additional reason for the relative obscurity of this poem.

Engaging the reader

As the central issue of this paper, I have situated the question of literary evaluation in relation to the act of reading. I have argued that it is the formal qualities that chiefly distinguish "Frost at Midnight" from "To the Rev. George Coleridge" and that have promoted it to its current canonized status. In particular, the later poem invites the reader to participate in the affective processes of the poem in a way that the earlier does not. Moreover, the meanings developed by "Frost at Midnight" appear to be at a level that enables almost any reader competent in the English language to experience and participate in the poem's processes; no special knowledge is required of Coleridge's life or situation, or of the place of the poem in literary history. This, however, is not because the poem wears its meaning on its face, as it were. While the poem reflects on issues of central significance in the emotional life of any reader,[15] the key to the effectiveness of the poem is the consistency with which these issues are confronted, developed, and (at least in part) resolved. The poem can be said to recreate the reader's feelings in its own image. The poem's agency in this respect depends upon several fundamental properties of feeling (cf. Miall 1989, 1995).

First, feeling is self-referential. When a specific feature of the poem, whether a passage textured by alliteration, an image of a sleeping child, or a wish to find companionship in an inanimate object, invokes a feeling in the reader, that feeling is significant because it embodies some current concern or striving of the self (Klinger 1978; Emmons 1986). Through our feelings we mediate what is of current importance to the self, monitoring experience moment by moment, and adjusting responses and expectations in line with the self that the feeling projects. Readers are thus drawn to find resonances with their own situations within the poem, although the specific experiences or memories in question may remain below the

---

15. As Eldridge puts it, the poem "presents in a compressed and accessible form a picture of how one might go about meditating on one's moods in the hope of uncovering general subjunctive features of human life" (p. 215). Although my method in reaching this conclusion has been, to follow van Peer's terms, a *hermeneutic* analysis of the properties of each poem and the processes of reading they promote, it is here, in the affective relation to the reader, that we might look for a *nomothetic* law of canon formation, within the framework proposed by van Peer (1997).

level of awareness. This first process is, in itself, necessary but insufficient. It is the power that the poem has to recontextualize the reader's feelings that raise it to significance as a specifically *literary* experience. For example, I pointed to the series of reflective images in "Frost at Midnight," which answer to the speaker's need for a participatory relation to the wider world. In each, the feeling of isolation and bafflement is situated in a context that offers to overcome it: only another feeling is capable of this outcome, thus we see the speaker testing a succession of feelings. First, the reaching towards a moving but inanimate object; second, the context provided by remembering his excitement at the sound of church bells; third, the anticipated future transcendence of his child in nature. While only the third appears fully satisfactory, at each stage the reader's own feeling of isolation is placed in these informing contexts, serving to call it into question and suggest alternative meanings for it. The devices of the poem, in other words, work to defamiliarize the feeling, while at the same time they point to possible avenues for reconstruing it through the perspective of another feeling.

This is perhaps the most central, but by no means the only example of this process in the poem. Almost every three or four lines contain devices that initiate similar processes. For example, in "that solitude, which suits / Abstruser musings" (5–6), musing (daydream is a favourite topic of Coleridge's) is contextualized by the adjective "abstruser" and by the succession of /u/ sounds (five in all), a narrow back vowel. Although musing seems an appropriate activity for Coleridge late at night alone in his cottage, its positive connotations are challenged by the cloistered, even claustral, implications of this form of expression (the narrowness of the /u/ sound is thus an example of what has been termed phonetic symbolism: Fónagy 1989). That musing is unsustainable, once the owlet's cry has been heard for the second time, being too narrow or fragile in the face of the anxiety that the speaker then develops (the silence "vexes meditation"), anticipates a related sense of narrowness at other key moments of the poem – the schoolroom, being "pent" in the city – but more importantly, it projects the constrictedness of the speaker's predicament which apparently prevents a relationship with the wider world outside the cottage. Having read the phrase on "musing," and been made uncomfortable, shall we say, by the defamiliarizing effect of the diction, a reader senses in the feelings it has evoked a possible context for understanding why musing is inadequate, a context that is glimpsed but not yet instantiated. The feeling, in other words, is the reader's agent for locating an appropriate context for understanding this part of the poem, and, as I have suggested, the sense of narrowness will recur and be elaborated as the poem continues to unfold. The reader is thus positioned by the poem's structure to find what is sought for,[16] although what is sought becomes richer and more far-reaching the further the reader progresses into the poem. In this respect, feeling is anticipatory: at any given point in the poem it projects forward to meanings that are about to be developed or that are fulfilled later in the poem.

The coherence of "Frost at Midnight" for the reader is due in large measure to this fulfilment of a feed-forward process that is continually being initiated or renewed in every line or two of the poem. In the reader it constitutes the presence of an interactive agency, prompting hesitations and questions about the meaning of the reader's own feelings. That is, while the poem is being read or reread, the reader is able to recognize feelings that embody some significant aspect of the self. Through the agency of the poem, however, these become newly delimited; unfamiliar connections may form between these feelings and hitherto unrelated feelings or experiences. It is because this process in the reader has a characteristic integrity and completeness that we have tended to identify its agent, the poem, as possessing aesthetic unity. It does not imply an integrity in the reader, however (the process might precipitate disunity, when a reader recognizes a feeling that conflicts with a major belief system previously in place).

In conclusion, it has been the argument of this paper that, like "Frost at Midnight," the texts we have come to value highly operate on the reader to evoke feelings central to the reader's self concept, and to initiate a process of questioning and re-contextualization of those feelings through the text's rhetorical, figurative, and aural structures. While each literary text will deploy a different and partly unique array of such structures, what characterizes value in literature is the power of such texts to make each of us inquirers into the meaning of our experience (whether personal, social, cultural, or historical). We are participants in the unfolding processes of the poem, having made those processes relevant to the fate of our own feelings.[17] As we read, we are caught up in processes of defamiliariza-

---

16.   This phrase is borrowed from Kierkegaard's account of poetic inspiration, which seems to offer an instructive parallel to the reading process (1971, I.48).

17.   The present argument, that the highly valued text speaks to us about our own concerns as individuals, may seem plausible only in relation to relatively recent works (e.g., Romantic and post-Romantic), where little or no background knowledge may be required. Critics such as George Steiner (1972) have claimed that the modern reader lacks the shared culture that enables an informed reading of Shakespeare or Milton. As a teacher I have found this claim frequently controverted in practice. With a little background information (required for most pre-Romantic texts) and some annotations, I have found introductory level students are often as excited and moved by *Beowulf*, Donne, or Milton, as they are by any more recent work. Its seems likely, from the nature of their responses, that the formal qualities of the text provide an important gateway to their initial understanding.

tion and re-contextualization, focusing on issues that are of central interest to us as individuals; yet those same issues are amenable to different readers in different contexts across different epochs of time. Whereas a lesser text makes a requisition on our feelings or confines us to being a witness of its processes, the literature that becomes most highly valued arises from the interaction of a structurally powerful text and a responsive reader. Such a text makes us a performer (Attridge 1999) of the processes it embodies, an instrument for reflecting on and reconstruing what we are.

References

Abrams, M. H. (ed.). 1960. *English Romantic Poets: Modern Essays in Criticism*. New York, NY: OUP.

Ashton, R. 1996. *The Life of Samuel Taylor Coleridge*. Oxford: Blackwell.

Attridge, D. 1999. Innovation, Literature, Ethics: Relating to the Other. *PMLA* 114: 20–31.

Austen, F. 1989. *The Language of Wordsworth and Coleridge*. Basingstoke: Macmillan.

Clark, J. & Colin Y. 1990. *An Introduction to Phonetics and Phonology*. Oxford: Blackwell.

Coleridge, S. T. 1956–71. *Collected Letters of Samuel Taylor Coleridge*. E. L. Griggs (ed.). Oxford: OUP.

Coleridge, S. T. 1969. *The Friend*, B. E. Rooke (ed.). Princeton, NJ: Princeton University Press.

Coleridge, S. T. 1971. *Lectures 1795: On Politics and Religion*. L. Patton & P. Mann (eds.). Princeton, NJ: Princeton University Press.

Coleridge, S. T. 1981. *Logic*. J. R. de J. Jackson (ed.). Princeton, NJ: Princeton University Press.

Coleridge, S. T. 1983. *Biographia Literaria*. W. J. Bate & J. Engell (eds.). Princeton, NJ: Princeton University Press.

Eldridge, R. 1983. On Knowing How To Live: Coleridge's 'Frost at Midnight'. *Philosophy and Literature* 7: 213–228.

Emmons, R. 1986. Personal Strivings: An Approach to Personality and Subjective Well-Being. *Journal of Personality and Social Psychology* 51: 1058–1068.

Everest, K. 1979. *Coleridge's Secret Ministry: The Context of the Conversation Poems: 1795–1798*. Sussex: Harvester Press & New York, NY: Barnes and Noble.

Fónagy, I. 1989. The Metaphor: A Research Instrument. In *Comprehension of Literary Discourse*, D. Meutsch and R. Viehoff (ed.), 111–113. Berlin: Walter de Gruyter.

Freud, S. 1955. The Uncanny [1919], In *The Standard Edition of the Complete Psychological Works of Sigmund Freud*, Vol. XVII, J. Strachey (ed.). London: The Hogarth Press.

Fulford, T. 1991. *Coleridge's Figurative Language*. Basingstoke: Macmillan.

Harper, G. McL. 1925. Coleridge's Conversation Poems. *Quarterly Review* 244: 284–298.

Holstein, M. E. 1979. Poet into Priest: A Reading of Coleridge's 'Conversation Poems'. *University of Toronto Quarterly* 48: 209–225.

House, H. 1953. *Coleridge: The Clark Lectures 1951–52*. London: Rupert Hart-Davis.

Jakobson, R. 1987. *Language in Literature*. K. Pomorska and S. Rudy (ed.). Cambridge, MA: Harvard University Pres.

Kierkegaard, S. 1971. *Either/Or*, trans. D. F. Swenson. Princeton, NJ: Princeton University Press.

Kirchoff, F. 1979. Reconstructing a Self: Coleridge's 'Frost at Midnight'. *The Wordsworth Circle* 10: 371–375.

Klinger, E. 1978. The Flow of Thought and Its Implications for Literary Communication. *Poetics* 7: 1–25.

Lamb, C. & Lamb M. A. 1975. *The Letters of Charles and Mary Anne Lamb*. E. W. Marrs (ed.). Ithaca, NY: Cornell University Press.

Landsberg, M. E. 1995. Semantic Constraints on Phonologically Independent Freezes. In *Syntactic Iconicity and Linguistic Freezes: The Human Dimension*. M. E. Landsberg (ed.), 65–78. Berlin: Mouton de Gruyter.

Lau, B. 1983. Coleridge's Reflective Moonlight. *Studies in English Literature 1500–1900* 23: 533–548.

Magnuson, P. 1998. *Reading Public Romanticism*. Princeton, NJ: Princeton University Press.

Marks, E. R. 1981. *Coleridge on the Language of Verse*. Princeton, NJ: Princeton University Press.

McKim, A. E. 1992. 'An Epicure in Sound': Coleridge on the Scansion of Verse. *English Studies in Canada* 18: 287–300.

McKusick, J. 1986. *Coleridge's Philosophy of Language*. New Haven, CT: Yale University Press.

Miall, D. S. 1989. Beyond the Schema Given: Affective Comprehension of Literary Narratives. *Cognition and Emotion* 3: 55–78.

Miall, D. S. 1989. The Displacement of Emotions: the Case of 'Frost at Midnight'. *The Wordsworth Circle* 20: 97–102.

Miall, D. S. 1995. Anticipation and Feeling in Literary Response: A Neuropsychological Perspective. *Poetics* 23: 275–298.

Miall, D. S. & D. Kuiken. 1999. What is literariness? Three components of literary reading. *Discourse Processes* 28: 121–138.

Mukarovský, J. 1964. Standard Language and Poetic Language. In *A Prague School Reader on Esthetics, Literary Structure, and Style*, P. L. Garvin, (ed.). Washington, DC: Georgetown University Press.

O'Grady, W. & M. Dobrovolsky. 1989. *Contemporary Linguistics: An Introduction*. New York, NY: St. Martin's Press.

Pinker, S. & Birdsong D. 1979. Speakers' Sensitivity to Rules of Frozen Word Order. *Journal of Verbal Learning and Verbal Behavior* 18: 497–508.

Plug, J. 1993. The Rhetoric of Secrecy: Figures of the Self in 'Frost at Midnight'. In *Coleridge's Visionary Languages*, T. Fulford & M. D. Paley (eds.). Rochester,NY: Boydell & Brewer.

Purves, A. C. 1962. Formal Structure in 'Kubla Khan'. In *Studies in Romanticism* 1: 187–191.

Sharp, R. A. 1985. The Structure of Coleridge's Nature Poetry. *Papers on Language & Literature* 21: 28–42.

Steiner, G. 1972. In a Post-Culture. *Extraterritorial: Papers on Language and Literature*. London: Faber & Faber.

Stillinger, J. 1994. *Coleridge and Textual Instability: The Multiple Versions of the Major Poems*. Oxford: OUP.

Tsur, R. 1987. *The Road to Kubla Khan: A Cognitive Approach*. Jerusalem: Israel Science.

Tsur, R. 1992. *What Makes Sound Patterns Expressive? The Poetic Mode of Speech Perception*. Durham, NC: Duke University Press.

van Peer, W. 1997. Two Laws of Literary History: Growth and Predictibility in Canon Formation. *Mosaic* 30: 113–132.

Wheeler, K. M. 1981. *The Creative Mind in Coleridge's Poetry*. London: Heinemann.

Wu, D. (ed.). 1994. *Romanticism: An Anthology*. Oxford: Blackwell.

Yarlott, G. 1967. *Coleridge and the Abyssinian Maid*. London: Methuen.

Zöllner, K. 1990. 'Quotation analysis' as a means of understanding comprehension processes of longer and more difficult texts. *Poetics* 19: 293–322.

CHAPTER 7

Evaluation and stylistic analysis

Mick Short and Elena Semino

Stylistics is normally concerned with providing accounts, mainly via linguistic analysis, of readers' interpretations of, and responses to, particular works and texts in general. In this chapter we show how stylistic analysis can also be applied in the discussion of text evaluation, and in particular to comparing different versions of (part of) the same literary work. We begin by reflecting on the process of evaluation generally, and literary evaluation in particular. We then explore some specific dimensions of evaluation by comparing different versions of three poems by William Blake, Ted Hughes and T. S. Eliot. Finally, we carry out a comparative analysis of two equivalent extracts from the two editions of John Fowles's *The Magus*. We use this analysis to explain in detail why, somewhat surprisingly, we prefer the earlier version of the passage to the later one (though that does not mean that we would necessarily make the same judgment in relation to the two editions in their entirety). Our overall conclusion is that stylistic analysis can contribute to a better understanding of the bases for the valuing of texts and of the process of literary evaluation more generally.

1. Introduction

Stylistic analysis (sometimes known as literary linguistics or linguistic criticism) is an approach to the analysis of literary works which involves a detailed and systematic account of their linguistic properties, linked to what we know about the details of the reading process, in order to arrive at a detailed account of how readers understand particular texts in the ways they do (see, for example, Fowler 1986; Herman 1995; Leech 1969; Leech & Short 1981; Semino 1997; Short 1996; Simpson 1993, 1997; Toolan 1988).

In this paper, however, we will focus not on the use of stylistics in critical interpretation, but on the relationship between stylistic analysis and evaluation. In Section 2 we examine some general properties of the activity of evaluation, and of literary evaluation in particular. Then, in Section 3, using small-scale examples from 'The Tyger' by William Blake, 'October Dawn' by Ted Hughes and the beginning of T. S. Eliot's 'Little Gidding', we explore the different domains with respect to which evaluation can apply, and outline, as we see it, the general relationship between stylistic analysis and evaluative activity.

The discussion of Blake's 'The Tyger' compares two different extant versions of its first stanza, and in Section 4 we extend this comparative approach to the evaluation of fictional prose. We explore how stylistic analysis can be used as a basis on which to compare and evaluate two equivalent small-scale extracts from the two editions of *The Magus* by John Fowles. The functions of the passages from which the smaller extracts are taken appear to be roughly equivalent, and so, by looking at textual detail in relation to these functions, we can state clearly which piece of writing we prefer and why. Interestingly, our analysis suggests that, in respect to these extracts at least, the first edition of the novel is to be preferred over the second, something which Fowles presumably would not agree with, as otherwise he would not have made the changes he did. This judgement is only made with respect to small-scale extracts from the novels, however, and so even if we are correct in our assessment of these extracts from the two editions, the assessment of the two editions as a whole might still be the other way round (see Sections 2 and 4.3 for more consideration of this matter).

2.   The relation between evaluation and interpretation, and different domains of evaluation

In spite of the fact that most critics would see the evaluation of literary texts as the end-goal of their endeavour, 20th century literary criticism has, by and large concentrated on the *interpretation* of texts. This is also true of stylistic analysis, the logical terminus of approaches like I. A. Richards's practical criticism.[1] That criticism has, in general terms, tackled interpretation before evaluation is not altogether surprising. Indeed it would appear to be sensible in terms of establishing a research programme for working out how we evaluate literary texts. The eval-

---

1.   If you decide that literary understanding comes about through the interaction between readers and texts, close examination of the linguistic structure is essential to good criticism. It then soon becomes clear that it is not enough just to read texts very carefully, but that you have to analyse the various aspects of language structure in a text in order to see how the text plays its part in the reader-text interaction. Modern stylistic analysis, however, is not formalist, in spite of claims to this effect by some other critics. Because interpretation is the product of an interaction between reader and text, it is just as important when building and/or arguing for a particular interpretation to take into account what we know from psychologists and other researchers about the interpretative processes which readers employ in textual understanding. Modern stylisticians examine carefully both textual and processing factors, and indeed, earlier stylisticians, if one examines their writings carefully, also took such factors into account informally, even when they were claiming to be formalist in their orientation.

uation of any human activity or its product must be related to its purpose(s) or function(s), and to properly understand the functions of particular texts we must already have interpreted them.

Indeed, we can to some degree learn lessons about aesthetic evaluation by considering how evaluation works in non-aesthetic fields. If we evaluate two different word-processing programmes, factors like the following will need to be taken into account: (i) how easy it is for non-experts (e.g. business people or humanities scholars) to operate them in their range of applications, (ii) whether they automatically save documents from time to time (because humans sometimes forget to do this, and so lose their work if there is a power cut), (iii) how many different sorts of thing they let you do relevant to writing tasks (e.g. writing texts in dual columns as well as single columns) and so on. Which features of the programs we focus on are thus related to some assumed overall function. If we look for analogues of this kind of evaluative activity in literature, we can ask questions like how literary works affect us emotionally, help us to see the world differently, help us to understand the human condition better, and so on. And to answer these questions with respect to some particular text, that means relating our evaluation to our understanding of the text. Final evaluation is thus dependent on our arriving at an overall understanding.

Of course we come to provisional understandings, and hence possible provisional evaluations, during the reading process itself, but we cannot sensibly confirm either our overall interpretation or our overall evaluation until we have got to the end of a text and thought it through. The same is true, note, of evaluating word-processing packages. You may not like a particular feature of a new piece of software on your first encounter (e.g. the availability of shortcuts to pull-down menu commands you frequently use), but your final evaluation would have to be more thorough and all-encompassing.

The word-processing package is a complex object with more than one function, and this means that the process of its evaluation is also complex. We may prefer particular aspects of word-processor 1 to word-processor 2 but still decide that, overall, 2 is the better piece of software. To decide between the two pieces of software we are thus involved in comparing localised pros and cons of sub-parts of the packages, combining them and examining closely the functional interaction of the various sub-parts. This shows us that evaluative activity can operate with respect to a series of different domains, local, intermediate and global. Moreover, it may be that the two different word-processors were not designed with exactly the same balance of functions in mind. For example, one could be designed primarily for humanities academics, and so have a wide range of fonts and be good at footnotes and altering reference lists to suit different publishing styles, and another might be targeted at mathematicians and so be better at inserting mathematical equations. A third package might be a compromise between the two. In this respect, evaluating word-processing packages involves *comparing objects which are alike in some respects but not in others*. Finally, our comparison might be not between two actual pieces of software, but between a particular existing package and a hypothetical word-processor which has added advantages. Evaluation must be a comparative activity – if there really is only one way of doing something there is no point in trying to evaluate it – but the alternative possibilities can be *potential* as well as actual.

The evaluation of literary works is similarly complex. We can rate very highly particular lines or stanzas of one particular poem about the horror of war (or indeed one extant manuscript version of one poem, for example Wilfred Owen's 'Anthem for Doomed Youth') while still preferring overall another poem on the same theme, even though it may have no lines as outstanding as those we picked out in the first text. We can compare for evaluative purposes two texts which are similar in some functions, but not all (for example we can prefer one novel by Conrad to another even though they are not about the same thing). This means that we do not have to have two texts with *exactly* the same intents in order to evaluate them with respect to one another, but merely texts which are close enough in function to make it sensible to compare them. Hence we are not committed to the fashionable view that it is impossible to evaluate texts in relation to one another because they all have different purposes, though we would, of course, prefer to compare texts that are as similar in function as we can find. The evaluation of texts which have no close extant counterparts is also possible, of course, through a 'comparison' in relation to a hypothetical alternative version of that text.

3.   Stylistics and evaluation in poetry

Traditionally, stylisticians have mainly confined themselves to issues relating to the description and interpretation of texts (but see Short and van Peer 1988 for some consideration of evaluation). They have left matters relating to evaluation to the critics and philosophers on the grounds that there is more than enough for them to do in trying to explain in detail how readers get from text to understanding. But in some respects stylistic analysis is a good platform from which to look at the process of evaluation. Because it examines in such minute detail how texts come to mean what they do, it provides the basic evidence upon which relatively small texts (e.g. poems) and local parts of larger texts can be evaluated (see also Coulthard 1994 for a discussion of this issue in relationship to non-literary texts). Moreover, although a complete stylistic analysis of a long text like a novel or a play is so daunting that it will almost never be carried out, it is likely that examining in detail the processes of evaluation that are at work in localised text-parts will help us to see better what happens when we evaluate texts more globally.

(a) 'The Tyger' by William Blake

We will begin with a consideration of two different versions of the first stanza of a very well known poem, 'The Tyger' by William Blake. Version B is the final version, and A is a previous draft of the first stanza:

Version A	Version B
Tyger! Tyger! burning bright	Tyger! Tyger! burning bright
In the forests of the night,	In the forests of the night,
What immortal hand <u>and</u> eye	What immortal hand <u>or</u> eye
<u>Dare</u> frame thy fearful symmetry?	<u>Could</u> frame thy fearful symmetry?

There are only two words (those which are underlined) which are different in the two versions. With respect to both differences, we would want to argue that the final version is the best. Overall, the poem portrays the Tyger as something so fearful that even God, its creator, was afraid of it, and a significant contributory factor in the portrayal of it as something to be feared is its unknowable quality and the resultant lack of certainty for the addresser in the poem, and hence the reader. We do not have the space to provide extended stylistic analyses of the texts from which the extracts we discuss in this section come, but a few details concerning the poem's organisation will serve to illustrate the point we are making here. Every sentence in the poem is a question apparently addressed to the Tyger, none of which is answered. The presuppositions behind the questions in stanza 4 (see below) suggest that the Tyger, which, in spite of its unusual spelling, we would assume to be animate, has been forged from metal (though these references could conceivably be metaphorical):

> What the hammer? what the chain?
> In what furnace was thy brain?
> What the anvil? what dread grasp
> Dare its deadly terrors clasp?

Moreover, most of these questions are so elliptical as to become difficult to interpret with certainty. 'Wh-' questions typically have only one 'focus' of interrogation, the explication of the referent of the 'wh-' word. For example 'What was the hammer used for?' assumes that some person used the hammer as an instrument for some purpose, and asks what that particular purpose was. But 'What the hammer?' gives us too little propositional form to allow unambiguous interpretation and therefore to work out with certainty the 'focus' of the question. The use of 'or' as opposed to 'and' in line 3 of the first stanza also helps to increase this aura of uncertainty, and so contributes towards the general effect which Blake is working towards. As only people are normally assumed to have hands, 'What immortal hand and eye / Dare frame thy fearful symmetry?' apparently presupposes that some anthropomorphic possessor of the immortal hand and eye did so dare, and asks, metonymically, for the identity of that being. The search for identity would then fail, thus leading to the standard 'rhetorical question' inference, namely that no being would so dare. The use of 'or' instead of 'and' would appear to have all of these resultant effects plus at least two others: there is the issue as to whether it was the hand or the eye which was involved, and, as a consequence, the comfortable assumption that the creator was anthropomorphic is also undermined.

The other difference in the two versions of the first stanza is 'Dare' versus 'Could' in the last line. The 'could' modal relates to ability, and 'dare' to courage in the face of fear. So at first sight it might appear that 'dare' is the better choice here. But we also need to remember that the first stanza of this poem is repeated as the last stanza. In the first version, we have an exact repetition, but in the final one, the 'Could' of the first stanza becomes 'Dare' in the final stanza. In other words, the first version brings up the fear/courage issue at the beginning and merely repeats it at the end, whereas the final one first brings up the issue of ability at the beginning, and then, after we have read the rest of the poem, raises the fear/courage issue separately at the end. The final version thus increases the extent of the doubt in relation to the increasing insecurity and fear of the addresser as the poem unfolds, and challenges more explicitly two assumptions that Christians normally make in relation to a creator, namely his/her/its omnipotence and, consequently, the irrelevance of the issue of fear, and so courage, for such a being.

In the above discussion of a small part of Blake's 'The Tyger', we have compared an earlier version of the poem with Blake's final version, to show why, in two respects, the final version is preferable. This process could be re-applied to different aspects of this poem and its earlier drafts. In the remaining poetic examples, we will not have two different extant versions of a text to compare. Instead, though, we can carefully compare texts with alternatives which we can imagine with the help of detailed stylistic analysis, and use these analyses as the basis for evaluative judgements.

(b) 'October Dawn' by Ted Hughes

In our view, 'October Dawn' is a good poem which is rather let down by its last stanza. It is an exploration, in half-rhyming couplets, of how October can be seen, not just as the end to summer and the beginning of winter, but as the beginning of a threatening process which could, if that process was not impeded, result in the establishment of a new ice age. A description of interesting rhythmic and phonetic effects in relation to interpretation in the middle of this poem can be found in Short (1996: 146–9). At the end of the poem we are told that the prehistoric ice-age beasts will celebrate being reunited:

... while a fist of cold
Squeezes the fire at the core of the world,

Squeezes the fire at the core of the heart,
And now it is about to start.

(Ted Hughes, 'October Dawn')

The final stanza is bound to be prominent just because it is the end of the poem. In addition, it is the only stanza which has a couplet with a full rhyme ('heart'/'start'). This internal deviation in the poem's rhyme scheme further foregrounds the last stanza, leading us to expect appropriate effects in terms of significant content. But the last line merely says explicitly something we have known throughout the poem. The resultant effect is what traditionally is referred to as bathos. The organisation of the poem leads us to expect something new and significant at the very end, but no such item of significance occurs, and so we feel let down. If Hughes could have thought of a better last line, our overall evaluation of the poem would have been higher.

(c) The opening of 'Little Gidding' by T. S. Eliot

The last of T. S. Eliot's famous *Four Quartets*, 'Little Gidding' is arguably one of Eliot's greatest poems, and we would not want to disagree with such a judgement. However, we do want to suggest that it is not completely beyond improvement, by pointing out, with the help of stylistic analysis, a small problem with the opening:

Midwinter spring is its own season
Sempiternal though sodden towards sundown,
Suspended in time, between pole and tropic.
When the short day is brightest, with frost and fire,
The brief sun flames the ice, on pond and ditches,   5
In windless cold that is the heart's heat,
Reflecting in a watery mirror
A glare that is brightness in the early afternoon.
And glow more intense than blaze of branch, or brazier,
Stirs the dumb spirit: no wind, but pentecostal fire   10
In the dark time of the year. Between melting and freezing
The soul's sap quivers. There is no earth smell
Or smell of living thing. This is the spring time
But not in time's covenant. Now the hedgerow
Is blanched for an hour with transitory blossom   15
Of snow, a bloom more sudden
Than that of summer, neither budding nor fading,
Not in the scheme of generation.

> Where is the summer, the unimaginable
> Zero summer   20
>
>   (T. S. Eliot, 'Little Gidding')

The subject matter of these opening lines, which in many ways prefigure the rest of the poem, is St Lucie's day, the year's shortest day and therefore the darkest day of the year in the calendrical cycle. But the particular St Lucie's day which Eliot describes is sunny, and he uses this opposition at the beginning of the poem as part of a systematic series of related contrasts: bright *vs.* dark, hot *vs.* cold and, a few lines later, life *vs.* death. The idea of sunlight (light, warm) on the shortest day of the year (dark, cold) is thus used as a metaphorical vehicle for the consideration of life and death. Even at the darkest, coldest, and so, by implication, the most dead part of the year, sunlight, and so light, warmth and life are still present, to begin the part of the cycle which moves through spring to summer, when the life force is at its strongest.

This general kind of metaphorisation is not new, of course. The consistent basis for this grouping of textual metaphors is the conceptual metaphor LIFE IS A FLAME which, as Lakoff and Turner (1989:87–8) point out, is a composite of two other cognitive metaphors, LIFE IS LIGHT and LIFE IS HEAT. The obvious converses of these basic metaphors are DEATH IS DARK and DEATH IS COLD. To point out that the metaphor grouping which Eliot explores is common in English is not, however, to deny his considerable poetic invention. What is innovative is the creation of new and striking instantiations of these basic metaphors and how he links them together in a complex way which is consistent both with the 'underlying' conceptual metaphors from which they are 'derived' and the development of his paradoxical textual theme.

There are many aspects of this paradoxical thematic development in the poem's opening. For example, if we look at just a few of the verse paragraph's complex noun phrases, we can see that 'spring' is premodified by 'midwinter' in line 1 and 'cold' is postmodified by a relative clause 'that is the heart's heat' in line 6. Similarly, 'glare' is postmodified by 'that is darkness in the early afternoon', 'blossom' is postmodified by 'of snow' in lines 15–16, and so on.

But the aspect of this development which we want to explore in detail is a system of 'grammatical rhyme' which Eliot employs to the same thematic end. The prepositional phrase at the end of line 3, 'between pole and tropic' (with the structure: 'preposition + "noun and noun"'), is paralleled, at the end of the following line, by 'with frost and fire'. In both cases, the noun pairs also exhibit alliterative parallels.[2] Structural parallelism, as stylisticians have pointed out, often push readers towards interpretations which involve similar or opposed meanings (see, for example, Short 1996: 13–15, 22–3 and 63–8). The two pairs of grammatically co-ordinated, but semantically opposed nouns form a clear example of the effect of parallelism. Internally, each noun + noun parallelism holds a semantic opposition, and externally the overall prepositional phrases, which are structurally parallel to one another, can be seen as embodying similar oppositions (cold/hot). This 'parallelism of oppositions' is then picked up in another grammatical rhyme, this time involving verbal nouns, at the end of line 11, 'Between melting and freezing' and finally, a few lines later, (line 17) by 'neither budding nor fading', which, although it is not a prepositional phrase, and so does not parallel the prepositional phrases at the end of lines 3 and 4, does parallel 'Between melting and freezing' because of the shared use of co-ordinated present participle verbs. The grammatical rhymes of lines 3 and 4 are thus connected to 'neither budding nor fading' of line 17 by the intermediate structure at the end of line 11, which rhymes both with lines 3 and 4 and with line 17. Moreover, it is this 'developing grammatical rhyme' device which Eliot uses to connect together the light/dark and hot/cold oppositions with the other opposition of life/death. It is clear, then, that Eliot was intuitively alive to the detailed structural and meaning potentials of the grammatical rhymes he creates, and employs them to useful thematic effect. Indeed, our stylistic description leads fairly easily to a positive evaluation for this aspect of Eliot's writing. He is articulating a complex developing set of thematic interrelations in a controlled and precise way.

But this same aspect of his writing can also be seen as ameliorable. The first two grammatical rhymes which we have pointed out have the cold/dark element first and the hot/light element second. But in lines 11 and 17 the order is reversed. We can see no obvious reason why the ordering could not have been kept consistent throughout, thus reinforcing the developmental parallelism and making it easier for the reader to perceive. This is a pretty fine discrimination, but it would appear that, on the basis of his already considerable achievement, it is possible to construe an instantiation of Eliot's poem which is a little better than the extant version. After all, although we would not put ourselves in the same category, Ezra Pound's advice on early drafts of *The Waste Land* resulted in considerable improvements on Eliot's original.

Moreover, there is another aspect of Eliot's system of grammatical rhyme which we have not yet considered. At the end of line 5, the line immediately after the grammatical rhyme with which we began this discussion, there is another

---

2. We use 'alliteration' here to include the use of phonetically similar, as well as identical phonemes. For a discussion of alliteration which indicates our general theoretical position, see Short (1996: 107–11).

'preposition + "noun and noun"' structure, 'on pond and ditches', which, like those of the previous two lines, also exhibits alliterative connections (although weaker ones) between the nouns. The psychological pressure related to processing this parallelism is likely to have the unfortunate effect, on some readers at least, of inducing them to try to include this prepositional phrase in the set of interconnected grammatical rhymes we have already discussed. Indeed, when we have discussed this extract in class on past courses on the stylistics of poetry, this is precisely what our students have tried to do. They have suggested, for example, despite the lack of evidence, that ponds are naturally colder than ditches. In some cases, they have wanted to make such an interpretative move, even when the difficulty we have outlined is pointed out to them, precisely because they find it difficult to accept the idea that a great poet like Eliot could 'make mistakes'. In other words, Eliot's continuation of the structural parallelism has led some of our students up an 'interpretative garden path'. This problem could have been avoided, without obvious harm in other respects, by using, for example, 'on frozen ditches' instead of 'on pond and ditches'. It is not so much that Eliot has 'made a mistake' here, but rather that it is possible to construe richer, preferable alternatives which could add to an already valuable text.

What general lessons can we draw from this rather detailed discussion? First of all, even the best of poems (or indeed other literary works) do not have to satisfy us in every minute detail to want to praise them very highly. 'Little Gidding' is still a wonderful poem, even if we notice a few minor details that do not work as well as they might. Indeed, absolutely perfect literary texts, in the sense that the form of the text leads us unerringly to a complete understanding of the complex whole without any unnecessary difficulties, seem unlikely, and the more unlikely the longer the text becomes, if only because there is more material to control. So, when we come to considered evaluations, absolute perfection is too high a standard to demand, even though we may hope for it.

Secondly, it would appear that the assumption that authors are in complete control of their textual output *does* have to be made during the interpretative phase of criticism, even if it has to be weakened eventually. For example, it is noticing the details of the changes in the pattern of grammatical rhymes from lines 3/4 to 11 and 17, and then trying to find an explanation for the pattern of linked similarity and difference, that allows us to frame the aspect of interpretation of 'Little Gidding' that relates the hot/cold and light/dark oppositions to life/death. Another example would be the religious lexis which occurs in the above verse-paragraph. We would have to assume that Eliot had not made a mistake in including such vocabulary items in what is otherwise a description of nature, but that it was included to help the reader infer a connection between religious belief and the cycle of the seasons. At the end of an attempt at interpretation, critics may well still find aspects of the text unaccounted for, even if they appear to have achieved a good interpretation. At that point, logically they would have to say, other things being equal, that an interpretation of the text which explained what they had explained *plus* any other aspects would have to be a superior interpretation.

Thirdly, it will be helpful to notice that these details help us to see how evaluation is always relative to interpretation. Other things being equal, an account of 'Little Gidding' which accounted interpretatively for what we have explained and also came up with a way of integrating successfully the aspects with which we have difficulty would not just have improved on our interpretation. At the same time it would have improved the overall valuation of the poem because there would be less 'interpretative residue', as it were (cf. the chapter by Harald Fricke in this volume).

4. **Stylistics and evaluation in prose fiction: A comparison of two versions of the same scene from the two editions of John Fowles's *The Magus***

We now want to explore the use of stylistic analysis in helping to substantiate judgements about fictional prose. John Fowles wrote two different versions of his novel *The Magus*. The first edition was published in 1966, the second in 1977.[3] In the foreword to the second edition, he states that:

> Though this is not, in any major thematic or narrative sense, a fresh version of *The Magus*, it is rather more than a stylistic revision. A number of scenes have been largely re-written, and one or two new ones invented.   (Fowles 1977:5)

The Magus is about a young man, Nicholas D'Urfe, who leaves London to teach English in a school on a small Greek island. There, he meets a man called Conchis, who, in god-like fashion, creates a series of real-life tableaux and masques in which Nicholas becomes enmeshed. Nicholas is continually involved in a quest to find out the truth behind Conchis's illusions, but each 'truth' is later seen as yet another illusion which Conchis has created in order to fool him. In particular, Nicholas is tricked again and again concerning the identities and roles of the beautiful young women Conchis engineers him to become involved with. Nicholas meets someone called Lily, who he thinks is Conchis's mistress. But she turns out to be called Julie, and playing the part of Conchis's dead fiancé in one of Conchis's tableaux. Julie also has a twin sister who is at first called Rose, and who we later know as June. In the scene on which we are concentrating, Nicholas and Julie have just been in bed together after June has 'lured' Nicholas to the hotel where Julie is waiting for him. Men suddenly rush into the hotel room and assault Nicholas. In the first edition of the novel, the attack comes at the end of Chapter 58 (pp. 443–4) just as

---

3.   In this article, all references to the first edition are to the World Books edition (1967). All references to the second edition are to the Jonathan Cape edition (1977).

Nicholas and Julie are about to make love. In the second edition, the attack is at the very beginning of Chapter 59 (pp. 488–9), immediately after their love-making has taken place. In both cases, the woman, who he has been getting to know in the most intimate terms, tells him just before the attack that she is not Julie after all. We do not have the space below to quote both passages extensively, but instead will quote the smaller extracts from the passages on which we concentrate most of our more detailed analysis. In each version, (a) Nicholas is quickly overpowered and tied up, and (b) Conchis then comes in and administers a tranquillising drug to him. Below, we will compare how these two events are portrayed in the two editions of the novel.

The overall mode of narration is the same in the two versions of the novel: a homodiegetic first-person narrator tells the story some time after it happened (although it is not clear *how long* after it happened (see Loveday 1985: 38–9; Wolfe 1979: 84)). In both versions of the scene the narrator tries to represent the sense of shock, disorientation, helplessness and anger that he experienced at the time. As a consequence, in both cases we have access to the viewpoint of the 'I'-as-character, experiencing these disconcerting and frightening moments at first hand. However, there are also some major differences between the two passages. The first edition is told much more consistently from the viewpoint of the 'I'-as-character, whereas the second version mixes together the different perspectives of the character's (experienced) event-time and the narrator's coding-time memories. As a consequence, much of the sense of immediacy and drama in the first edition is lost. Ho (2007) systematically compares the two editions of *The Magus*, using a combination of qualitative and corpus-based stylistic analysis, and suggests why Fowles might have wanted to sacrifice drama for ambiguity in the novel as a whole.

4.1   Nicholas is overpowered

Let us begin by looking in detail at the openings of the two descriptions of the attack, up to the point before the character Conchis enters the room. There are two main differences in terms of the detail of the plot. In the first version Julie covers herself with a bathrobe and remains in the room for some time, while in the second version she leaves the room immediately and is apparently comforted by someone just outside. The other difference is the addition of a third character ('the blond-headed sailor') in the second version. All further differences are to do with the way in which the same events are told, and it is this that we will focus on in our analysis.

Here is the opening of the first version. (Sentence numbers have been inserted at the end of each sentence and accompanied by the letter 'a' to indicate the first version. The letter 'b' will be used for the numbers of the sentences in the second version.)

The door was flung wide open, the light came on, there were two black figures, two tall men in black trousers and shirts (1a). One was the Negro and the other was 'Anton' (2a). Joe came first, so fast at me that I had no time to do anything but convulsively grip the bedspread over my loins (3a). I tried to see Julie, her face, because I still could not accept what I knew: that she had turned the key and opened the door (4a). Anton flung her something she caught and quickly put on – a deep-red towel bathrobe (5a). Joe flung himself at me just as I was about to shout (6a). His hand clapped violently across my mouth and I felt the weight of him; a whiff of shaving-lotion, or hair-oil (7a). I was in no fit state to struggle (8a). What fighting I did was mainly to try to keep the bedspread over me (9a). Anton gripped my legs (10a). They must have had loops of rope ready prepared, because in fifteen seconds I was tied up (11a). Then I was gagged (12a). I got one stifled beginning of what I felt out at Julie (13a).

'You –' (14a)

But then I was silenced (15a). The two men forced my arms back, so I was lying flat, straining my neck up to see Julie (16a). She turned, tying the ends of the belt (17a).

(Fowles 1967:443)

A number of linguistic features are used here to anchor the viewpoint as that of Nicholas-the-character, *at the time of the event*, rather than as that of Nicholas-the-narrator, looking back with the benefit of hindsight. These features relate particularly to what Leech and Short (1981) have called 'psychological sequencing' – a technique whereby we find out details about the fictional world not in logical or chronological order, but in the order in which they are experienced by the character whose viewpoint is privileged. Short (1996) refers to choices relating to the presentation and sequencing of events in the narrative as 'event-coding', and provides an analysis of part of the extract above as illustration (Short 1996:275–6).

As we will show below, some linguistic features connected with event-coding are retained in the second version to suggest the psychological sequencing of Nicholas-as-character. Such devices are used less consistently, however, and the perspective of Nicholas-as-narrator is much more prominent. Here is the opening of the second version of the scene:

Three men, all in dark trousers and black polo-neck jumpers – they came so quickly that, paralyzed in everything but instinct, I had no time to do anything but grab the bedspread over my loins (1b). The one in the lead was Joe, the Negro (2b). He flung himself at me just as I was about to shout (3b). His hand clapped brutally over my mouth and I felt the strength and weight of him throw me back (4b). One of the others must have turned on the bedside lamp again (5b). I saw another face I knew: the last time I had seen it had been on the ridge, when the owner had been in German uniform, playing

Anton (6b). The third face belonged to the blond-headed sailor I had seen twice at Bourani that previous Sunday (7b). I tried as I struggled under Joe to see Julie – I still couldn't accept that this was not some nightmare, like some freak misbinding in a book, a Lawrence novel become, at the turn of a page, one by Kafka (8b). But all I glimpsed was her back as she left the room (9b). Someone met her there, an arm went round her shoulders as if she had just escaped from an air disaster and drew her out of sight (10b).

I began to fight violently, but they had obviously anticipated that, had loops of rope ready (11b). In less than half a minute I was tied up and lying on my face (12b). I don't know if I was still shouting obscenities at them; I was certainly thinking them (13b). Then I was gagged (14b). Somebody threw the bedspread over me (15b). I managed to twist my head to see the door (16b).

(Fowles 1977: 488)

We will now compare the language used in the two versions in more detail.

(a) Passives, intransitives and agent deletion

Four passives are used in the first sixteen sentences of the first version of our scene: 'The door was flung wide open . . .' in sentence (1a), '. . .I was tied up.' in sentence (11a), '. . . I was gagged . . .' in sentence (12a), and '. . .I was silenced.' in sentence (14a). In all four cases the agent is deleted. The choice of the passive in sentence (1a) is clearly due to the fact that at that point Nicholas-the-character does not know who opens the door, but perceives the opening of the door before realising who is responsible for it. The reader is thus put in the same position as the character, rather than benefiting from the narrator's superior *post-hoc* knowledge. The other three uses of the passive are somewhat different, in that, by now, Nicholas knows who the people acting upon him are. However, the use of these passives with agent deletion is consistent with the assumption that, due to his state of disorientation, he does not realise exactly which individual ties him up, gags him and silences him. After all, most of these actions are carried out from a position behind his back.

A grammatical device similar in effect to the use of the passive with agent deletion is used in the first sentence to reinforce the character's surprise at what is happening around him. In the clause '. . . the light came on . . .', an intransitive verb is used with an inanimate subject. The subject, in this case, is not the agent, but the entity affected by the action. Again, because Nicholas-as-character does not immediately know who puts the light on, we do not get a transitive structure such as 'X switched the light on', since the identity of 'X' is not known to him when he experiences the event.

In the second version, only two passives are used: '. . . I was tied up . . . 'in sentence (12b) and '. . . I was gagged.' in sentence (14b). No reference is made at the beginning to Nicholas's perception of the door opening or the light coming on without his knowing who the relevant agents are. Indeed, the first sentence begins with a reference to the agents themselves. Only the opening left-dislocation ('Three men [...] – they ...') and the adverb phrase 'so quickly' are used in the second version to suggest Nicholas's surprise.

(b) The introduction of new referents
In the first version, Nicholas-the-character's state of disorientation at the time of the attack is conveyed in part by the way in which new referents are introduced. Appositional structures are used to suggest changing perceptions on Nicholas's part: from blurred, indistinct perception to more precise identification. In sentence (1a) the two people who burst into the room are introduced as ' ... two black figures, two tall men in black trousers and shirts'. The noun 'figures' makes a vague reference to human beings, who are not even identified in terms of their sex, but only in terms of colour. And at this stage it is not even clear exactly what 'black' specifically relates to (clothes?, skin?, the visual effects associated with the light being suddenly switched on?), a fact which correlates with Nicholas's state of disorientation. This is followed by a noun phrase where the invaders are described in terms of their size ('tall'), their sex ('men'), and the nature and colour of their clothes ('black trousers and shirts'). It is only in the following sentence that the two individuals are identified by name (or nickname), so that, as readers, we find out, along with Nicholas, that they are not strangers at all. The strategy of following a less specific noun phrase by a more specific one referring to the same thing is also used in sentence (5a) to refer to the object that Anton throws to Julie: 'something she caught and quickly put on – a deep-red towel bathrobe.' The object is first referred to by means of an indefinite pronoun ('something'), and is only subsequently identified and described in detail by means of a fully-fledged noun phrase. Finally, in 'I tried to see Julie, her face ...' of sentence (4a), the second element, 'her face' indicates the precise part of Julie that Nicholas wants to see – the part of her which is most likely to give evidence of her attitude and feelings. If we compare this with the more simple 'I tried to see Julie's face' we can see that the clause Fowles uses suggests a sequence in which a generalised intention becomes more specific in the process of its realisation.

The use of these techniques is diluted in the second version. We still have two stages in the perception of the invaders, from 'Three men ...' to full recognition. The first reference, however, is much more precise than in the first version. We immediately know the sex of the three people ('three men'), and we are given a very precise description of their clothes. 'Polo-neck jumpers' suggests a clear, detailed perception, and the colour of the trousers ('dark') is distinguished rather subtly from that of the jumpers ('black'). The provision of such minute detail weakens the sense of fast, blurred impressions conveyed by the first version. No reference is made in the second version to a bathrobe being provided for Julie, although indefinite pronouns are used on two occasions to suggest the limitations of Nicholas's perceptions: 'someone' in sentence (10b) and 'somebody' in sentence (16b). The psychological sequencing effect in relation to Julie's face is also removed in the second version ('I tried as I struggled under Joe to see Julie . . .').

(c) Other differences

In the first version of the scene, a number of other linguistic features suggest the viewpoint of Nicholas-as-character and his varying degrees of certainty about the events told in the story. In terms of 'social' deixis (Short 1996: 272–4), it is interesting to note the use of 'scare quotes' in reference to the character calling himself 'Anton'. These scare quotes highlight Nicholas's uncertainty about the true identity of this person and some of the other characters in the story (the same device is used in relation to Julie later in the passage). Similarly, the use of the modal verb 'must' in sentence (11a) highlights the sense of epistemic uncertainty in which the character finds himself: the proposition *They had loops of ropes ready prepared* is not presented as a directly experienced 'fact', but as an inference based on the speed with which Nicholas was tied up. In the first version of the scene, we are also brought very close to Nicholas-the-character's event-time experience by means of references to (i) minute physical sensations, such as Joe's smell in sentence (7a), (ii) his cognitive struggle to make sense of events, such as his reluctance to accept the validity of his deductions in sentence (4a), and (iii) his intentions, such as in sentence (4a) ('I tried to . . .').

In the second version, no scare quotes are used for Anton's name, but an explicit reference is made in sentence (6b) to the fact that Nicholas had last seen him while he was 'playing Anton'. As in the first version, the modal auxiliary 'must' is used in sentence (5b) to indicate an inference on Nicholas's part, and the modal adverb 'obviously' is used in the same way in sentence (11b). What is different, however, is that in sentence (13b) we find an expression of epistemic uncertainty ('I don't know') which relates to Nicholas-as-narrator, rather than as-character. The use of 'certainly' in the same sentence also seems to relate to the narrator. Whereas in the first version any uncertainty belonged to the perspective of Nicholas-as-character, in the second version we have a mixture of the character's and the narrator's uncertainty. The second version also has fewer physical details relating to Nicholas's sensations: no reference is made to smell, for example, and this also eliminates the uncertainty about the *source* of the smell conveyed by 'a whiff of shaving-lotion, or hair-oil' in sentence (7a). On the other hand, we still have some indication of Nicholas's thought processes, as in sentence (8b) ('I still couldn't accept this was not some nightmare'), and his intentions, as in sentence (16b) ('I managed to twist my head to see the door'). What is added in the second version is, firstly, some additional background information, for example the reference to the exact circumstances in which Nicholas had last met Anton (sentence

6b) and the blond sailor (sentence 7b). Secondly, we find a new simile in sentence (8b), recasting Nicholas's experience in terms of his knowledge of different literary novels (see also Loveday 1985: 38; Palmer 1974: 56–8; Wolfe 1979: 89). Both types of addition lessen the sense of 'being there' with Nicholas-the-character during his disconcerting experience, and instead emphasise rather more the presence of Nicholas-the-narrator, reflecting on his past experience and providing contextual information for the reader.

4.2 Conchis drugs Nicholas

Another interesting contrast between the two versions in terms of viewpoint is provided by the description of the way in which, after Nicholas has been sub-dued by his henchmen, Conchis injects a tranquilising drug into his arm. The two versions of this event are given below (using the same conventions as in 4.1, the sentences are numbered to take account of the unquoted intervening text between these extracts and the previous ones):

> Conchis came forward from doing something by the table (39a). He leant over me (40a). 'Nicholas, we shall not frighten you any more (41a). But we want you to go to sleep (42a). It will be convenient for us and less painful for you (43a). Please do not struggle (44a).'
> The absurd memory of the pile of exam papers I had still to mark flicked through my mind (45a). Joe and Anton held my left arm like a vice (46a). I resisted for a moment, then gave in (47a). A dab of wet (48a). The needle pricked into my forearm (49a). I felt the morphine, or whatever it was, en-ter (50a). The needle was withdrawn, another dab of something wet (51a). Conchis went back to his table (52a).   (Fowles 1967:444)

> 'Anton' held out a small open case to Conchis (27b). He took out a hypo-dermic syringe, checked it was correctly filled, then leant over me a little and showed it (28b).
> 'We shall not frighten you any more, young man (29b). But we want you to go to sleep (30b). It will be less painful for you (31b). Please do not struggle (32b).'
> The absurd memory of the pile of examination papers I still had to mark went through my mind (33b). Joe and the other man turned me on my back again and gripped my left arm like a vice (34b). I resisted for a few moments, then gave in (35b). A dab of wet (36b). The needle pricked into my fore-arm (37b). I felt the morphine, or whatever it was, enter (38b). The needle was withdrawn, another dab of something wet (39b). Conchis stood back, watched me a moment, then turned and replaced the syringe in the black medical case it had come from (40b).   (Fowles 1977:489)

First of all, there are some obvious similarities in the content of the two scenes, notably what Conchis says to Nicholas, Nicholas's memory of the marking he has to do, the way in which he is held still, and the description of his sensations during the injection. The differences are, once again, to do with the way in which the events are 'coded'.

In the first version Nicholas is unaware of what Conchis is going to do until he does it, so that the reader also has to infer, step by step, what is happening to him. In sentence (39a), Conchis's activities at the table are referred to by means of the indefinite pronoun 'something'. As a consequence, the first indication of what he is about to do can only be inferred from the fact that he says '. . . we want you to go to sleep' in sentence (42a). In the following paragraph, the fact that Conchis is giving Nicholas an injection can be inferred from increasingly stronger clues: the way in which Nicholas's arm is being held, the 'dab of wet', the reference to the needle pricking his arm, the liquid going in, and so on.

The second version is rather different. Here Nicholas is aware from the very beginning of what is going to happen, and so, of course, is the reader. After the reference to Anton holding out 'a small open case' for Conchis in sentence (27b), we have the explicit mention of 'a hypodermic syringe', which Conchis checks and shows to Nicholas before speaking to him. As a consequence, the sense that Nicholas is not just helpless, but also partly unaware of what is going on, is lost in the second version. The reader's life is also made easier, since less inferential work is needed to understand what is going on.

4.3 Overall comments

Overall, our analysis has shown that the first version of our scene from *The Magus* represents very consistently the viewpoint of Nicholas at the time that he experiences these rather disturbing events. A number of linguistic choices are used to maximise effects of immediacy, confusion and helplessness, and to show Nicholas's gradual move from shock and uncertainty to awareness and understanding. Because readers experience the scene from the point of view of Nicholas-as-character, they are, to some extent, put through the same ordeal of struggling to come to terms with what is going on in the fictional world (see Salami 1992: 77–8). They therefore have to do a considerable amount of inferential work in order to understand some elements of the narration (e.g. Why are scare quotes used around Anton's name? What is Conchis about to do to Nicholas in sentence 39a?).

On the other hand, the second version oscillates between the perspective of Nicholas-as-character and as-narrator, and is therefore less consistent in terms of point of view. Although some parts of the scene are still presented from Nicholas's viewpoint at the time he experienced the events, the effects of immediacy, involvement and confusion are much weaker than in the first version. Although at times readers are brought close to Nicholas's original experience, at other times they are given the narrator's more detached and better-informed perspective. As narrator, Nicholas provides more background information about the characters (e.g. he reminds us explicitly about the issue to do with Anton's identity), makes intertextual connections between his story and other stories, and uses his hindsight to make up for his confusion at the time. A different element of uncertainty is introduced, however. The narrator does not appear to be sure about his memory of the events (sentence 13b), so that it may sometimes be difficult to decide whether non-factive expressions should be attributed to the character or the narrator (see also Loveday 1985: 35–6).

The reason why we prefer the evocation of the scene from the first edition is that we value and enjoy its consistency, the immediacy and sense of mystery associated with the presentation of the perspective of Nicholas-as-character and the consequent reader involvement. It is conceivable that other readers will prefer the second version because of its greater detachment and use of inter-textual references, perhaps *via* the kind of critical move which Loveday (1985: 46) wants to make. He points to the possibility that the kinds of inconsistencies in the narration which we have highlighted in detail, along with various other kinds of inconsistency, suggest that '... *The Magus* reminds us that it is illusion.' It is not clear whether Loveday's characterisation of the novel in terms of his suggestion of the functions of mixed viewpoint can be coherently sustained when it is examined in more detail, and, in any case, trying to decide between competing large-scale evaluations of whole novels is well beyond the scope of this paper. Well-informed judgements on matters of this sort need a much better account not just of how we evaluate small-scale textual parts, but of how we integrate a host of such small-scale judgements into a large-scale evaluative whole. The point of our discussion in this section has been much more limited: to show how it is possible to use linguistic analysis to explain in detail the motivation for our evaluation of less than a couple of paragraphs of what is, after all, a very long novel.

5.   Concluding remarks

Unfortunately we have not had the space to examine any examples from drama in our discussion of the relationship between stylistics and evaluation. However, we believe that in general terms the kinds of arguments we have put forward in relation to poetry and prose are also applicable to play texts. We have looked in considerable detail at the small-scale extracts from poetry and prose which we have chosen to discuss because we believe that such careful analysis should be an essential cornerstone of criticism, whether it be for interpretative or evaluative purposes.

When textual interpretation is being considered, it is often said that stylistic analysis, because it is so detailed, and hence time-consuming, works best on short texts, like poems. There is clearly considerable truth in this. Detailed stylistic accounts of *whole texts* are only feasible when the texts are short. The same point can be made about stylistics and evaluation. But a detailed linguistic stylistic examination of textual extracts can be illuminatingly related to larger-scale interpretative remarks, as the stylistic work to date on the novel and drama has demonstrated. And it should also be clear, from our discussion in 4 above, that the same point can be made in relation to stylistic analysis and the evaluation of longer literary works. Moreover, we hope to have shown how the kind of detailed care which stylistic analysis brings to the act of critical interpretation can help us not just to uncover part of the basis for the judgements of particular works, but also to understand the procedures by which we evaluate literary texts in general. It is not surprising that plenty of work still needs to be done before we understand how we evaluate literary texts. After all, considerably more critical effort has been expended on how to interpret texts, and there is still much to be done there. But we hope that we have shown how stylistic analysis can be of use in literary evaluation as well as in interpretation.

References

Coulthard, M. 1994. On analysing and evaluating written text. In *Advances in Written Text Analysis*. M. Coulthard. (ed.), 1–11. London: Routledge.

Eliot, T. S. 1963. *Collected poems, 1909–1962*. London: Faber and Faber.

Fowles, J. 1966 [1967]. *The Magus*. London: World Books.

Fowles, J. 1977. *The Magus*. 2nd edn. London: Jonathan Cape.

Fowler, R. 1986. *Linguistic Criticism*. Oxford: OUP.

Herman, V. 1995. *Dramatic Discourse: Dialogue as Interaction*. London: Routledge.

Ho, Yufang. 2007. *A qualitative and quantitative stylistic comparison of the two editions of John Fowles's 'The Magus'*. Unpublished Ph.D. thesis: Lancaster University, UK.

Hughes, T. 1982. *Selected Poems 1957–1981*. London: Faber and Faber.

Lakoff, G. & M. Turner. 1989. *More than Cool Reason: A Field Guide to Poetic Metaphor*. Chicago IL: University of Chicago Press.

Leech, G. N. 1969. *A Linguistic Guide to English Poetry*. London: Longman.

Leech, G. N. & M. H. Short. 1981. *Style in Fiction: A Linguistic Introduction to English Fictional Prose*. London: Longman.

Loveday, S. 1985. *The Romances of John Fowles*. London: Macmillan.

Palmer, W. J. 1974. *The Fiction of John Fowles: Tradition, Art, and the Loneliness of Selfhood*. Columbia MI: Missouri University Press

Salami, M. 1992. *John Fowles's Fiction and the Poetics of Postmodernism*. London: Associated University Presses.

Semino, E. 1997. *Language and World Creation in Poems & Other Texts*. London: Longman.

Simpson, P. 1993. *Language, Ideology and Point of View*. London: Routledge.

Simpson, P. 1997. *Language Through Literature: An Introduction*. London: Routledge.

Short, M. 1996. *Exploring the Language of Poems, Plays and Prose*. London: Longman.

Short, M. & W. van Peer. 1988. Accident! Stylisticians Evaluate: Aims and Methods of Stylistic Analysis. In *Reading, Analysing and Teaching Literature*, M. Short (ed.), 22–71. London: Longman.

Toolan, M. J. 1988. *Narrative: A Critical Linguistic Introduction*. London: Routledge.

Wolfe, P. 1979. *John Fowles: Magus and Moralist*. Lewisburg: Associated University Presses.

CHAPTER 8

The value of Juvenal

Walter Nash

Written in the early 1990s, in response to Professor van Peer's then developing views of literariness and the literary canon, this paper considers the status of Juvenal (Decius Junius Juvenalis c.80–c.130) as a canonical presence in English literature, focusing particularly on the Augustan age (17th–18thC), when Juvenal was valued as a model of socio-political rhetoric. The problem of translating Juvenal's distinctive style, a mix of the low and the lofty, is considered, and the free-verse hexameters of a modern translator, Peter Green, are presented in contrast to the rhyme-bound pentameters of the Augustans. The paper closes with a discussion of tradition, literary merit, and the canonicity of Juvenal.

I

There must be veterans still in Britain, men of riper years, as the cliché goes, who will remember subscribing in their pre-war schooldays to a periodical called *The Boys' Own Paper*, and who may recall that magazine's proud Latin motto: *Quicquid agunt pueri nostri farrago libelli* – helpfully translated by the editor as "Whatever boys do makes up the mixture of our little book". The boyish activities in question were such as might make for the service of Country, King and Empire: manly sports, useful hobbies, clean living, ripping adventures, honour, duty, playing the game. Few of the paper's young readership could have known -nor did the editor reveal – that *Quicquid agunt pueri*, &c., was a wonderfully inappropriate revision of some lines in Juvenal's 1st Satire, reading *Quicquid agunt homines, votum, timor, ira, voluptas/ Gaudia discursus nostri farrago libelli est*: "Whatever men do, whatever they pray for, whatever they fear, whatever makes them angry, their pleasures as they take them, their joys as they pursue them – these things are what my hotchpotch poetry is all about." Juvenal's word, *farrago* means, strictly, "cattle cake", or "mash", and it defines from the outset a characteristically subversive attitude. He derisively rejects the traditional and the respectable, the safe moral refuge, the stylistic convention. To evoke his patronage as big brother of good British boys was an extraordinary act. It was as though the scoutmaster had taken a tip from the town tearaway.

And indeed, Decimus Junius Juvenalis, comfortably Englished as Juvenal, was a tearaway of a writer. There is no word that will accurately characterise him, no single pronouncement that will comprehend him. You can say all sorts of things about him, and you will contradict yourself at every other moment. He is elegant, but he is coarse. He is noble and spiteful. He is deeply in earnest, though cynical. He is a profane moralist. He is bawdily misogynistic, angrily xenophobic, lewdly homophobic. He rarely appears to like anybody; but then he has a tenderness for children – *maxima debetur puero reverentia*, he says – above all else show respect for a child – which may perhaps provide something in the way of an excuse for the editor of the *Boys' Own Paper*. He affects to hate Rome, yet is inveterately Roman. He is a bundle of passions, prejudices and vehement contradictions, and in all these things appears as the master of a style so brilliant, so quick-stepping, of such deadly precision, that the reader, though possibly suspecting that this is a not altogether *nice* man, is still ready to forgive him – almost – anything.

No one could call him Politically Correct, as we now understand that term. If some stern modern censor were to propose a league of the ideologically dubious, Juvenal would have to be nominated as a candidate for presidency. But his work survives; beyond the mutable fortunes of ancient manuscripts, it survives quite simply because he could write; because Time, as W.H. Auden puts it, "worships language, and forgives / Everyone by whom it lives":

> Time, that with this strange excuse
> Pardoned Rudyard Kipling's views,
> And will pardon Paul Claudel,
> Pardons him for writing well.
>
> ("In Memory of W. B. Yeats", Auden 1950:66)

Auden's "him" refers to Yeats, but the judgement applies equally to Juvenal.

How writers survive, and play a part in the formation of literary traditions beyond their own time and place, is a question worthy of more attention than current literary theory might wish to allow. There are fashions, we know; poets fall into obscurity only to re-emerge, perhaps after a long period, into the fashionable light. Often, the death of the artist brings the first darkness over his work, a fate which appears to have befallen Juvenal's *Satires* in the hundred years after his death in 140 AD, or thereabouts. Peter Green makes the interesting suggestion that this initial neglect is understandable, "since both the vices and the literary fashions which Juvenal castigated became increasingly popular with the Imperial Court towards the close of the Antonine period" – an assessment which puts Juvenal among the opponents of power, the subversives of the existing order. (Green 1976:9) Green further points out the ironic circumstance that it was the Christian apologists of the fourth century who "rediscovered" Juvenal as a writer applicable to their purposes. Thereafter follows European posterity, in its variety of nations, societies, schools.

In Britain, for example, he has enjoyed a measure of esteem over several centuries, but his price has fluctuated. Anyone interested in the current evaluation might try the supermarket test and count the entries for Virgil, Horace and Juvenal in that Almanac of All Things British, *The Oxford Dictionary of Quotations*. Lyrical Horace scores 177; wise Virgil, 111; but button-bright Juvenal, wit of wits, only 32.[1] The explanation for that could well be that Horace and Virgil wrote a great deal more, and have enjoyed a long life as curriculum authors, routinely studied – at least until recently – in colleges and secondary schools. But they have been "routinely studied" because they are perceived as unquestionably *valuable*; by them we judge, as generations before us have judged, of standards in a craft. Virgil in particular is one of those great admonitory figures who stand always before us when the talk is of literature and literary values. Juvenal's position is less certain; it changes from generation to generation, as writers find uses for his poetry. This perhaps defines the status of the very good minor poet; he does not set immutable standards, he is not an unbudging keeper of the keys, but he shows brilliantly how some things can be done, how certain effects can be encompassed. The work of such a poet is potentially valuable in two ways. It may be seen as valuable because of the light it throws on our present experience (though this may often be a deceptive, "willed" light); and it may be valuable for its power to keep alive in us the creative spirit – the *wit* – of language.

II

In both of these senses, there was a time when English writers clearly found a value in Juvenal: roughly, the period from 1660 to the 1740s, that era of letters urban and urbane, loosely called by examination candidates "the Augustan age". The Juvenalian spirit irradiates the writings of the Augustan age, as a way of discoursing, mocking, attacking, in verse or prose. There are many passages in which Swift recalls Juvenal; the Juvenalian bravura turns up intermittently in *Hudibras*; even *The Beggar's Opera* has something in it of Juvenal, if only because MacHeath's London is not dissimilar, in the darkness and cynicism of its underworld, to Domitian's Rome. But the principal use of Juvenal during these decades was to stand sponsor, along with Horace, to the genre of poetic satire.

John Dryden found in Juvenal a congenial spirit, preferring him on the whole to Horace, a superbly accomplished writer, much in favour among English wits,

---

1.   This count is based on the listings in the 2nd edition (1954).

but, as Dryden apparently saw him, always bland, never really dangerous, a rough smoothie, basically an Establishment man. Dryden appreciated the Horatian urbanity, and paid high tribute to the subtleties and refinement of Horatian language; and yet he loved most the stylistic daring, the masculine aggression, of Juvenal. His characterisation of Juvenal's style, typically delivered in a concrete metaphor, is acute: "Horace is always on the amble, Juvenal on the gallop, but his way is perpetually on carpet ground".[2] "Galloping on carpet ground" fairly characterises his own work. He was certainly influenced by Juvenal, gave him a high place in the classical canon, and translated several of the Satires.

What may seem the oddest of oddities to a modern observer, however, is that, given his shrewd perception of Juvenal's style, its long rhythmic lines, its rhetorical-colloquial gallop, he should have chosen to render him into tersely rhyming decasyllabic couplets. But in his own day and his own casually authoritative way, Dryden fostered opinions about rhyme (and, concurrently, poetic metre) to which our modern sensibilities are perhaps not acutely attuned. One of his more striking suggestions was that rhyme in English served as an equivalent to syllabic quantity in classical prosody. "The case is the same in our verse, as it was in theirs", says Neander, Dryden's representative in the essay *Of Dramatic Poesy*; "rhyme being to us in lieu of quantity to them."

By this he meant that quantity in the one case and rhyme in the other were disciplines, and therefore heuristic challenges, guiding the shaping of the verse (particularly in dramatic dialogue), the evolution of the metre, the precise placing of word and emphasis. Beyond this feeling for the structural importance of rhyme, Dryden saw it as a heightening, a mark of the separateness and dignity of verse in certain genres – for example, in epic poetry and tragedy. Blank verse, suitable enough for some discursive purposes, was after all a *sermo pedestris*, "a poetic prose...most fit for comedies, where I acknowledge rhyme to be improper". In any case, couplet writing could be given a semblance of prose through proper management of the metre, with "breaks in an hemistich, or running the sense into another line – thereby making art and order appear loose and free as nature". Rhyme is then to be further esteemed because of its "sweetness", the pleasurable chime that can offset the variations of prosody, and attractively define the cadence of each distich.[3]

These opinions on rhyme and metre, propounded by Dryden more or less as they occurred to him, became the established aesthetic of discursive poetry in the first half the eighteenth century. At the same time there emerged some notions of

---

2.   By "carpet ground" Dryden means soft ground, or turf.

3.   Dryden's views on rhyme and metre are quoted from his essay *Of Dramatic Poesy*; see Ker 1926. For a conspectus of Dryden's views on rhyme and prosody, on translation, and on Juvenal, see Aden 1963, *passim*.

verse translation, aired sporadically in critical writings. Augustan and eighteenth century opinion viewed *translation* as a super-ordinate object attainable only on certain subordinate terms. The word *transfusion* appears commonly as a general term for the process of finding new words for old, or, as the ancient saying goes, putting old wine into new bottles. Dryden defines methods ranging from strict word-by-word rendering to a free cross-cultural adaptation:

> First, that of metaphrase, or turning an author word by word, and line by line, from one language into another...The second way is that of paraphrase, or translation with latitude, where the author is kept in view by the translator, so as never to be lost, but his words are not so strictly followed as his sense; and that too is admitted to be amplified, but not altered...The third way is that of imitation, where the translator (if now he has not lost that name) assumes the liberty, not only to vary from the words and sense, but to forsake them both as he sees occasion; and taking only some general hints from the original, to run division on the groundwork, as he pleases.   (See Aden 1963, under *translation*)

In other passages he reveals a dislike of "imitation", seeing it as a way of exalting the translator at the expense of the author, and disparages "metaphrase", considering it dull and uncreative. He favours the middle way of paraphrase, or, sometimes, a compromise between paraphrase and metaphrase. His own translations bear out his theoretical principles, if indeed "theory" is a word to be much associated with a writer whose circumstances were so very much those of the practical, professional man of letters. Dryden always looked to the job in hand; but in doing it, he was able to demonstrate how authors of earlier ages and societies, representatives of the classical canon, might be "re-canonised" (so to speak), and established in the tradition of another aesthetic and another culture. In this way a vernacular canon is created; and while Dryden's own renderings of Juvenal may not quite have achieved canonical status, at least they paved the way for the undisputed canonicity of Samuel Johnson.

III

Johnson published two great poems, based on the texts of Juvenal's third and tenth Satires, and presented to the public as *Imitations*. One, entitled *London*, (imitating the third Satire) was published to great acclaim in 1738, in the same year as Pope's *Epilogue to the Satires* – "so that", the adoring Boswell observes, "England had at once its Juvenal and Horace as poetical monitors".[4] Noting that Johnson was a mere 29 years old when *London* came out, Boswell calls it his "juvenile poem"

---

4.   Chapman (1980:92). Pope's poem was at first published under the title *One Thousand Seven Hundred and Thirty-Eight*. To read it in conjunction with *London*, or with *London* as

(which I take to be a pun of sorts).[5] Eleven years later, in 1749, Johnson published his second great English satire *The Vanity of Human Wishes*, (imitating the tenth Satire), which some readers found less spirited, less pointed in style, indeed more difficult than the popular *London*. David Garrick (Boswell relates) "observed in his sprightly manner, with more vivacity than regard to just discrimination" (go down, Garrick), that when Johnson "saw a good deal of what was passing in life, he wrote his *London*, which is lively and easy. When he grew more retired he gave us his *Vanity of Human Wishes*, which is as hard as Greek. Had he gone on to imitate another satire, it would have been as hard as Hebrew". (Chapman 1983: 138).

Thus the great actor, on a poem which Boswell describes as having "less of common life, but more of a philosophick dignity than his *London*". (ibid.) The perception of "philosophick dignity", like that of being "as hard as Greek" may be attributed to the stretching, perhaps even overstretching, in *The Vanity of Human Wishes*, of the reasonable bounds of "imitation". In *London*, Johnson sports with Juvenal's material; but in the later poem, he often slips the parent text and creates his own, at some length, frequently prompted to "run division on the ground-work", as Dryden puts it. There is a diagnostic symptom of this in the annotations of the early printings, for example in Hawkins' 1787 text, where an apparatus of footnotes guides the reader, with line references or quotations, to those passages in the Latin text which Johnson is "imitating".[6] The *London* text supplies enough of the Latin for the reader to see how Johnson manipulates his original, sometimes expanding his model, sometimes contracting or compacting quite drastically the narrative sense, taking considerable liberties, particularly of excision, but all the same never wandering too far from Juvenal's mandate.

The footnotes to *The Vanity of Human Wishes*, by contrast, are bare line-references. The reader who follows them, studying Johnson's "coverage" (as it might be called) of Juvenal's text, will discover many passages that go past or round

---

a supplementary text, is to gather some notion of the political tendency of Johnson's poem. Boswell (Chapman 1980, *loc.cit.*) records that the two poems came out on the same day, and that *London* – published anonymously – was enthusiastically received by the undergraduates of Oxford).

5.   Chapman (1980: 94). Boswell remarks that "Johnson's juvenile poem was naturally impregnated with the fire of opposition, and on that account was universally admired". By "juvenile poem" he clearly means, in the first instance "the poem of a young man"; but unless I am mistaken the sense of "Juvenalian" lurks playfully here.

6.   The Johnson quotations are from Sir John Hawkins' (1787) edition of the *Works*. In the footnotes to successive episodes of *London* the Latin text is cited to indicate the lines that are "transfused"; on the basis of these, Johnson expands the English sense. These citations are a good guide to the selectiveness of Johnson's "imitation". There is an excellent account of the two Johnsonian poems, in their making and in their relationship to Juvenal's text, in Rudd 1981.

Juvenal, beyond paraphrase, into inventions "after the manner of", original reflections on a literary model. It is an instructive exercise to study side by side the passage in the tenth Satire beginning *da spatium vitae, multos da, Iuppiter annos*, in which Juvenal expatiates on the miseries of a protracted existence, and the Johnsonian equivalent starting with the line "Enlarge my life with multitude of days". Juvenal's text runs (or gallops) to just over 100 lines (lines 188–289). Johnson reduces this to 64 lines, that is, 32 end-stopped rhyming couplets. On the one hand is a close-constructed sermon and on the other is a great sprawling tirade; how to compare them? But the difficulty of making comparisons is not a matter of finding where and how Johnson has made cuts and condensations. The problem is, in effect, to find Juvenal. There are many places in which Johnson's writing is – to use one of his own favourite adjectives - *powerful*; but it is a power displayed in Juvenal's absence. Take, for instance, these lines:

> But grant, the virtues of a temp'rate prime
> Bless with an age exempt from scorn or crime;
> An age that melts with unperceiv'd decay,
> And glides in modest innocence away;
> Whose peaceful day Benevolence endears,
> Whose night congratulating Conscience cheers;
> The gen'ral favourite as the gen'ral friend;
> Such age there is, and who shall wish its end? [291–8]

Ah no, Juvenal's ghost might protest, such age there is not; for there is nothing quite like this passage in Juvenal's poem, and indeed it runs counter to the strain of satiric fervour in which he writes about rheumy old, gloomy old, doomy old, put-upon old men. This is Johnson, that pious and "philosophick" sage, taking the occasion to enforce a righteous reading, bent on creating a Johnsonian Juvenal.

We know from Boswell's testimony that Johnson liked Juvenal and had virtually memorised his works. When Boswell asked why, after the success of *London* and *The Vanity of Human Wishes*, Johnson had not considered further translations from Juvenal's Satires, "he said he probably should give more, for he had them all in his head; by which I understood that he had the originals and correspondent allusions floating in his mind, which he could, when he pleased, embody and render permanent without much labour. Some of them, however, he observed were too gross for imitation." (Chapman 1983: 138.) Having "the originals and correspondent allusions floating in his mind" (*floating* is a happy choice of word) aptly expresses the Johnsonian way of imitating. Creative, or "free" translation was for him a way of testing the strength of a poem – translations otherwise being for the benefit of the uneducated. "We must try its effect as an English poem", he said of a translation of Aeschylus; "that is the way to judge of the merit of a translation."

(Chapman 1983:921) This would suggest that the poetry was to come first, the techniques of "transfusion" later.

He shrewdly perceived the fruitful contradictions of Juvenal's style, observing in his *Life of Dryden* that "the peculiarity of Juvenal is a mixture of gaiety and stateliness, of pointed sentences and declamatory grandeur." Dryden and his collaborators, he felt, had succeeded in conveying the gaiety but had fallen short of stateliness. "It is therefore perhaps possible to give a better representation of that great satirist", Johnson concluded, "even in those parts which Dryden himself has translated." (Johnson 1821: 424) If we did not know that those words were written in the late 1770s, long after Johnson had published his own "representations", we might almost suppose him to be modestly putting himself forward as one for whom it was "perhaps possible" to do a better Juvenal, with more scope for declamatory grandeur.

His resources as a translator are those described by Dryden as "metaphrase", "paraphrase" and "imitation". He does not make great use of the closer techniques, but rather, as the texts "float" in his mind, works outward, from a few phrase-by-phrase renderings, through many broader instances of paraphrase, and so, most freely, to "imitations" of two kinds. One, the stricter sort, is a rehabilitation of the original text, using equivalent allusions, personages, or social features – so "translating" from culture to culture. The other, freer, sort of imitation is the invention of new or additional matter, in a style thought to be representative of the original author. (Such imitations are a species of pastiche).

One of Johnson's most successful metaphrases is a line he valued so highly that he had it printed in capitals:

SLOW RISES WORTH BY POVERTY DEPRESS'D

This, from his *London* (line 177), comes fairly close to Juvenal's wording in the third Satire (lines 164/5):

> Haud facile emergunt quorum virtutibus opstat
> Res angusta domi

It would be hard to devise a closer rendering, and at the same time a verse that stands up in its own merit; indeed the English line, in its compression and pointedness, has attained almost proverbial status.

A more usual resort is paraphrase, and in this Johnson displays wit of a kind that would certainly have attracted Garrick's praise for "lively and easy" composition. Take, for example, some lines from the third Satire on the successful industry of the Greek immigrants, whom the racist Juvenal vehemently detested:

> Grammaticus rhetor geometres pictor aliptes
> Augur schoenobates medicus magus, omnia novit
> Graeculus esuriens: in coelum iusseris, ibit (III, 76)

("Grammarian, rhetorician, geometer, painter, trainer, soothsayer, physician, magician – your hungry little Greek does it all. Tell him to fly – he's up and away"). Now this is what Johnson supplies, in humorous paraphrase:

> They sing, they dance, clean shoes, or cure a clap:
> All sciences a fasting Monsieur knows,
> And bid him go to hell, to hell he goes. [114–16]

Here the *Graeculus esuriens* ("hungry Greekling", "half-starved Greekie") becomes the "fasting Monsieur" (London had its population of *emigré* Frenchmen); the Greekie's "sciences" – soothsayer, tightrope walker, quack, magician – are translated into trades more likely to be encountered round the streets of London – though "cure a clap" is a sly rendering of Juvenal's *medicus*; but the best of the paraphrase is in the rendering of *in coelum iusseris, ibit*, "tell him to fly and he flies", "say take off, and off he takes". However one chooses to translate this smart directive, the core-phrase, apparently, is *in coelum*, "up to heaven" (or more freely, "into the blue"). But Johnson impishly reverses the direction of travel: *in coelum iusseris*, "send him to heaven" becomes "bid him go to hell", a rendering all the more amusing, and convincing, because it sounds like something your bluff exasperated Brit might actually say ("go to hell, Froggy"). This is paraphrase at its most effective. It keeps the original wording in sight and does not stray from or distort the original meaning; but it gives something of its own -and in that respect "paraphrase" begins to border on "imitation".

But imitation in the sense defined by Johnson in his Dictionary – "a method of translating...in which modern examples and illustrations are used for ancient" – opens up a new creative field, a release from the obligations and constraints of the parent text. One of the most widely admired imitations in Johnson's Juvenal is the passage in *The Vanity of Human Wishes* describing the military glory and downfall of Charles XII of Sweden. (Charles was killed by a stray bullet in 1718, at the "petty fortress" of Fredrikshald, and so in 1749 was still a recent instance, an allusion as modern as poetic imitation might hope to find). This passage corresponds to Juvenal's account, in the tenth Satire, of the rise and fall of Hannibal (dead by his own hand in 183 BC, three hundred years before Juvenal's time, not at all a recent instance). The two extracts are roughly of a length – Johnson makes 32 lines out of Juvenal's 26 – and thanks to Johnson's inspired choice of a modern parallel to the ancient event, there are striking similarities between the two military biographies: the ambition for conquest, the irresistible military prowess, the catastrophic defeat in battle, the retreat into exile and obscurity, the death in sordid or suspicious circumstances. The content of one passage is well imitated in the other. The difference between them, and it is a huge one, is stylistic. See how grandly Johnson begins:

> On what foundation stands the warrior's pride,
> How just his hopes, let Swedish Charles decide; [191–2]

Note there, as a matter of prosodic importance, that "his" must be accentuated – "how just *his* hopes" – because military pride is being contrasted with other kinds of vain emulation. Now here is Juvenal (tenth Satire, line 148):

> Expende Hannibalem: quot libras in duce summo invenies?

("Put Hannibal on the scales – how many pounds do you reckon *that* 'supreme commander' will amount to?"). Any close translation, or "transfusion", should catch at the abrupt, almost slangy opening of Juvenal's character-sketch. *Expende Hannibalem* – weigh him, weigh him up, size him up, the beggar (supreme commander, indeed!); this sprightly manner is so different from the august, almost marmoreal solemnity of "let Swedish Charles decide". As one reads on, it becomes clear that Johnson is striving (with great effect, it must be said) for the "declamatory grandeur" which he missed in the translations made or sponsored by Dryden. But the Hannibal episode in Juvenal is designedly averse to declamation; it moves briskly along to its jeering conclusion:

> I demens et saevas curre per Alpes,
> Ut pueris placeas et declamatio fias. [X, 166–7]

("Go on, you madman, storm those cruel Alps, and all for the benefit of little boys and their speech-day exercises"). Declamatory grandeur is not in Juvenal's programme for this episode; oratory is a vacuous, even a dangerous pursuit (look at what happened to poor old Cicero, he tells us, in another section of the poem); and mere speechifying of the classroom kind is all that is left of the great Hannibal and his soldierly career.

So Johnson's imitative impulse will sometimes betray Juvenal's intention. This aberrancy becomes more noticeable in those passages which Johnson interpolates, or for which there is no firm voucher in Juvenal's text, or where he in effect censors Juvenal. A notable instance is his rendering of a passage at the end of the tenth Satire, a passage containing the phrase *mens sana in corpore sano*, frequently quoted and invariably misapplied by sporting schoolteachers and bar-room wags. Juvenal's closing recommendation to his readers begins a little earlier than the line *Orandum est ut sit mens sana in corpore sano*. ("What you must pray for [as you grow old] is that your mind will stay sound and your body healthy"). It begins with some disparaging comments on the futility of religious ritual.

Here is *mens sana, &c* in its wider context:

> Ut tamen et poscas aliquid, voveasque sacellis
> Exta et candiduli divina tomacula porci,
> Orandum est ut sit mens sana in corpore sano.
> Fortem posce animum et mortis terrore carentem;
> Qui spatium vitae extremum inter munera ponat
> Naturae, qui ferre queat quoscumque labores;
> Nesciat irasci, cupiat nihil, et potiores
> Herculis aerumnas credat saevosque labores
> Et Venere et coenis et plumis Sardanapali.
> Monstro quod ipse tibi possis dare; semita certe
> Tranquillae per virtutem patet unica vitae.
> Nullum numen habes, si sit prudentia: nos te
> Nos facimus, Fortuna, deam, caeloque locamus. (X, 354–366)

These lines are accurately and beautifully rendered by Peter Green:

> Still, if you must have something to pray for, if you
> Insist on offering up the entrails and consecrated
> Sausages from a white pigling in every shrine, then ask
> For a sound mind in a sound body, a valiant heart
> Without fear of death, that reckons longevity
> The least of Nature's gifts, that's strong to endure
> All kinds of toil, that's untainted by lust and anger,
> That prefers the sorrows and labours of Hercules to all
> Sardanapalus' downy cushions and women and junketings.
> What I've shown you, you can find by yourself: there's one
> Path, and one only, to a life of peace – through virtue.
> Fortune has no divinity, could we but see: it's we,
> We ourselves, who make her a goddess, and set her in the heavens.
>
> [Green 1976:217]

That is about as emphatic a declaration as one might expect to find of the belief that life's single resource and comfort can only be Stoic virtue. Ritual religion – oh, those *divina tomacula*, those consecrated sausages a-sizzle on the shrine! – will do you no harm, and no good either. Your help and salvation must lie within you.

But that is not how Samuel Johnson, a Christian, a churchgoer, a devout believer in revealed religion, cares to read these lines. His poem ends with a passage that bears only occasional and vague resemblances to the Juvenalian model:

> Yet when the sense of sacred presence fires,
> And strong devotion to the skies aspires,
> Pour forth thy fervours for a healthful mind,

Obedient passions, and a will resigned;
For love, which scarce collective man can fill;
For patience, sovereign o'er transmuted ill;
For faith, that panting for a happier seat
Counts death kind Nature's signal of retreat:
These goods for man the laws of heav'n ordain,
These goods he grants, who grants the pow'r to gain;
With these celestial Wisdom calms the mind,
And makes the happiness she does not find. [357–368]

This is all very abstract and *philosophick*; the *mens* is present, but the *corpus* has retired (or perhaps may be glimpsed in those "obedient passions"); Dame Fortune, who cuts such a fine figure in Juvenal's closing distich, has gone away and left Wisdom (note, *celestial* Wisdom) to take over the conclusion;[7] there are obscure, non-Juvenalian lines (e.g. "for love, which scarce collective man can fill") that Garrick might well have found "as hard as Greek".

The most telling point of contrast, however, is that Johnson virtually deletes Juvenal's sardonic allusions to the observances of household religion, and in doing so obscures a crucial stylistic shift, when Juvenal moves out of his habitually astringent, burlesque manner into a vein of serious, even lofty address. Johnson ignores the burlesque, or rather, turns it into respectable sentiment. The reek of the domestic altar's holy smoke becomes the "sense of sacred presence" that "fires" the devotee, the "strong devotion" that "aspires" heavenward. Juvenal's fires are smelly and real, Johnson's are polite theological metaphor. By this act of deletion and transference, he robs Juvenal's conclusion of its Stoic force, and imposes on it his own, essentially Christian, message. Juvenal says, let the gods alone, don't pester them, forget your ridiculous offerings and libations, they'll decide what's what in their own sphere and their own time; your business here and now is the pursuit of virtue. But Johnson's conclusion is, submit yourself in prayer to the will

---

7.   Johnson's rendering of the last two lines of the Satire was quite possibly directed by a variant reading in his Latin text, that is, 'nullum numen abest' for the more familiar 'nullum numen habes'. (For evidence of this, see Chapman 1980:1206). The now generally accepted reading, 'nullum numen habes si sit prudentia', is defiantly addressed to Fortune – "you have no power over us, Fortune, if we have wisdom" (that is, the wisdom to perceive that Fortune is a human construct); whereas 'nullum numen abest si sit prudentia' signifies "divine help will not be denied if we have wisdom" (that is, the wisdom to put our faith in a deity). The latter reading may well support Johnson's invocation of "celestial Wisdom" which "calms the mind" and "makes a happiness". In conversation with Boswell (Chapman *loc.cit.*) Johnson remarked that although 'nullum numen abest' etc. "does not always prove true, we may be certain of the converse of it, 'nullum numen adest, si sit imprudentia' ("there is no divine help if we are unwise"). 'Nullum numen abest' was a reading in general accordance with Johnson's moral-theological stance.

of God ("he ... who grants the pow'r to gain") while you await your translation to "a happier seat".

It is a comfortable sort of ending: if we are good, all will be well and we all go to heaven when we die (something that Johnson, who had a horrid fear of hell and damnation, desperately needed to believe). Juvenal's ending is not exactly happy, offers no comfortable assurances, no transcendent hopes; his closing lines are defiant, unresigned, a call to that glittering Roman fortitude that faces death without fear and without expectations. This attitude is not truly represented at the close of *The Vanity of Human Wishes*; Juvenal has quit the scene; there is no more use for him in this five-beat couplet show. Samuel Johnson has imitated him almost out of reach, and in doing so has created two great poems – for *London* and *The Vanity of Human Wishes* are indeed great poems – to stand forever in the eighteenth century repertoire.

IV

After Johnson, Juvenal ceases to be a major presence in English literature, or indeed in British sensibility. Literary fashions change, verse forms change, the status of verse as a political instrument, or "monitor", to use Boswell's revealing expression, changes. The poetic temper of the second half of the eighteenth century does not much favour urban satire in decasyllabic couplets; still less do the writers of the nineteenth century cultivate this kind of monitorship, though something like the Juvenalian spirit is discernible in Byron's poetry and in the novels of Dickens. (In a fine introductory essay to his volume of translations, *The Sixteen Satires*, Professor Green reflects on a most fruitful paradox, that "George Orwell's essay on Dickens is the most illuminating introduction to Juvenal in existence"). (Green 1976:27–8) But after the eighteenth century the powerful presence of the old atrabilious master is less solidly felt. Old poets never die – they crumble into quotations; and a few heel-ends of phrases – *mens sana in corpore sano, res angusta domi, rara avis, quis custodiet ipsos custodes* – seem, at times, to be all that remains of Juvenal.

Nevertheless, there is much of substance that is left to us. First, we have Johnson's canonical poems, and very fine they are, so tall and upstanding in their humanity. But they are of the eighteenth century. Their aesthetic is Augustan; they render Juvenal's hexameters into end-stopped rhyming decasyllabic couplets. And they are imitations, refurbishing the old texts with modern examples and ideas, though by now their "modernity" has something of the patina of respectable age. And they present, or imply, notions and "ideologies" (my, such a word) which the Roman writer would scarcely have recognised (at the same time eliminating, or curiously "deflecting" some Juvenalian sentiments not altogether agreeable to the eighteenth century sensibility). Indeed, they occasionally suggest the covert operation of something analogous to Political Correctness, though Johnson did not know the term and would very probably have laughed at the idea. They are in fact not very like Juvenal, although their authority is now such that the name of Juvenal is most likely to suggest to the British student these Satires translated, or "imitated", by Dr Johnson. Johnson's Juvenal is our canonised Juvenal, our honoured eighteenth century notion of a frequently misunderstood poet. With the passage of time these texts are in their turn slipping away from us, and will before long seem as remote as Juvenal himself.

To stay in touch with Roman Juvenal, uncensored and unrhymed, most of us, whatever the state of our Latin, must rely on translations that abandon the ambitions of the imitator, and depend on the skill of paraphrase and metaphrase. Such a translation is Peter Green's text, quoted elsewhere in this essay. Green's translations are both metaphrastic and paraphrastic; in their word-for-word faithfulness, indeed, they often challenge Dryden's disparaging comments on the uncreative pedantry of mere metaphrase. For a random example, take the following passage from the third Satire (a passage which, incidentally, finds no equivalent in Johnson's *London* imitation, quite certainly because it is irrelevant to his political purpose). Juvenal's topic is the wearisome hierarchical significance of dress in Roman society, beginning with the fact that in Rome all free citizens were obliged to wear the cumbersome toga, with its appropriate marks of status:

> Pars magna Italiae est (si verum admittimus) in qua
> Nemo togam sumit nisi mortuus. Ipsa dierum
> Festorum herboso colitur si quando theatro
> Majestas, tandemque redit ad pulpita notum
> Exodium, cum personae pallentis hiatum
> In gremio matris formidat rusticus infans;
> Aequales habitus illic, similemque videbis
> Orchestram et populum; clari velamen honoris,
> Sufficiunt tunicae summis Aedilibus albae.   (III, 171–9)

Two Juvenalian characteristics are to be noted here: that on the one hand the phrasing is laconic and compact, in places almost elliptical (see for example the intricate construction from *ipsa dierum ... majestas*); and on the other that the hexameters flow freely, almost chattily, one into the other, not at all like end-stopped rhyming couplets. The tone is the stylish-colloquial which this poet so often affects, without apparent effort (though the labour of polishing can only be imagined). A prose rendering might read like this:

> There are large tracts of Italy where – let's face it – nobody wears a toga until he's dead. Even on big occasions, on feast days held in the grassy theatre, when the old familiar farce is put on yet again, and the peasant child in his mother's lap is scared stiff by the gape of the actor's white mask – there you'll see everybody in

town, from the people in the best seats to the folk on the back row, dressed in the same way. White tunics will do, a garment good enough even for their worships the Magistrates.

Now here is Peter Green's versification;

> Throughout most of Italy – we
> Might as well admit it – no one is seen in a toga
> Till the day he dies. Even on public holidays,
> When the same old shows as last year are cheerfully staged
> In the grassgrown theatre, when peasant children, sitting
> On their mothers' laps, shrink back in terror at the sight
> Of those gaping, whitened masks, you will find the whole
> Audience – top row or bottom – dressed exactly alike;
> Even the magistrates need no better badge of status
> Than a plain white tunic. [Green 1976:93]

That is excellent paraphrase, one might say *close* paraphrase; in its closeness it answers well to Dryden's definition of metaphrase, "turning an author word by word, and line by line". The reader who takes the trouble to check Green's translation against the original text must be struck by the consistency with which the "transfusion" is carried out. And yet this is not dull, pedantic, artless translation. It has its own rhythm and flair, and an idiom that, despite its colloquial modernity, gives full and reliable access to the Roman Juvenal. No one reading Green's translations could subsequently claim to be ignorant of the content of Juvenal's verse; or would be able to allege that the poet had been misrepresented through omissions, additions, or impermissibly "free" renderings; or would want to deny that these close-reading paraphrases carry the reader along in the pleasurable swing of something that must be called English verse, since there is no other word for it. But if there is pleasure in these transfusions, it derives from Peter Green's creation of his own aesthetic, based on a rhythm generally mimetic of Juvenal's free-pacing verse movement, but also mimetic of modern English talk. The translations adequately *represent* Juvenal, verbally and aesthetically, while they *appeal* to an audience whose notions of rhythmic pulse and sinew exist at some distance from the model of the rhymed pentameter.

V

At length, then, we come to the question raised by way of a title – *the value of Juvenal*; and it is apparent that the title is ambivalent, or double-bottomed, because it implies firstly some evaluation of the Latin poems and their author, but then also an evaluation of the evaluations of Juvenal, that is, of his English imitators and translators. The original Juvenal has been evaluated, over the centuries, with some diversity. John Dryden seems to have read him as a sturdy proponent of Republican virtue in crass Imperial times; Samuel Johnson found in him the makings of a Tory and a Christian. No one has as yet completely repudiated him on account of his livid hostility to gays, to the liberated woman (see the shameless obscenities of the sixth Satire), and to ethnic minorities, but these are familiar preoccupations of our own time, and anyone setting out to read him now must come to terms with the fact that this author, seen from where we stand, is often Politically Incorrect. If that calls for an excuse, there is only this to say, that when he takes it into his head to dislike something, he is then helplessly driven to dislike practically everything. His hatreds have nothing to do with ideologies; they are the fears of a man who feels that he and his kind are being cornered into irrelevance. He is pathologically resentful – in which respect he is resembled by that other displaced and indignant person, Jonathan Swift. But still, these people can write, and in possession of that power are hardly to be put down.

So let us now evaluate our evaluators, and in particular two works of translation, presenting respectively the methods of "imitation" and the closer technique of "paraphrase". Why do I read Samuel Johnson? Not to find out what is in Juvenal's third and tenth Satires, for which purpose he would be at best an irregular guide; and certainly not for guidance and support when the Latin text eludes my infirm grasp. I read *London* and *The Vanity of Human Wishes* as poems. They are no doubt poems deeply involved with eighteenth century politics and ethical concerns – *London* in particular is a political poem, and was received as such by the audience of 1738; yet it never occurs to me to read and enjoy it as an assault on an unpopular administration. Its ideological content – if one may call it that – is long since obscured, and it has little of what current critical fashion calls "relevance", at least not of the socio-political sort.

Its aesthetic, too, is old-fashioned. We have some difficulty nowadays in responding wholeheartedly to the standard eighteenth century couplet, particularly when, as in Johnson's case, the writer never takes up Dryden's suggestion of "breaking an hemistich, or running the sense into another line". We are not wholly convinced of the centrality of rhyme to English verse, and have but a dim perception of Augustan notions of "ruggedness", "strength", "sweetness" and "musicality". But after all, it is the majesty of language, the sustained declamatory power that has kept Johnson's Juvenal alive for two and a half centuries: that, and his ability to evoke, beyond the local concern, the particular event, the current idea, some universals of human experience and feeling. Certain lines dwell in the mind, and gather significance with each new reading; certain passages speak incessantly about human life at large.

Translations like those of Peter Green present a different appeal and a different merit. To them, indeed, I go for information; to them I have resort when an obscure reading in the original leaves me frowning and baffled; from them, because I can read them rapidly, at the poet's own speed, without my finger in the text, I can form an overview of Juvenal's creative design. These are not imitations: they are attempts at a close reading of the Latin text, and in them Juvenal, not Green, is still the sovereign, directive power. Green takes no mandate to proceed at large and create his own Juvenal. This does not mean that his translations offer no aesthetic satisfactions. He solves the principal problem, of "transfusing" not only the *meaning* but also the *feeling* of Juvenal, by working out his own prosody – a "variable six-stress line", as he calls it – enabling him to mimic Juvenal's expansiveness, the run-on lines, the evolution of the verse in paragraphs rather than in lines or couplets. His six-stress line, an accentual line, cannot be a true equivalent to the quantitative metrics of the hexameter, but he is right in supposing it to be a better device, for purposes of translation, than blank verse or rhyming decasyllabics.

What he gives us is a representation of a man speaking, grumbling, intoning, declaiming – a theatre of monologue (with occasional dialogue) such as indeed we find in Juvenal. Green's translations, furthermore, usefully and pleasingly remind us of the parts of Juvenal that Johnson did not care to reach, because they had no bearing on his moral and social purposes. Juvenal is not all declamations and aphorisms. He is capable of showing us more vividly, perhaps, than any other Roman poet, the ordinariness, the violence, the oddity of Roman life – the crowd at a provincial theatre, the snake spewing and drowning in a wine-vat, the benighted walker being mugged by a drunk, the mob making haste to establish their political correctness by kicking the ribs of Sejanus' corpse. Such episodes *live* in a good translation, and such translations contribute something to a literary tradition.

"Tradition" here is an important word. These reflections on Juvenal and his imitators have been governed by the idea of a poetic power being passed down and turned to use, across times and places, at different stages of culture, sometimes fading, sometimes transmuted, then rehabilitated. The study of a tradition is one of the most important of literary processes; it is the scholarship of pleasure. Currently, however, this important word, *tradition*, is being overtaken by a busier term. The talk is of the *canon*, a word which, as it happens, is tainted with ambiguity. There are at least three meanings of *canonical* in literary usage, thus:

1. "This is a canonical work"
    = This is a text, the authenticity of which, as the product of a particular writer or school, is attested by scholars.

2. "This is a canonical work"
    = This is a work of such power to move and delight, such scope to live through mutations and interpretations, that it has been accorded a permanent and prominent place in literary history.

3.   "This is a canonical work"
     = This is a work regarded as ideologically acceptable to an influential class, whose interests it represents.

Of these meanings, the first, and narrowest, is hardly relevant to the present discussion of Juvenal, although scholars may continue to discuss the authenticity of certain lines or short passages in the Satires. The second sense of *canonical* coincides or meshes with the idea of *tradition*; writings become canonical (aesthetically) as their importance in shaping and transmitting a tradition is perceived. The third sense is political, and nearly always amounts to wilful nonsense.

It certainly will not fit Juvenal in his original or in any of his transmuted forms. It will not fit his kind of satire, for satire is never ideologically acceptable to an influential class. It subverts all kinds of ideologies – that is, if it can be thought to have any practical consequences. For poetry, as Auden says, "makes nothing happen":

> it survives
> In the valley of its saying where executives
> Would never want to tamper: it flows south
> From ranches of isolation and the busy griefs,
> Raw towns that we believe and die in; it survives,
> A way of happening, a mouth.
>   (Auden 1950:65)

Such survival, it could be added, depends on not caring about being Politically Correct; but caring about many things with an intensity that can turn the Politically Incorrect into the Poetically Correct. About many things; about the *farrago* of living, with all its pains, passions, irrationalities, contradictions; and not at all about certitudes fit only for *The Boys' Own Paper*.

References

Auden, W. H. 1950 *Collected Shorter Poems, 1930–1944*. London: Faber & Faber. (Now in *Collected Shorter Poems, 1957*).

Aden, J. M. 1963. *Critical Opinions of John Dryden: A Dictionary*. Nashville TN: Vanderbilt University Press.

Boswell. J. 1980. *Life of Johnson*, ed. by R. W. Chapman. Oxford: OUP.

Chapman, R. W. (ed.). 1980. *James Boswell, Life of Johnson*. Oxford: Oxford University Press.

Green, P. 1976. *Juvenal: The Sixteen Satires*. (transl.) Harmondsworth: Penguin Classics.

Hawkins, Sir J. 1961. *Life of Samuel Johnson*, London 1784, 2nd edn 1797. London: Jonathan Cape.

Ker, W. P. 1926. *Essays of John Dryden*, selected and ed. by W. P. Ker. Oxford. Clarendon Press.

The Oxford Dictionary of Quotations. 1956. 2nd edn, 3rd impression. Oxford: OUP.

PART II

Theoretical reflections

CHAPTER 9

Some correlates of literary eminence

Colin Martindale

Two independent but highly correlated measures of permanent fame and a measure of contemporary fame were investigated for a sample of 50 eminent poets.
The greater the permanent fame of the poets, the more they avoided references to
concepts and emotions and the more they focused upon concrete images. Permanent fame was related to estimated intelligence but unrelated to wealth or social
class. Contemporary fame was found to be unrelated to permanent fame and
could not be predicted by the variables investigated. It is apparently based upon
different criteria in different epochs. For neither permanent nor contemporary
fame was there any evidence that rich white men have any advantage in becoming
famous.

There has recently been controversy about the canon of great works of Western literature. It has been argued that one must be a rich, preferably dead, white man in
order to gain admittance. This argument is rather fatuous. Some poor white men
such as Robert Burns somehow got admitted. Some women such as Jane Austen
also managed to get in. Even Phyllis Wheatley, a black woman, has been in the
canon of American poetry for several hundred years. It certainly does help to be
a dead white man to be included in the canon, but examples such as those cited
above show that this is not a necessary condition. It is most certainly not a sufficient condition to be a dead white man. The vast majority of dead white men who
tried their hand at literature have been justly consigned to oblivion. If they ever
were in the canon, their names have been expunged.

Another criticism of the canon has been that one's works must uphold the
status quo in order to be admitted. If I understand Marxism, Feminism, and the
New Historicism, the main business of society is to oppress poor people, women,
and people of colour. It has also been held that we want to oppress 'the other'.
Because it is never made very clear who 'the other' is, I would guess that these are
rather difficult people to find, let alone oppress. Herrnstein Smith (1988) argues
that canon formation is a political process. One must say what the ruling class
wants to hear or he or she will have no chance of being admitted to the canon. We
are left to wonder how a poet such as Ezra Pound made his way into the canon. He
certainly didn't say anything that the American ruling class wanted to hear. Van

Peer (1996, see also Chapter 1 in this volume) compared versions of the Romeo and Juliet story by Shakespeare and Arthur Brooke. Shakespeare's version went against the mores of the ruling class, whereas Brooke's version conformed with them. Why is Shakespeare in the canon and Brooke forgotten? One imagines that the reason has to do with literary quality.

In the past, the ruling class may have taken some interest in literature. At least in Western Europe and North America, this has not been the case for quite a while. They are too busy making money to have the slightest interest in literature. To take the most extreme case, no one at all reads contemporary poetry with the exception of other poets and teachers of literature (Auden 1948). Canon formation may be political, but it is academic politics. Like much in academia, arguments as to who should or should not be in the canon are pointless, as the canon is literally cast in concrete. Martindale (1995) did a study of how many books the Harvard University libraries have about the 602 poets listed in the various *Oxford Book of English Verse*. Shakespeare came in first with 9,118 books about him. Milton was a distant second with 1,280 books devoted to him. At the other end of the scale, no books at all were devoted to 134 of the poets. The top 25 poets accounted for 64.8% of the books. These are certainly canonical authors, and nothing is going to change that. Even the relative ordering is unlikely to change. For Milton to surpass Shakespeare, 78 books about Milton would have to be written in each of the next 100 years. This seems quite unlikely.

One could certainly argue that if no one reads the books about Shakespeare and Milton, then the numbers I have cited count for nothing. However, we shall see below that contemporary fame is a fleeting thing unrelated to permanent fame. The canon refers to permanent fame. How does one obtain permanent fame? One supposes by the literary quality of his or her works. The beauty of one's poetry is not in the colour or one's skin or one's social class but in the quality of what he or she has produced. Beauty is most certainly not in the eye of the beholder. I have done dozens of studies in which people were asked to rate works of art or literature. The most relevant is Martindale and Dailey (1995). We replicated I.A. Richards's (1929) experiment and used statistical methods to measure agreement amongst subjects. Richards was simply wrong. People agree perfectly well as to the meanings of poems. The only way to explain this is to postulate that there is something in the poems that people perceive in the same way. It is well to re-call Hume's (1757) comment: "Whoever would assert an equality of genius and elegance between Ogilby and Milton...would be thought to defend no less an ex-travagance, than if he had maintained a mole-hill to be as high as Tenerife, or a pond as extensive as the ocean."

One would suppose that literary quality is determined by the way an author puts together words. However, a moment's thought reveals that which words are combined is also important. A sonnet sequence on the joys of trading pork bellies on the Chicago Mercantile Exchange would not be well received. Computers are not very good at determining a well turned phrase, but they have no trouble in tallying words or classes of words. A few computer studies concerning the difference between good and bad literature have been carried out.

Forsyth (1998) compared poems by 54 eminent British poets with poems by 54 long-forgotten British poets. He found that the poetry by good poets tended to be simpler. Most notably, it used shorter words and was most likely to begin with initial lines composed only of monosyllables. Because only two groups were examined, it was not possible to look for curvilinear trends. In a study of classical musical themes, Simonton (1980) found an inverted-U relationship between thematic fame and unpredictability. The best known themes were neither too simple nor too unpredictable.

Simonton (1989) studied Shakespeare's 154 sonnets, which are reliably judged to differ in literary quality as gauged by the number of times they have been anthologized. In contrast to Forsyth's findings, quality was positively correlated with linguistic complexity. It was also correlated with specificity of the themes dealt with, the number of different themes dealt with, and amount of primary process content (see below). Smith (1935) provides estimates of contemporary and permanent fame for a number of British poets on a scale of 1 (moderate quality) to 4 (supreme quality). For other purposes, I (Martindale 1990) had gathered random samples of about 3,000 words from the poetry of 50 of these poets. The poets are listed in Table 1.

As a check on Smith's ratings of permanent fame, I also tallied the number of pages devoted to each poet in the relevant *Oxford Anthology of English Verse* (Chambers 1932; Grierson & Bullough 1934; Hayward 1964; Sisam & Sisam 1970; Smith 1926). The latter correlated .76, $p < .0001$ with Smith's estimates of permanent fame. Contemporary fame correlated with neither of these measures. The correlations were .10 for Smith's estimates and .09 for the *Oxford* estimates. None of the measures of fame was correlated with birth date. Thus, there was no need to correct for temporal trends in fame.

The computer program COUNT (Martindale 1973) was used to analyze the textual samples with several dictionaries. The Regressive Imagery Dictionary (Martindale 1975) tallies words falling into the categories of primordial content (such content indicates the concrete sort of thought found in dreams and reveries – e.g. references to drives and sensations), conceptual content (such content indicates the abstract sort of thought found in normal waking consciousness – e.g. references to time, restraint, abstractions, moral imperatives, and social and instrumental behaviour), and emotions (e.g. references to love, sadness, anxiety, aggression, and positive emotions). Factor analytic studies have shown that primordial and conceptual content are polar opposites on the same continuum and that emotional content lies at the midpoint of this continuum. COUNT was also

Table 1. Information on poets included in the study.

Name	Contemporary Fame	Permanent Fame	Pages in Oxford Anthologies
WYATT	1	2	31.50
VAUX	3	1	3.75
SURREY	1	2	12.50
SPENSER	3	3	96.00
DANIEL	3	2	54.50
DRAYTON	3	2	53.25
SHAKESPEARE	3	4	69.25
DONNE	2	3	58.50
JONSON	4	2	33.50
HERBERT ,G.	1	2	27.50
MILTON	2	4	104.00
CRASHAW	1	2	35.00
COWLEY	4	2	24.00
MARVELL	1	2	29.00
VAVGHAN	1	2	28.00
DRYDEN	3	3	57.50
ROCHESTER	2	1	11.50
PRIOR	3	2	16.25
POMFRET	3	1	5.50
SWIFT	2	2	26.25
ADDISON	3	1	8.00
GAY	3	2	14.50
TICKELL	2	1	9.75
POPE	4	3	53.00
THOMSON, J.	3	2	29.25
JOHNSON, S.	2	1	10.00
GRAY	3	3	24.25
AKENSIDE	2	1	11.50
COLLINS	1	2	17.50
GOLDSMITH	3	2	15.00
CHURCHILL	3	1	4.75
COWPER	3	2	37.00
BEATTIE	3	1	3.75
CRABBE	3	2	10.00
BLAKE	1	2	14.50
BURNS	3	3	49.00
WORDSWORTH	3	3	57.25
SCOTT	4	2	20.75
COLERIDGE	2	3	37.00
MOORE, T.	3	2	14.50
BYRON	3	3	37.00
SHELLEY	2	3	29.25
CLARE	3	1	25.00
KEATS	2	3	49.25
TENNYSON	4	3	53.75
BROWNING	3	3	54.00
MEREDITH	3	2	14.50
ROSSETTI, D.G.	3	2	13.75
SWINBURNE	2	2	36.00
THOMPSON	3	3	8.00

Table 2. Sample Harvard III Psychosociological Dictionary Categories, Sample Words, and Correlations with Permanent Fame and Oxford Fame

Category (Sample words)	Permanent Fame	Oxford Fame
Ideal Value (ability, able, beauty)	−.44**	−.25
Pleasure (cheer, delight, funny)	−.31*	−.26
Guide (aid, allow, benefit)	−.31*	−.19
Attempt (aim, apply, bid)	−55.***	−.29*
Move (pull, put, run)	−.33*	−.36**

*: $p < .05$
**: $p < .01$
***: $p < .0001$

used to apply the *Harvard III Psychosocial Dictionary* (Stone et al. 1966) to the texts. This is a general-purpose dictionary that, if we ignore function words, categorizes 80–90% of texts into one of its 55 categories. Categories, along with sample words, that correlated significantly with Oxford eminence or permanent fame are shown in Table 2.

SEMIS (Martindale 1974a) works somewhat differently than COUNT. Rather than just counting words in various categories, it assigns weights to each word. Osgood, Suci, and Tannenbaum (1956) found that the connotative meaning of words can be described by where they fall in a three-dimensional space defined by the orthogonal axes Evaluation (good versus bad), Potency (strong versus weak), and Activity (active versus passive). Heise (1965) gathered ratings for the 1,000 most frequent English words on these dimensions. SEMIS was used to apply these norms to the texts. For each text, it computed an average – based upon words found in the dictionary – Evaluation, Potency, and Activity score. The standard deviation of each of these three scores was also computed. SEMIS was also used to apply ratings on the Imagery, Concreteness, and Meaningfulness of 925 frequent English nouns gathered by Paivio, Yuille, and Madigan (1968) to the texts. Meaningfulness as they defined it refers to the number of word associations elicited by a word. SEMIS was also used to apply these norms to the texts. For each of the three measures, both the mean and the standard deviation were computed. LEXSTAT (Martindale 1974b) was used to assess the lexical diversity of the texts. LEXSTAT computed 12 measures of word frequency, word length, and phrase length.

Fame was also correlated with several non-literary variables provided by Smith (1935): father's social class, education, wealth, and source of wealth. Cox (1926) estimated the IQ's of a large number of historical figures based upon the age at which they accomplished various tasks. She provided two estimates: AI is the estimate based upon all available information. Because amount of information varies tremendously, she also made an estimate which she called AII. AII represents her IQ estimate correcting for varying amounts of biographical information.

Table 3. Significant correlates of Smith's Permanent Fame and of Oxford Eminence

Variable	Permanent Fame	Oxford Fame
Emotion (RID)	−.36**	−.33*
Secondary Process (RID)	−.30*	−.08
Activity (Semantic Differential)	−.42**	−.18
Imagery (Paivio et al. norms)	.31*	.17
Concreteness (Paivio et al. norms)	.34*	.17
Meaningfulness (Paivio et al. norms)	.33*	.32*
Average sentence length	.10	.31*
Standard deviation of sentence length	.32*	.48***
Coefficient of variation of sentence length	.35*	.36**
Cox AII estimate of IQ	.41	.51*

*: $p < .05$
**: $p < .01$
***: $p < .001$

To summarize, I correlated the three measures of fame with 88 variables. This virtually guarantees that some significant correlations will be found. This is indeed a problem. By convention, a correlation is considered to be statistically significant if $p < .05$. What this means is that we would only find a correlation this large 5 times out of 100 purely by chance. To put this another way, if we have 100 correlations, we would expect 5 of them to be significant at $p < .05$ merely by chance. For 88 correlations, we would expect about 4 to be significant at $p < .05$. By extension, for 100 correlations, we would expect 1 to be significant at $p < .01$. For 88 correlations, we would expect .8 to be significant at this level. Because a correlation is either significant or not, we would round up and expect 1 correlation to be significant at this level.

Given the considerations set forth in the prior paragraph, I cannot predict contemporary fame with the variables at hand. Only 3 correlations significant at $p < .05$ were found. This is less than we would expect by chance. For the record, contemporary fame correlates with the standard deviation of Evaluation – $r(48) = -.32$; the Harvard III If category (sample words: almost, chance, else) – $r(48) = .29$; and father's social class – $r(48) = -.28$. The last means that the lower one's father's social class, the more contemporary fame he had. I assume that these are just spurious correlations. One might be able to predict contemporary fame, but not with the variables that I had available.

A quite different picture emerges when we turn to eminence as measured by either Smith's (1935) estimates or by the Oxford estimates. Significant correlations are shown in Table 2 above and in Table 3.

We see that there are far more significant correlations than would be expected by chance. Furthermore, the correlations tend to be consistent with one another. If we turn to Table 3, we see that the more eminent a poet is, the more he avoids references to emotions. Note also the negative correlation with references to Pleasure in Table 2. This should be no great surprise. Contrary to the views of the layperson, poetry has not dealt with the expression of emotion for several centuries (Martindale 1997). Contemporary British and American poetry by eminent poets contains about the same amount of emotional content as is found on the front page of the *New York Times* (Martindale 1990). While eminence does not correlate significantly with primary process content, it is correlated with the inverse measure, secondary process content. This is consistent with Simonton's (1989) findings with Shakespeare's sonnets. Great poetry does not deal with concepts or ideas or actions. This contention is borne out by the negative correlation of eminence with Activity, Ideal Value, Guide, Attempt, and Move; and the positive correlations with Imagery and Concreteness. Great poetry, at least for the present sample, deals with the depths of the mind and with concrete objects as opposed to thought or action.

Eminence was not correlated with variability of word frequency or of word length. As may be seen in Table 3, more eminent poets tend to use longer sentences on average, but tend to intermix long and short sentences. This intermixture is picked up by the correlations of eminence with the standard deviation of sentence length and the coefficient of variability of sentence length. The coefficient of variability of a measure is its mean divided by its standard deviation. The correlation with Meaningfulness is consistent with findings concerning sentence-length variability. Words with more associations are potentially more ambiguous than those with few. These findings coincide with Simonton's (1989) findings but contrast with Forsyth's finding that great poets use simpler language than bad poets. The reason for the difference may be that all of the poets in the present sample are eminent, while Forsyth contrasted eminent with downright bad poets. As for the correlation with AII, it is certainly not counterintuitive that the more intelligent one is the better poetry he will be capable of producing.

We see that there are quite specific and objectively measurable types of content that correlate with poetic eminence. It is interesting to note what eminence is not correlated with. Just as "money can't buy you love," it can't buy you fame either. Several *caveats* are in order. Without further empirical work, we cannot be sure if the findings reported in this chapter are specific to British poets or have cross-cultural validity. Second, one cannot become a great poet simply by avoiding references to thought, emotion, and action and talking only of concrete objects. However, one can more or less guarantee that he or she will not become a great poet by writing poetry concerned with such topics.

References

Auden, W. H. 1948. Squares and Oblongs. In *Poets at Work*, C. D. Abbott (ed.). New York NY: Harcourt Brace Jovanovich.

Chambers, E. K (ed.) 1932. *The Oxford Book of Sixteenth Century Verse*. London: OUP.

Cox, C. 1926. *The Early Mental Traits of Three Hundred Geniuses*. Stanford CA: Stanford University Press.

Forsyth, R. S. 1998. Pops and Flops: Some Properties of Famous English Poems. In *Proceedings of the XV Congress of the International Association of Empirical Aesthetics*, P. Bonaiuto, A. M. Giannini, C. Martindale, H. Hoege, P. Machotka & G. C. Cupchik (eds.), 41–42. Rome: Edizioni Universitarie Roma.

Grierson, H. J. C. & G. Bullough (eds). 1934. *The Oxford Book of Seventeenth Century Verse*. London: OUP.

Hayward, J. (ed.) 1964. *The Oxford Book of Nineteenth Century English Verse*. London: OUP.

Heise, D. R. 1965. Semantic Differential Profiles for 1000 Most Frequent English Words. *Psychological Monographs* 79: 1–31.

Hume, D. 1999. Of the Standard of Taste. In *Eighteenth-Century British Aesthetics*. D. Townsend (ed.), 230–241. Amityville NY: Baywood. (Orig. edn. 1757).

Martindale, C. 1973. COUNT: A PL/I Program for Content Analysis of Natural Language. *Behavioural Science* 18: 148.

Martindale, C. 1974a. The Semantic Significance of Spatial Movement in Narrative Verse: Patterns of Regressive Imagery in the Divine Comedy. In *Computers in the Humanities*, L. Mitchell (ed.), 57–64. Edinburgh: EUP.

Martindale, C. 1974b. LEXSTAT: A PL/I Program for Computation of Lexical Statistics. *Behavioural Research Methods and Instrumentation* 6: 571.

Martindale, C. 1975. *Romantic Progression: The Psychology of Literary History*. Washington DC: Hemisphere.

Martindale, C. 1990. *The Clockwork Muse: The Predictability of Artistic Change*. New York NY: Basic Books.

Martindale, C. 1995. Fame more Fickle than Fortune: On the Distribution of Literary Eminence. *Poetics* 23: 219–234.

Martindale, C. 1997. Is Poetry about Emotion? In *Emotion, Creativity, and Art*, Vol. 2., L. Dorfman, C. Martindale, D. Leontiev, G. Cupchik, V. Petrov & P. Machotka (eds.), 429–441. Perm: Perm State Institute of Arts and Culture.

Martindale, C. & Dailey, A. 1995. I. A. Richards Revisited: Do People Agree in their Interpretations of Literature? *Poetics* 23: 299–314.

Osgood, G. E., Suci, G. & Tannenbaum, P. H. 1956. *The Measurement of Meaning*. Urbana IL: University of Illinois Press.

Paivio, A., Yuille, J. C. & Madigan, S. A. 1968. Concreteness, Imagery, and Meaningfulness Values for 925 Nouns. *Journal of Experimental Psychology Monograph Supplement* 25: 1–25.

Richards, I. A. 1929. *Practical Criticism: A Study of Literary Judgment*. New York NY: Harcourt Brace & World.

Simonton, D. K. 1980. Thematic Fame and Melodic Originality in Classical Music: A Multivariate Computer-Content Analysis. *Journal of Personality* 48: 206–219.

Simonton, D. K. 1989. Shakespeare's Sonnets: A Case of and for Single-Case Historiometry. *Journal of Personality* 57: 695–721.

Sisam, C. and Sisam, K. 1970. *The Oxford Book of Medieval English Verse*. Oxford: OUP.

Smith, B. H. 1988. *Contingencies of Value: Alternative Perspectives for Critical Theory.* Cambridge MA: Harvard University Press.

Smith, C. P. 1935. *Annals of the Poets.* London: Charles Scribner's Sons.

Smith, D. N. (ed.). 1926. *The Oxford Book of Eighteenth Century Verse.* London: OUP.

Stone, P., et al. 1966. *The General Inquirer: A Computer Approach to Content Analysis.* Cambridge MA: The MIT Press.

CHAPTER 10

Macbeth through the computer

Literary evaluation and pedagogical implications[1]

Sonia Zyngier

Corpus linguistics offers tools and methodologies which may help uncover elements that respond for the linguistic quality of a text. In order to evaluate quality, we assume that it depends on two criteria: linguistic predictability and function. Corpus analysis also helps substantiate interpretations and contradict statements about texts previously taken for granted. In this chapter the language of *Macbeth* is seen against the Birmingham Shakespeare corpus and that of its source text to illustrate how claims on literary quality can be made. It is assumed that if literary texts work by discoverable rules, it is possible to recover them for pedagogical application. To this purpose, pedagogical applications are offered showing how this can be a very productive method in the classroom.

1. Introduction

This article suggests a move towards students' emancipation in reading, responding, interpreting and evaluating literary texts. It demonstrates how the computer can be a potent tool in providing an environment which enables students to think about language and produce justifiable evaluations of the text. Because they can do things with language, submission to the power of printed criticism is diminished. Finding out for themselves, students can challenge traditional readings and look for what is implicit rather than for what is stated. Evaluation is then possible because the reader makes inferential postulations about the language of the text.

Relativist perspectives and radical reader-response theories have argued that pattern perception is a cultural event which depends on a socially constructed convention of relations. It is true that interpretation may vary from group to group of the same language speakers and from generation to generation. However, a text's properties also constrain interpretations and may answer for its quality. Based on Augustine, Eco (1990:65) rightly notes that "any interpretation given of a certain

---

1. This chapter is dedicated to the memory of John McH. Sinclair, who introduced me to corpus linguistics and to whom I greatly owe.

portion of a text can be accepted if it is confirmed by, and must be rejected if it is challenged by, another portion of the same text. In this sense the internal textual coherence controls the otherwise uncontrollable drives of the reader". This argument may be quite helpful for literary education. Students may not be fully competent linguistically and may not be sophisticated readers with a rich framework of reference but may nonetheless bring new and stimulating perceptions to the discussion if these can be justified within the linguistic framework of the text.

2.   Some theoretical assumptions: The literary text and value

The reader who picks up this book may anticipate he or she will find in one of the essays collected here a convincing answer to the question of literary evaluation. I must warn this reader that the task is impossible. One can suggest, bring up possibilities, persuade, but the answers should be taken as a temporary solution. To deal with evaluation is to swim in troubled waters.

One of the reasons for this claim is that literary evaluation is deeply involved with social and cultural factors. A text is considered literary according to what a given community considers worth preserving. However, this claim does not invalidate the possibility of establishing some working assumptions and criteria, even if on a provisional basis. In this chapter, I will assume that the language of a literary text is arranged in such a way that it brings into focus values and ideas which are treasured by the community of readers.

In its simplest terms, a literary text is a collection of linguistic signs produced and received within a cultural context operating on at least three dimensions: the existential, the self-reflective and the functional. On the existential level, the reader perceives the mapping out of an individual's perception of the world. This existential level is brought about by the content of the text, or what it deals with. The self-reflective dimension takes into account the making of the text and the questions raised about its constituent material. Culler (1983: 35–36) points out that "In so far as literature turns back on itself and examines, parodies, or treats ironically its own signifying procedures, it becomes the most complex account of signification we possess". Literary texts provide a critical language in which to view systems of thought. In other words, they are the metalanguage of culture. Thirdly, the literary text functions in society. Every culture produces its own texts (written or oral). They are handed down from generation to generation following sets of rules and conventions established by communities. To summarise the discussion so far, then, literary texts are products of the individual as an epistemic and a social being.

3.   Criteria for literary evaluation: Predictability and function

Deciding on which texts are worth valuing is not a simple issue. Quality varies with taste and depends largely on cultural agreement. Here I will argue that quality depends at least on two criteria: predictability and function.

Cognitive psychology and information theory have suggested that what draws a reader's attention to an event is the degree of its unpredictability (cf. Bruner et al. 1951; Luria 1976). For instance, newspaper headlines break the routine of daily events by making something news. The intention is to have the reader reflect upon the novel situation, compare it to a former set of expectations and, once realising the difference, insert it in the repertoire as a new item. Gombrich (1986) shows how the function of an outdoor poster is to draw the viewer's attention to the improbable and hold it so that the process of interpretation is prolonged. Accommodation follows and this new state of affairs turns into part of the reader's experience.

Granted that predictability is closely associated with frequency of occurrence (Sinclair 1982; Willis 1990), I argue that the possibility of knowing in advance that a word, sentence, pattern, etc. will happen has a major influence in setting the value of a text. Developments in computer research and the building of corpora have done much and can still do much to help researchers make empirical statements about such predictability.

The notion of textual predictability depends largely on studies on collocation. Sinclair (1991) argues that words do not occur at random in a text and that the occurrence of a word or structure points ahead to the next realisation, thus reducing the possibility of choice. He postulates that lexis, syntax and semantics are closely linked and function in such a way as to allow the reader to predict what will come next.

However, there is always room for ambiguity. The same structure can yield more than one sense. This fact does not pose a problem in everyday communication, as the text will tend towards disambiguation. In literature, it can be used for stylistic effects. Therefore, if sense and structure are not either inseparable or independent, they must be closely associated. Sinclair proposes two principles: the *open choice principle*, where a structure opens a slot that may be filled with any word, the only restraint being grammatical options (slot-and-filler model) and the *idiom principle*, or the simultaneous choice of two or more words. He summarises: "Most normal text is made up of the occurrence of frequent words, and the frequent senses of less frequent words. Hence, normal text is largely de-lexicalized, and appears to be formed by the exercise of the idiom principle, with occasional switching to the open-choice principle" (1991: 113). In other words, non-literary texts undergo progressive de-lexicalization. Their language becomes predictable and non-reflexive. The reader pays less attention to the language itself.

Contrarily, literary texts tend towards lexicalization, where more attention is given to the language. In fact, in a literary text, words may become over-lexicalized on the discourse level (Carter 1987). They may allow two or more meanings at the same time. Quite the opposite occurs in everyday conversation, where meaning is generally negotiated for disambiguation.

If there is a tendency towards de-lexicalization in everyday use of language, the following hypothesis can be formulated: the literary quality of the language used in a text can be determined by the open-choice principle. If the idiom principle prevails, the reader should look for stylistic reasons which may justify this fact. I am aware that there are some difficulties here. First, it is hard to check intuitively the frequency of combinations. Then, deciding on what to investigate, that is, isolating relevant features for processing implies a subjective choice. Furthermore, predictability in terms of most probable collocations is at present very difficult to sustain in non-contemporary texts.

Adding to that, linguistic predictability alone does not provide a substantial argumentation. A crucial factor is the conventional expectations of the reader – the "as if" behaviour (van Peer 1986:137) which answers for the treatment the reader will give to the text. Readers generally expect poems to contain rhyme and rhythm, to be more compressed in the use of language, and to display figurative language. Similarly, documents are expected to bear a closer relationship to a certain state of affairs in the real world and avoid ambiguous or conflicting interpretations. However, these expectations can be modified. Readers may look at advertisements not to be persuaded by a product but to find aesthetic manifestations in the language. In this case, they will be subverting the function of a specific genre and developing new dimensions not initially intended by the producer of the text. If one reads an advertisement as a poem, "new effects become possible because the conventions of the genre produce a new range of signs" (Culler 1975:162).

4.   What can corpus analysis do?

Corpus Linguistics is not a new branch of linguistics like psycholinguistics or sociolinguistics. It is a methodology by means of which we use the computer to organise large stretches of language in ways which allow us to perceive things we would not normally see or which we would not be able to account for. A *corpus* is a collection of pieces of language that have been selected and ordered according to explicit linguistic criteria in order to be used as a sample of language. According to Sinclair (1991:17) "One of the principal uses of a corpus is to identify what is central and typical in language". In this case, one may argue that corpus linguistics would not apply to the study of the language of literary texts precisely because writers tend to innovate and so literary texts cannot be considered "sample texts". Each text is then unique.

The issue of creativity in literary language is complex. As discussed above, a text is considered literary according to many conditions and values established by a given community at a certain time and not only because its language may be creative. In addition, not every instance of creative language is literary (cf. ads and jokes). Like other instances of language use, creativity depends on interpretability. From this standpoint, the less effort expended in interpretation, the less creative the text. Here, the notion of semantic reversal forwarded by Sinclair (1997) may be . illuminating. He explains that a given stretch of language depends on two meanings: the precise meaning of a word as determined by a lexicon (or by the frequency of its use) and the meaning produced by the verbal environment in which the word is inserted. Non-creative language is built on the accumulation of each successive meaningful unit as expected. This is what makes the text highly predictable: the two meanings – the one created by the environment and the one created by each item individually are expected. However, in a more creative use of language (metaphors, irony, etc.) the meaning generated by the textual environment is distant or even clashes with the meaning of the item, requiring the reader/addressee to exercise his/her interpretive skills. Here corpus linguistics may point out the environment of certain lexical items as used by an author and allow us some statements about possible interpretations which are demonstrable. This specific use may also be set against contemporary texts so as to verify the degree of creativity. This is easily done with 20th century literature, where access to all sorts of written materials is available. Although in the experiment I describe below I did have access to a 17th century corpus (The Helsinki Corpus), the language of the type of texts which compose that corpus does not give us enough coverage of language usage, which may mislead our conclusions. In the case of non-contemporary texts, when the written mode was not as widespread as today and when there was no means of recording spoken language, it is important to bear in mind that we are limiting the investigation to a corpus which contains centrally the writer's productions and peripherally that of his contemporaries.

Notwithstanding these limitations, the literary text may still be studied empirically against some sort of norm. Whether this norm is a collection of other texts from the same period or region, or whether it is the collected works of the same author, we may use the methodology of corpus linguistics for more objective analysis. In the case of Elizabethan/Jacobean English, it is hard to talk about corpora, as I did not have access to a large collection of texts in electronic form. But at the moment we can think of a Shakespeare corpus consisting of a collection of all of his works, the Helsinki Corpus, which is diachronically organised and brings some of the texts written at the time, and Holinshed's *Chronicles*.

Even if we are not dealing with large samples of language and are rather looking at features of a text from a small collection of works, we may still borrow the methodology and tools corpus linguistics offers. My assumption is that the computer may help us assess literary texts in ways which have not been available so far, thus providing more substantiation to intuitive interpretations and to decisions on literary evaluation. This method of investigation may help contradict statements about texts which have been taken for granted and, based on the observation of the language used, determine to a large extent the literary quality of the text. The question then is finding out what properties of an observation distinguish it from the rest as having interpretative importance. In this case, both overall frequency of occurrence, which may establish internal patterns of usage, and semantic reversal could account for these properties.

5. The experiment

In this section, I demonstrate an exercise carried out with *Macbeth* to verify whether a corpus approach to a non-contemporary literary text may bring new kinds of evidence and help validate and/or privilege certain interpretations. I also contrast the language of the play to its source text to illustrate how claims on literary quality can be made.

The research method adopted here is both quantitative and qualitative, since I both produce numerical accounts (the frequency lists) and from the list pick out some items to assess their behaviour within their context in the corpus. By reporting the experiment step-by-step my intention is to make it replicable and useful for pedagogical purposes.

a. Getting started: Frequency lists

The first step was to use the Shakespeare Corpus at the University of Birmingham to produce a frequency list of all the word-forms both in *Macbeth* (**MAC**) and in the Shakespeare Tragedy Corpus (**STC**) in order to decide where to start the investigation from.[2] According to Sinclair (1996: 80–81), "... the use of numerical methods is normally only the first stage of a linguistic investigation... [where] ... the focus is on repeated events rather than single occurrences". Repeated events provide a decisive framework by means of which we can investigate single occurrences. The intention was to verify which lexical items would draw our attention and which we would consider worthy of investigation. This decision was ultimately

---

2.   I would like to thank Geoff Barnbrook for these initial lists and for the most pleasant and enlightening conversation during a two-day stay in Birmigham in July 1997 sponsored by the Fundação de Amparo à Pesquisa do Rio de Janeiro (FAPERJ).

subjective but may not invalidate the general point. In order to establish evaluative significance, the investigation followed a pragmatic orientation, one in which priority was given to the effect the text has on the reader, a view in line with theories which assume the existence of structures which may not be immediately apparent to the reader but are accountable for the literary effect. It is possible that this effect is achieved either by frequency of the use of certain lexical items, by the unpredictability of single occurrences, or even by the absence of some of the items, of what has not been selected.

Starting very informally from a point I had heard before that Macbeth was a man of "shoulds" and "woulds" and that the play was future-oriented, I decided to look at the verb-forms in the play to check whether any form would capture my attention. Using a not too sophisticated apparatus (a 486 personal computer and MicroConcord as the software), I ran the Electronic Edition of *The Complete Works of Shakespeare* through the computer. Here is the frequency list of **verbs** comparing the most frequent occurrences:

Table 1. Frequency list of verbs

	MAC 17,839 tokens		STC 101,352 tokens	
	Occurrences	%	Occurrences	%
Is	190	1.06	1,072	1.05
Be	139	0.77	730	0.72
Have	122	0.68	672	0.66
Do	84	0.47	572	0.56
Enter	76	0.42	295	0.29
Will	75	0.42	513	0.50
Are	74	0.41	420	0.41
Shall	68	0.38	373	0.36
Come	67	0.37	328	0.32
Hath	52	0.29	231	0.22
Was	48	0.26	252	0.24
Would	47	0.26	261	0.25

Setting a comparison between the frequency list of verbs in the entire Shakespeare corpus (**STC**) and in *Macbeth* (**MAC**) did not lead me too far in terms of whether this play would differ significantly from the other tragedies as regards verb choices. Verbs like **will** or **shall** that could be relevant in terms of the question of time were not characteristically more frequent in *Macbeth* than in the Shakespeare Tragedy Corpus. Of course one could argue that time is not exclusively conveyed by these verbs. There may be other markers of time in the play which one could investigate. What this search did was to rule out the possibility of it being conveyed by **will** or

shall. What was interesting was to check why **enter** was more frequent in *Macbeth* than in the other tragedies. Such a frequency, especially in the stage directions, indicates that this is a dynamic play with a lot of movement on the part of the actors, especially Macbeth, who does most of the enterings. The following table shows the most frequent verbs in **MAC** as opposed to the most frequent ones in the **STC**:

Table 2. Comparative list of order of verb frequency

	MAC	STC
1	Is	Is
2	Be	Be
3	Have	Have
4	Do	Do
5	Enter	Will
6	Will	Are
7	Shall	Shall
8	Come	Come
9	Hath	Enter
10	Was	Let
11	Would	Would
12	Make	Am

This table confirms the relevance of "enter" and points out a significant difference between "make" in MAC and "am" in STC. Not quite knowing where to go from here, I decided to look at a frequency list of nouns:

Table 3. Frequency list of nouns

	MAC (17,830 tokens)		STC (101,352 tokens)	
	Occurrences	%	Occurrences	%
Time	46	0.25	146	0.14
King	36	0.20	197	0.19
Lord	35	0.19	448	0.44
Man	30	0.16	189	0.18
Sir	29	0.16	259	0.25
Sleep	26	0.14	54	0.05
Blood	26	0.14	68	0.06
Son	26	0.14	73	0.07
Thane	25	0.14	*not included in the 400 most frequent occurrences	
Heart	22	0.12	122	0.12

The order of frequency in which these words appear is the following:

Table 4. Comparative list of order of noun frequency

	MAC	STC
1	Time	Lord
2	King	Sir
3	Lord	Love
4	Man	King
5	Sir	Man
6	Sleep	Time
7	Blood	Father
8	Son	Heart
9	Thane	Night
10	Heart	Heaven

If we check the most frequent nouns in **MAC** against those in the **STC**, we will notice that five stand out conspicuously. Because **time, sleep, blood, son, thane** are not the most frequent words in the **STC**, they could be telling us something particular about *Macbeth* ("lord" and "thane" would seem to be selecting from the same lexical set and would still be less than the normal percentage of usage in the corpus). Would one of the keys to interpretation lie in these words and their patterning?

b. Selecting from the list
The next step was to produce a concordancing of these words to check whether the patterns they helped produce would be worth pursuing.

Time
This word is twice more frequent in *Macbeth* (46 cases, 0.257%) than in *Othello* (30 cases, 0.095%), *King Lear* (27 cases, 0.087%), and *Romeo and Juliet* (30 cases, 0.103%). Compared to *Macbeth*, it is 40% less frequent in *Hamlet* (47 cases, 0.127%). However, the order of frequency of the words presented in Table 4 above is the following in *Hamlet*: Lord (225), King (210), Sir (76), Love (70), Father (69), Man (60), Time (47), Heaven (44), Night (37), Heart (30). This order not only shows that *time* is not the most frequent word in the play but is also illuminating if we consider the protagonist's conflict between his loyalty to the ruler and the need to carry out the revenge demanded by his father's ghost. In terms of textual quality, if we compare Shakespeare's and Holinshed's use of the word, we can see that most of the 19 cases in Holinshed are highly predictable and require little effort to interpret. Here, *time* is used mostly in adverbial positions preceded by *at, in, for a long* or collocates with predictable items such as * *and place, tarie a* *. In

Shakespeare's text, not only is *time* invoked and personified, but it also collocates with a variety of different nouns (*seeds of* *; *master of his* *, *expense of* *, *bank and shoal of* *, *spy o' th'* *, *gaze o' th'* *), of adjectives (*blessed* *, *best* *, *olden* *, *recorded* , *woeful* *), and of verbs (*mock the* *, *fill up the* *, *rue the* *, *beguile the* *, *grant the* *), which answer for the creative use Shakespeare makes of the word (see Appendix I).

Thane

The concordancing showed that **thane** collocates mostly with the titles of the characters referred to in the play (Thane of Cawdor; Thane of Fife; Thane of Glamis; etc.). In 8 cases, they are part of noun phrases of honorific titles, in 6 cases they are placed in a positive semantic prosody and only in 3 cases they have negative connotations. By semantic prosody here, we mean "a consistent aura of meaning with which a form is imbued by its collocates" (Louw 1993: 157). There were 8 cases which I considered general and non-specific. If we add the 7 instances of honorific titles and the 6 cases where **thane** has positive connotations, we can see how we are made to look through Macbeth's perspective, the honorific title thus seen in a positive light as the object of his desire. It is interesting here to see that out of the 25 instances, in 8 cases there are pronouns in the near vicinity ("I am"; "me"; "to me"; "my"; "our"; "thee"; "thy"; "thine") and in 5 instances we find "worthy", which helps build the dramatic tension created by Macbeth's desire and support the quality of Shakespeare's text. In Holinshed, however, this doesn't occur. There are no underlying implications in the attributions of the titles. This becomes even clearer if we contrast "All haile, Makbeth, thane of Glammis!" (**HOL**), where the title comes immediately after the name, as a logical consequence, to the impact of "All hail, Macbeth! Hail to thee, Thane of Glamis."(**MAC**), where "thee" stands as the centre of reference, a bridge between Macbeth and what he will become.

Son

A concordancing of this word shows that in 15 cases, it occurs in the speech directions for MacDuff's son. As they are not in the spoken text and if we remove the other stage directions, we are left with only 9 occurrences, 5 of which have the meaning of progeny. Not a very exciting finding in itself, but relevant when put together with the treatment of the word **woman** (see below). It is interesting to notice that many of the characters have sons in the play (Duncan has two, Banquo, MacDuff, Siward have one each). There has even been speculation in traditional literary criticism about possible children Macbeth may have had, but as this speculation is not confirmed by the language of the play, I decided to leave it for what it is. The child-theme has already been given much emphasis (see Knights 1933, among others). Therefore, I decided to concentrate on the words **blood** and **sleep.**

c. Narrowing down: A concordancing of two items

blood

Macbeth is definitely the bloodiest of the tragedies. The following table shows the frequency of this word as compared to *Hamlet* (**HAM**), *Othello* (**OTH**) and *King Lear* (**LRQ**),[3] the Helsinki Corpus of English of compiled documents during Shakespeare's lifetime (**HCE2**) and my Holinshed corpus (**HOL**). If compared to the whole tragedy corpus (0.06%), **blood** is 2.08 times more frequent in *Macbeth*:

Table 5. Occurrence of "blood"

MAC	HAM	OTH	LRQ	HCE2	HOL	STC
0.14%	0.05%	0.04%	0.04%	0.01%	0.01%	0.06%

In terms of colligation, there is little to say about the patterning of the occurrences. Shakespeare seems to prefer **blood** in rhematic positions, generally preceded by a preposition (*with* *, *in* *). There are very few occurrences in thematic position. However, semantic preference is more telling. Blood is used in relation to a baboon, a sow, and a bat to add the exotic aspect of witchcraft, but this is not what distinguishes its use in this play from the other tragedies. Whereas in the other plays, the meanings are mostly metaphorical, a concordancing of **blood** in *Macbeth* indicates that it deviates from Shakespeare's use of the word, as there are 15 literal uses and 11 metaphorical ones, thus adding to the visual impact and the violence of the play. The following table indicates how the literal to the metaphorical ratio is much higher in *Macbeth* than in the other texts:

Table 6. Meaning of "blood"

	Metaphorical	Literal	Total	L/M ratio
MAC	10	15	25	1.5
HOL	16	8	24	0.5
HCE	16	6	22*	0.37
HML	17	2	19	0.11
LRQ	12	4	16	0.33
OTH	10	2	12	0.2

Apparently most of these instances come from religious documents.

With regard to collocates, in **MAC**, most of them occur before the node.[4] There is a semantic preference for profusion, especially in N-3 and N-2 positions

---

3. i.e., the Quarto edition. LRQ is the file name in the *Oxford Electronic Edition*.

4. "The node word in a collocation is the one whose lexical behaviour is under examination" (Sinclair 1991: 175). A span is "the measurement, in words, of the co-text of a word selected for

(all, ocean, much, fountain, pour). For instance, we can contrast "gouts of blood" (MAC) to "that drop of blood" (HAM). In HOL, 5 instances out of the 8 literal ones have the idea of profusion ("cakes of blood", "beraied with blood", "great effusion of blood", "blood ran about ") but it still does not compare to the preference of the literal use of the word in MAC. In addition, the association of "blood" and "gold" in "His silver skin lac'd with his golden blood"[5] and "gild the faces of the grooms" in MAC produce a semantic preference for richness, for something treasured, which does not occur in HCE, LRQ, HAM, OTH or HOL. The fact that Shakespeare prefers the literal sense to the metaphorical does not diminish the play's literary quality. If we compare his use of "blood" to Holinshed's, where its use, although mostly metaphorical, is highly predictable, we can perhaps start seeing why Shakespeare's text is richer. In Holinshed, most cases are connected to progeny and to religion – a highly predictable use. In Shakespeare, we find it in alliterations ("blood-baltered Banquo"), in repetitions ("blood will have blood"), with a variety of adverbs of intensity, in unusual collocations, and placed in very concrete situations, appealing to the reader's senses ("smell of the blood", "thy blood is cold"). The variety of uses leads to a variety of experiences which transcend time and may here indicate a degree of quality when compared to Holinshed (see Appendix II). As van Peer (1997:223) notes, "by facilitating the process of imaginative engagement, [literature] affords readers the opportunity for emotional experimentation, intense contemplation, self-evaluation, and possible reorientation in the everyday world".

sleep
The frequency table of occurrences of this word in different plays is also interesting:

Table 7. Frequency of **sleep**

MAC	HAM	OTH	LRQ	HCE	HOL	STC
0.14%	0.03%	0.01%	0.02%	0.0%	0.004%	0.05%

Sleep is almost three times more frequent in *Macbeth* (0.14%) than it is in the tragedy corpus (0.05%). In addition, it is more common as a noun in *Macbeth* than in the other plays (MAC: 16 nouns/9 verbs; HAM: 4 nouns/8 verbs; LRQ: 4 nouns/4 verbs; OTH: 3 nouns/3 verbs).[6] How relevant is this finding? This

---

study. A span of –4, +4 means that four words on either side of the node word will be taken to be its relevant verbal environment" (Sinclair 1991:175). N–3 and N–2 refer to the third and the second word to the left of the node, respectively.

5.   cf. II.iii.119

6.   There was only one instance in HCE and 8 in HOL (3 nouns and 5 verbs).

evidence not only helps distinguish the quality of *Macbeth* as compared to the Holinshed corpus but may also give a different dimension to the sleepwalking scene, to the dream world and ambiguity in *Macbeth*. Holinshed's use of the word is commonplace ("passed that night without anie sleepe comming in his eies"; "could not sleepe in the night time"; "keepe him still waking from sleepe"; "as he lay sleeping"). The same applies to his description of the guards: and "awaked them out of their droonken sleepe". If we compare this description to the creative beastly imagery Shakespeare used ("when in swinish sleep/Their drenched natures be"), we can see how in *Macbeth* literary value is guaranteed by polysemy. "Sleep" is a concept, not a process. It is "the season of all natures". Shakespeare's use of **sleep** is much more complex than in the Holinshed corpus. There are two different kinds of sleep in the language of the play: the ones with negative semantic preference, like "Curtained sleep", "thralls of sleep", "swinish sleep", "equivocates him in a sleep", the one which makes one guard cry "Murder" in his dream, and the ones set in a positive semantic preference, such as "innocent sleep", "sleep in spite of thunder", "the benefit of sleep", the one which makes the other guard "laugh in his sleep". Here again "foul is fair and fair is foul" is reinstalled. Sleep can be either good or bad. It adds to the uncertain atmosphere of the play and supports the theme of equivocation. This evidence goes against Knight's statement that "sleep [is]... the gentle nurse of life ...'sleep' is twined with 'feasting'. Both are creative, restorative, forces of nature. So Macbeth and his Queen are reft of both during the play's action" (1968:148). The sleepwalking scene then is a further evidence of the breakdown of a strong bond between the two main protagonists. While one cannot sleep anymore, the other one falls into a continuous slumber. The couple loses common ground, once shared through letters and dialogues, and start inhabiting different worlds.

Producing this list also worked as a check on other traditional statements about the play. For instance, Knight (1968:139) claims that "throughout the main action of *Macbeth* we are confronted by fear. The word occurs ubiquitously. Fear is at the heart of this play". A frequency list shows that **fear** occurs 35 times (18 as verbs; 11 as nouns and 6 as objects of prepositions). If we look at their collocations, we notice that there is a semantic preference for actually denying **fear** rather than reinforcing it in 10 verb cases and in 7 of the nouns. So, in 50% of the cases, **fear** is denied or questioned (e.g. "Fear not", "What need I fear?" "Hang those that talk of fear", "nor shake with fear"). Knight also holds that **honour** "occurs throughout, strongly emphasised" (1968:139). However, **honour** actually occurs only 11 times in the play (cf. the most frequent nouns in Table 3 above).

An investigation of the occurrence of **fear** in *Macbeth* and in the Holinshed corpus also showed interesting data for evaluating the quality of the texts. Holinshed is less inventive in his patterning of the word. There are 29 instances, but differently from *Macbeth*, most of them are placed as objects of prepositions (17).

There are only 4 verbs and 8 nouns. His collocates to the left are highly predictable items such as "all", "sudden", "great", "stand in". As for personification, whereas Shakespeare produces original images ("the initiate fear that wants hard use"; "pale-hearted fear"), Holinshed remains banal ("his owne feare fantasieth"; "a sudden terror and deadlie feare").

d. Using a top-down approach

Instead of starting from a frequency list of all word-forms in the play, I then decided to look at Lady Macbeth's role as a woman in the play. What drew my attention was that in reading the play, I noticed that she always spurred Macbeth by questioning his masculinity. There are 34 instances where the word **man** is used. A concordancing of this lexical item shows that the most frequent collocates are **a** (14) and **of** (13), which indicates a tendency to the generic reference. In 10 instances, the verb **be** collocates with man and in 4, comparatives are used ("like", "as", "more"). An examination of the semantic area of collocates indicates that in 12 instances, **man** is related to *power* and in 6 to *temporality*. In Holinshed, the positive semantic prosody (Louw 1993) of man is very similar, but in many instances comparisons or associations to power and temporality are not drawn. The epithets only help characterise the person ("of great nobility", "of loftie courage", "well learned", "well languaged", "of great experience"). In the play, the use of the word **man** points at the Renaissance focus on man as the centre of reference, as a paradigm, although subject to temporality. In order to spur her husband into action, Lady Macbeth challenges his manhood. The word she uses most is *great* (Louw 1991: 172) and it generally acquires an ironic overtone. This finding contradicts Knight's (1968: 141) suggestion that "Lady Macbeth wins largely by appealing to Macbeth's 'valour'".

On the other hand, **woman** is taken for her capacity to reproduce and is presented in neutral semantic prosody. This is typical of the play and of Holinshed's representation of women. There are 13 occurrences of **woman** in MAC and the following list shows the most frequent collocations. *Right* and *left* here refer to the collocates as positioned in relation to the node:

Table 8. Collocates of "woman"

	MAC			HOL	
Right:		*Left:*		*Right:*	*Left:*
born = 4		of = 8		a = 10	any = 5
		born = 4		of = 8	borne = 3
		to = 3			poore = 3
		a = 3			

What is interesting here is the adjective *poore* in **HOL**. When not presented in their capacity to reproduce, women are shown as destitute, lacking, in contrast to man, whose collocates to the left are *everie* (16), *noble* (9), *great* (8), *anie* (7). Here, the adjectives *noble* and *great* stand out in opposition to *poore*, as *any* contrasts with *everie*. According to Quirk et al. (1980:365), *any* may express indefinite amount, whereas *every* is "unambivalently singular". Man is singled out as unique. In addition, there are two instances in *Macbeth* of **woman** with parts of body: *woman's breasts*; *woman's ears*, which does not occur in Holinshed. The following table illustrates the semantic prosody of **woman** in *Macbeth* as compared to the other three tragedies and Holinshed:

Table 9. Semantic prosody of "woman"

	Negative	Positive	Neutral	Total
MAC	4	0	9	13
HAM	5	0	3	8
OTH	5	7	4	16
HOL	4	5	8	17
LR(Folio)*	3	0	5	8

*Instead of the Quarto Edition, as in the other tables, the Folio edition was used, as it had one more instance

Would the semantic prosody of **woman** in *Macbeth* indicate that through Lady Macbeth's deeds Shakespeare would be condemning women who refused their role as procreators? Would this refusal be a hideous crime and turn Lady Macbeth into the fourth witch? This seems to be what Freud (1968:135) suggests, "I believe [in] Lady Macbeth's *illness*, the transformation of her callousness, by which she is convinced of her *impotence* against the decrees of nature, and at the same time reminded that it is through her own fault if her crime has been robbed of the better part of its fruits" (my italics). This statement seems to be contradictory. If she's impotent against the decrees of nature, if, as the corpus indicates, she is socially represented as a poor element of procreation, why won't she bear children? I believe that, on the contrary, she gets what she sets out to get. What she cannot measure are the consequences of her act. Her short-sightedness does not allow her to anticipate the effect of the murder on her husband and on herself. She does not realise that it has come between herself and her partner, who begins to avoid her. They move into different worlds and this is what makes her break. Her suicide is the result of the loneliness she experiences in her state of isolation. Corpus analysis helps us see that instead of the ambitious wife we find in Holinshed's text, Shakespeare's Lady Macbeth is linguistically represented as a much more psychologically complex character: an early example of the "madwoman in the attic" (Gilbert & Gubar 1988). The complexity of the woman portrayed, her relationship to the husband, and the dramatic tension created by Shakespeare's use of language as opposed to Holinshed's solutions help us determine the quality of the play over its source text.

6.   Pedagogical application

If we assume that an author's use of language can answer for the literary quality of a text, it will be possible to sensitise students to the value of a literary text if they perceive how the language has been chosen and patterned to disclose values and ideas which transcend time. Pedagogically, the best way to arrive at sensitisation is to promote an environment where students can exercise their intellectual interest by asking their own questions and finding the answers themselves. Ultimately, the goal of such an exercise is to empower students so that they become critical thinkers who act from reflection rather than from information handed to them.

We start from the premise that the language of literary texts is organised into devices, patterns, and structures. The devices can be rhetorical, such as those carried out by figures of speech (metaphors, paradoxes, antitheses, pleonasm, irony, etc.), generic, that is, accepted by conventions (for instance, specific rhyme schemes in sonnets; unities and divisions into acts in plays; or time sequence in novels, etc.) and collocational (how a certain word is positioned within the text). Devices are combined into various patterns such as repetitions. These patterns further combine into characteristic stylistic structures of parallels, symmetries, analogies, correspondences or contrasts. Now, if the assumption that literary texts work (at least substantially) by these discoverable rules is correct, it will then be possible to recover them for pedagogical purposes and to investigate the question of quality.

As a matter of illustration, the experiment described above can be translated into the following suggestions for students if they have access to a rather non-sophisticated computer and a software similar to *Microconcord*. The objective is to have students find out for themselves what may be worth investigating, having them produce their critical appreciation of the text and then be in a position to evaluate the quality of the text. This can be done by suggesting them to use the software in successive steps to observe the frequency, collocation of words of their own choice, classifying, interpreting, evaluating, and making generalisations of their findings. This can be followed by subsequent searches on other words and collocations based on the previous search. These procedures can then be applied to other plays by the same author or works from the same period (literary or not), comparisons can be made and conclusions drawn. In addition, the students can select statements from acknowledged critics and check them against the results of a corpus analysis. In this way they may be able to challenge or reinforce traditional interpretations. This discussion can be translated into the following suggestions:

1. Observe the occurrences of fear in *Macbeth* and in Holinshed's *Chronicle*.

    a. Classify these occurrences (nouns, verbs, etc.) and check which group is more frequent.
    b. Observe the environment of *fear* in each instance. Use d or c to indicate whether fear is denied or confirmed. Use x for the ones which are hard to classify.
    c. Compare your classification in a and b with that of your partner.
    d. Make a generalising statement about Shakespeare's use of *fear* in *Macbeth*.
    e. Make a generalising statement about Holinshed's use of *fear* and then compare your answer with the one in d.

2. Running the electronic texts you have of a playwright's production through Microconcord, prepare two frequency lists of verbs:

    a. in a particular play
    b. in the writer's whole production.
    c. Once the lists are ready, check whether any differences stand out and whether you think they are significant.

3. Run a list of nouns according to the same procedure above.

    a. Select some of the items you consider significant and produce a concordancing to check the textual environment of the word selected. Observe whether it has a negative or positive semantic prosody and check the implications of this finding against your interpretation of the work.
    b. Look into the syntactical patterns (colligation) in which the items you selected above appear. If you find any pattern(s) you consider significant, describe it and point out its relevance.
    c. Make a list of the collocates of one item and check their position in relation to the node word. The chart below is an example of some of the collocates of "blood" in *Macbeth*. Modify the chart below according to the core word you choose and observe whether any pattern(s) stand(s) out. If you see one, describe it and comment on its relevance.

4. Make similar charts for other lexical items you consider relevant in *Macbeth* and check the collocation of the same lexical items as used by Holinshed. Which text is more literary? Which criteria did you use?

5. Choose a statement on the work in question by a literary critic and decide whether your findings support or contradict the statement.

Table 10. Collocates of "blood"

N–4	N–3	N–2	N–1	NODE	N+1	N+2	N+3
Too	Much	Charged	With	blood	of	Thine	
	All	Badged	With	blood	,	So	Were
The	Sleepy	Grooms	With	blood	.		
The	secret'st	man	Of	blood	.		
Those	Clamorous	Harbingers	Of	blood	and	Death	.
And	Dudgeon	Gouts	Of	blood	,		
,	A	sip	Of	blood	,		
The	Smell	of	The	blood	still	.	
The	Fountain	of	Your	blood	Is	Stopped	,

As a matter of inquiry, corpus analysis can promote students' critical independence. The exercises above illustrate pedagogical strategies which allow students
to identify, describe, generalise, organise, compare, assign significance and finally
attribute value to the language of literary texts. In this sense, the computer helps
place the students at the centre of learning. As Miall (1991:7–8) remarks, "the
computer ... tends to foreground the act of inquiry, to require an active grasp of
the implications and limitations of particular research procedures... The flexibility
of the computer as a tool, together with the fact that attending to the screen shifts
attention away from the teacher, encourages students to engage more actively in
the debate that is central to the Humanities".

Conclusion

In this article I have tried to verify how the rapidly developing area of corpus linguistics can contribute to the evaluation of literary texts. The experiment was to
run a canonical text with a long history of critical literature through a software
which I hoped would organise the language of the text so that a fresh look could be
offered into the way the language choices are patterned. The texts were examined
according to two major criteria: predictability and function. The main objective
was to check whether some of the traditional readings could find linguistic evidence to support their arguments and whether new readings could be produced
which would bring out the quality of the text. It should be stressed, however, that
literary evaluation is a complex process and that the two criteria alone cannot answer for the quality of the text. Other parameters can be used, when asking, for
instance, why Shakespeare has become canonical whereas Holinshed is only of
historical interest. Corpus analysis should be supported here by other elements,
such as point of view or the analysis of the strategies of involvement present in the
play: the tension created by the two main protagonists' reluctance in carrying out

the murder, the more prominent role given to Lady Macbeth, and the access to their private world via the letters exchanged and read out to the audience. These are further elements which contribute to guarantee the quality of Shakespeare's treatment of the theme.

To conclude, I am aware that this analysis is tentative and far from comprehensive or exhaustive. It should be regarded as a preliminary exercise which has to be critically examined and contextualized. One way of doing this may be to build a corpus of the history of the text's reception and check the data against the language of the text. My provisional conclusion is that among its benefits, corpus linguistics allows scholars to ask new questions which may not correspond to the traditional notions of reading, interpreting, and evaluating texts. It offers a high degree of verifiability. It provides high speed access to and analysis of large amounts of data. One may have access to inter-textual levels of analysis, as comparisons between texts are made much easier. In the classroom, it promotes an environment where the focus shifts from the teacher to the students, where students themselves formulate the questions and decide on what is to be investigated, where they carry out group projects and benefit from discussions with their peers, where the teacher truly becomes another interlocutor and not a transmitter of pre-determined values. In a word, instead of looking at the discourse of one text, corpus linguistics allows the polyphony of discourses, a dialogue between texts which can be, if properly applied, an invaluable method for the teaching of literature.

References

Bruner, J. S., L. Postman & J. Rodrigues. 1951. Expectation and the perception of color. *American Journal of Psychology* 64: 216–227.

Carter, R. A. 1987. Vocabulary and second/foreign language teaching. *Language Teaching* January: 3–16.

Culler, J. 1975. *Structural Poetics*. London: Routledge and Kegan Paul.

Culler, J. 1983. *The Pursuit of Signs. Semiotics, Literature. Deconstruction.* London: Routledge and Kegan Paul.

Eco, U. 1990. Overinterpreting Texts. In *Interpretation and Overinterpretation*, S. Collini (ed.), 45–66. Cambridge: CUP.

Freud, S. 1968. Some character-types met with in psycho-analytical work. In *Shakespeare. Macbeth. A Casebook*, J. Wain (ed.), 139–46. London: Macmillan.

Gilbert, S. & Gubar, S. 1988. *The Madwoman in the Attic: The Woman writer and the nineteenth century literary imagination.* New Haven CT: Yale University Press.

Gombrich, E. H. 1986. *Art and Illusion: A study in the psychology of pictorial representation.* Washington DC: The Trustees of the National Gallery of Art.

Knight, W. G. 1968. The Milk of Concord: Life-themes in *Macbeth*. In *Shakespeare. Macbeth. A Casebook*, J. Wain (ed.), 125–53. London: Macmillan.

Knights, L. C. 1933. *How many children had Lady Macbeth? An essay in the theory and practice of Shakespeare Criticism*. Cambridge: The Minority Press.

Louw, B. 1991. Classroom concordancing of delexical forms and the case for integrating language and literature. In *Classroom Concordancing*, T. Johns & P. King (eds), *ELR Journal* 4: 151–178.

Louw, B. 1993. Irony in the text or insincerity in the writer? The diagnostic potential of semantic prosodies. In *Text and Technology*. M. Baker, G. Francis & E. Tognini-Bonelli (eds), 157–176. Amsterdam: John Benjamins.

Luria, A. R. 1976. *Cognitive Development: Its Cultural and Social Foundations*. Cambridge MA: Harvard University Press.

Miall, D. S. 1991. Introduction. In *Humanities and the Computer*. D. Miall (ed.), 1–12. Oxford: OUP.

Quirk, R. et al. 1980. *A Grammar of Contemporary English*. London: Longman.

Sinclair, J. McH. 1982. Lines about lines. In *Language and Literature*, R. Carter (ed.), 163–72. London: George Allen & Unwin.

Sinclair, J. McH. 1991. *Corpus, Concordance, Collocation*. Oxford: OUP.

Sinclair, J. McH. 1996. The search for units of meaning. In *Textus* IX(1): 75–106.

Sinclair, J. McH. 1997. The lexical Item. *Trust the Text: Language, corpus and discourse*, R. Carter (Ed.), 131–48. London: Routledge.

van Peer, W. 1986. *Stylistics and Psychology. Investigations of Foregrounding*. London: Croom Helm.

van Peer, W. 1997. Toward a Poetics of Emotion. In *Emotion and the Arts,* M. Hjort & S. Laver (eds.), 215–224. Oxford: OUP.

Willis, D. 1990. *The Lexical Syllabus*. London: Collins ELT.

Electronic Texts:

The Helsinki Historical English Corpus (ICAME CD-Rom).
Shakespeare, William, *The Complete Works*. Oxford Electronic Texts.
Scott, M. & T. Johns. *Microconcord*. OUP, 1993.

Appendix I

Collocations of time

a.   In Holinshed:

MicroConcord search SW: time
Sort : 1L/SW shifted 10 characters.

1 he thought with himselfe that he must tarie a	time, which should aduance him
2 maner of title and claime, which he might in	time to come, pretend vnto the
3 that he ought to take heed of Makduffe, who in	time to come should seeke to
4 would not haue his house slandered, but that in	time to come he might cleare him
5 he which bv order of linage hath now for a long	time inioied the crowne of Scotland
6 king. At length, hauing talked with them a long	time, he got him into his priuie
7 the hands of the wrongful vsurper. In the meane	time, Malcolme purchased such

8 [the King] not [I. iii.] sleepe in the night
9 a voice was heard as he was in bed in the night
10 be restrained.... . But about that present
11 me, so likewise did they promise it at the same
12 and forged allurements, that in a small
13 prophesie which he bad heard long before that
14 Donwald, about the
15 them, which gaue names to the owners for the
16 of them, that before were thanes, were at this
17 Manie new surnames were taken vp at this
18 they doubted to vtter what they thought, till
19 and, where Malcolme remained, till

time by anie prouocations that
time to take his rest, vttering
time there was a murmuring among
time vnto the posteritie of
time he had gotten togither a
time, of the comming of Birnane
time that the murther was in
time.
time made earles, as Fife,
time amongst them, as Cauder.
time and place should better
time that saint Edward the sonne

b.   in *Macbeth*

MicroConcord search SW: time
Sort : 1L/SW unshifted.

1 come what come may,
2 referred me to the coming on of
3 There would have been a
4 actual performances, what at any
5 keeps her state, But in best
6 chance I had lived a blesse\d
7 Let every man be master of his
8 that's fled Hath nature that in
9 th' expectation of plenty. Come in
10 ace We will perform in measure,
11 hath chanced, and at more
12 what was mine own, At no
13 Be so much more the man. Nor
14 If you can look into the seeds of
15 We shall not spend a large expense of
16 But here upon this bank and shoal of
17 hath been shed ere now, i' th' olden
18 Ay, my good lord. Our
19 To the last syllable of recorded
20 you with the perfect spy o' th'
21 d live to be the show and gaze o' th'
22 plenty And yet seem cold. The
23 tyrant's power afoot. Now is the
24 an redress, As I shall find the
25 forgot the taste of fears. The
26 Th' usurper's curse\d head. The
27 industrious soldiership. The
28 Away, and mock the
29 As far, my lord, as will fill up the
30 Too terrible for the ear. The
31 , as who should say 'You'll rue the

Time and the hour runs through the roughes
time with "Hail, King that shalt be!"
time for such a word. Tomorrow, and
time have you heard her say?
time we will require her welcome.
time, for from this instant There's
time Till seven at night. To make so
time will venom breed, No teeth for
time! Have napkins enough about you;
time, and place. So thanks to all at
time, The interim having weighed it,
time broke my faith, would not betray
time nor place Did then adhere, and
time And say which grain will grow a
time Before we reckon with your
time, We'd jump the life to come.
time, Ere human statute purged the
time does call upon 's.
time, And all our yesterdays have
time, The moment on 't; for 't must
time. We'll have thee as our rarer
time you may so hoodwink. We have
time of help.
time to friend, I will. What you
time has been my senses would have cooled
time is free. I see thee compassed
time approaches That will with due
time with fairest show. False face
time 'Twixt this and supper. Go not
time has been That, when the brains
time That clogs me with this answer.

32 would be planted newly with the

33 read strange matters. To beguile the

34 And take the present horror from the

35 Only it spoils the pleasure of the

36 business If you would grant the

37 beguile the time, Look like the

38 At what it did so freely? From this

39 , we will keep ourself Till supper-

40 say. One, two,_ why, then 'tis

41 Harpier cries "Tis

42 Harpier cries "Tis

43 of nature, pay his breath To

44

45 Within the volume of which

46 vents New-hatched to th' woeful

time, As calling home our exiled

time, Look like the time; bear

time, Which now suits with it. While

time. What man dare, I

time. At your kind'st leisure.

time; bear welcome in your eye,

time Such I account thy love. Art

time alone. While then, God be with

time to do 't. Hell is murky. Fie, my lord

time, 'tis time."

time, 'tis time." Round about

time and mortal custom. Yet my heart

Time, thou anticipat'st my dread

time I have seen Hours dreadful and

time. The obscure bird Clamoured the

CHAPTER 11

How scientific can literary evaluation be?

Arguments and experiments

Harald Fricke

This chapter discusses the philosophical question whether and how aesthetic judgments on literary value can be founded at all. Two questions require particular attention in this respect: what is the object of literary judgments and what is predicated about this object. Answers are given here in the light of the author's theory of 'Norm and Deviation' (Fricke 1981/Fricke 2000): poets deviate from linguistic norms at all levels and in all forms – but not arbitrarily. A deviation becomes poetic only by fulfilling a recognizable *function* (either an IF 'internal function' within a text, or an EF 'external function' between the text and further contexts, e.g. other texts or social facts). Based on this theoretical foundation, three empirical hypotheses (not normative aesthetic principles) are discussed: that literary estimation in the long run will grow, the more (a) poetic deviations, (b) internal functions and (c) external functions the reader can recognize within the elements and structures of this text. These three hypotheses are, as a kind of empirical pre-test, employed to experimentally constructed variations of modern responses to post-modern poems by John Keats, Emily Dickinson and Ulla Hahn as well as to some examples of 'Concrete poetry'.

There is hardly any area in which literary studies need interdisciplinary cooperation with the philosophy of language as that of literary evaluation. The reason for this is straightforward enough: while there is little or no agreement on the criteria or procedures for literary judgement, critical practice carries on without ever challenging the premises on which it is based, namely the philosophical question whether and how such judgements can be founded at all.

Two questions require particular attention in this respect: What is the object of literary judgements? And what is predicated about this object?[1] The former question becomes clear in comparison with evaluations of other artistic objects. For instance, in judging a painting, we can actually point at the object (in a museum, a gallery, or a private home). When evaluating literary works of art, the very thing

---

Compare, in this respect, Ellis (1974).

itself about which the judgement is made is much more complicated. There is no point in 'pointing' at a literary text when explaining its evaluation. Consider the following list of items that may qualify for the evaluation of a literary text:

- the material copy of the book,
- a particular edition of the text,
- the printed text in one of the extant editions,
- the reader's experience while reading,
- the general reception of the work in the culture at large,
- a group of works to which the text belongs (e.g. the author's complete works, or the genre or period in which it may be categorized), or, finally,
- the author and
- his act of writing.[2]

But neither the author's *écriture* nor the reader's *lecture* can grant intersubjectivity to literary judgements; nor could the problem be solved by the idea that in the simple utterance "This is a beautiful poem" one simultaneously draws in an evaluation of other texts, that I judge each text in comparison to all other texts I have experienced. This would lead to the fatal consequence that in matters of evaluation, each critic would be speaking about a different realm of experience. The implication of this is that the reconstruction of literary evaluation can only proceed systematically if the object of evaluation is a singular text, in the sense of identical strings of linguistic signs in two or more tokens of the same text.

However, this is not a sufficient description of the semantic structure or the pragmatic role of literary value judgements. Even simple predicates like "x is beautiful" or "x is a masterpiece" obscure the complexity of reference, which will always concern the evaluated artefact, but also the person making the utterance as well as its addressee. Depending on one's philosophical position one of these options may be foregrounded in debates over aesthetic issues: the fact that a literary work has particular objective qualities, that it stands in a particular relationship to the utterer of the evaluation, or that the totality of its readers relate (or should relate) to the work in a specific way. It follows that an aesthetic judgement always contains three components with distinct pragmatic functions.

(1) Every evaluation contains a *descriptive* part, i.e. a propositional reference to a particular literary state of affairs.

(2) There is also an *expressive* element in the judgement, in that you communicate your (personal) pleasure or dissatisfaction concerning a poem or story; this communication is never neutral: Nobody else could have uttered it in an equivalent way.

---

2.   see Weimar (1986) on this issue.

(3)   Finally, each value judgement also contains an aspect of *appeal*: We express
       not only our own pleasure, but also invite agreement of others to our asser-
       tion. Or – as Kant put it – we 'request from others their assent' to our aesthetic
       judgement.

The decisive point now is that (2) and (3) do not *follow* from (1) in any logically
compelling way. Rather, the descriptive aspect of a judgement provides only a *motivation* for our own evaluation, as well as a motivation for others to endorse our
judgement. This implies that, however correct and exhaustive a description of a
literary work may be, it will not provide a *scientific*,[3] but only a *rhetorical* basis for
the judgement.

From a scientist's point of view this may be regrettable. But we should not
overlook how welcome this circumstance is for us as *readers*, for it shows that no
one can ever impose a literary value judgement on us that we do not subjectively
share. In the present philosophical analysis this insight forms the linchpin of it all,
i.e. readers' fundamental right to *disapprove* of any literary work. However, this
does not lead to the position that literary scholars are not allowed to evaluate –
indeed, to disallow this would be inhuman and quite unnatural. They are only denied the legitimation to act as if they are able to mount the same degree of *scientific
validity* for their aesthetic judgements as they are able to muster for, say, their historical work. In evaluating literary works, they can only act as readers (albeit quite
experienced readers). On the other hand, what they can do as scientists with aesthetic judgements is something altogether different. They can (and should) *explain*
literary judgements, i.e. formulate hypotheses as to why particular literary works
are evaluated in the way they are. And they can empirically test these hypotheses.

Precisely one such hypothesis will be developed and tested in what follows.
It concerns the comparative study of reader evaluations of three experimentally
manipulated variations on the following poem by Ulla Hahn (1981:78).

Ars Poetica (A)

> Danke ich brauch keine neuen
> *Thanks I don't need new*
> Formen ich stehe auf
> *forms I'm standing on*
> festen Versesfüßen und alten
> *firm verse feet and old*
> Normen Reimen zu Hauf
> *norms rhymes on and on*

---

3.   Throughout this article the terms 'science', 'scientist', and 'scientific' are used as English
equivalents of the continental terms for 'Wissenschaft', 'sciences humaines' and the like.

zu Papier und zu euren
to paper and to your
Ohren bring ich was klingen soll
ears I bring what should sound
klingt mir das Lied aus den
when the song sounds out of my
Poren rinnen die Zeilen voll
tears the lines get full and round

und über und drüber und drunter
and over and above and under
und drauf und dran und wohlan und
and up and on and come on and
das hat mit ihrem Singen
that alone through her singing
die Loreley getan.
the Loreley did anon.

In three different ways, the experimentally manipulated versions B / C / D attempt to improve Ulla Hahn's text, and every reader is invited to judge whether these improvements were successful. The procedure consists in comparing each of these versions, B, C and D separately to the original version A. Hence no comparisons are made between the manipulated versions, but only between each manipulated version and the original. Let us start with version B:

Variation B

Danke ich brauch keine neuen
Thanks I don't need new
Strukturen ich stehe auf
structures I'm standing on
festen Versesfüßen und alten
firm verse feet and old
Normen Reimen zu Hauf
norms rhymes on and on

zu Papier und zu euren
to paper and to your
Ohren bring ich was klingen soll
ears I bring what should sound
klingt mir das Lied aus den
when the song sounds out of my
Drüsen rinnen die Zeilen voll
glands the lines get full and round

und über und drüber und drunter
> *and over and above and under*

und drauf und dran und wohlauf und
> *and up and on and well then and*

das hat mit ihrem Singen
> *that alone through her singing*

die Loreley getan.
> *the Loreley did anon.*

As can be seen, no more than three words have been exchanged against a synonym in this version: in line 2 "Formen" (forms) has been substituted by "Strukturen" (structures), in line 8 "Poren" (English version 'tears') by "Drüsen" (English lachrymal 'glands'), and in line 10 "wohlan" (come on) has been replaced by "wohlauf" (well then). The question readers are asked is: which of both versions is better, A or B?

In version C, just the final two lines of the poem have been replaced by a synonymous formulation:

Variation C

Danke ich brauch keine neuen
> *Thanks I don't need new*

Formen ich stehe auf
> *forms I'm standing on*

festen Versesfüßen und alten
> *firm verse feet and old*

Normen Reimen zu Hauf
> *norms rhymes on and on*

zu Papier und zu euren
> *to paper and to your*

Ohren bring ich was klingen soll
> *ears I bring what should sound*

klingt mir das Lied aus den
> *when the song sounds out of my*

Poren rinnen die Zeilen voll
> *tears the lines get full and round*

und über und drüber und drunter
> *and over and above and under*

und drauf und dran und wohlan und
> *and up and on and come on and*

der Gesang der Loreley nur
> *only the song of the Loreley*

nur der ist schuld daran.
only that is to blame for it.

Again readers are asked which text is best, A or C.

In the final version, D, an attempt was made to introduce a stronger metrical element ('firm verse feet') into Ulla Hahn's poem.

Variation D

Danke ich brauch keine neuen Formen
Thanks I do not need new forms
ich stehe fest ja auf
I'm firmly standing on
Versesfüßen und alten Normen
syllabic metric feet, old norms
und auf Reimen zu Hauf
and rhymes words on and on

zu Papier und zu euren Ohren
First to paper and then to your ears
bring ich was klingen soll
I bring what well should sound
klingt mir das Lied aus den Poren
whenever the song sounds out of my tears
rinnen die Zeilen voll
the lines get full and round

und drüber und drunter voll Schwingen
Over, above, and under full swinging
und drauf und dran und wohlan
and up and on and come on
und das hat mit ihrem Singen
and that alone by means of her singing
die Loreley getan.
the Loreley did anon.

Again the question is: which is better, A or D?

Convincing explanations should have predictive power, that is, they must make predictions that are empirically falsifiable. At least this is one of the fundamental insights of the analytic philosophy of science. The hypothesis submitted here yields the prediction of a clear 3 : 0 victory for the original version by Ulla Hahn. And this prediction has been borne out by all empirical investigations. The comparisons were made in the framework of several lectures and paper presentations, and this in a rather informal way.[4] In all cases a clear majority (first of poets and critics, later of German and Swiss students of literature) voted for the original poem as the best poem – with one remarkable exception: During a lecture for the Goethe Institute in 1983, a group of Soviet teachers of German expressed a slight preference for (the more 'traditional') variation D. Presumably this may be explained in terms of their being non-native speakers of German, or of a certain cultural formalism and conservatism in the former Soviet Union. This case clearly demonstrates how important it is in such empirical investigations to specify the range and scope of the hypothesis. For instance, does the hypothesis relate to (a) the author's contemporaries; (b) to us, readers of today; (c) to readers of all future generations; (d) to native speakers of the same language; (e) to its response in 'world literature'?

As stated before, the fact that reader reactions bear out the predictions of a particular hypothesis does not prove that such evaluations are 'right' – only that they are probable. In what follows, the question why nearly all readers preferred version A will be explored. We will return to this explanatory hypothesis shortly, but before we do so, it must be emphasized that the search for such an explanation should not be carried out on an ad hoc basis, but should instead be embedded in a theoretical framework, where various hypotheses are systematically related to each other. The theoretical model employed here is that of poetic deviation, as it has been developed in the theory of foregrounding or defamiliarization. For reasons of space, this model can be described only briefly here; but cf. Fricke (1981), Leech (1969), Martindale (1990), van Peer (1986), Zwaan (1993, esp. Chapter 5). There is also empirical evidence in favour of this theory, see, especially Hakemulder (2004, 2007), Miall & Kuiken (1994), van Peer (1992), van Peer, Hakemulder and Zyngier (forthcoming); van Peer, Zyngier and Hakemulder (forthcoming); Sopcak (2007); Zyngier, van Peer and Hakemulder (forthcoming). For the historical background of the theory, see Dolezel (1990), Erlich (1955), Galan (1985), Hansen-Löve (1978), Steiner (1984), Striedter (1989).

The idea behind the theory is the rejection of the view that literature can be understood in terms of norms, conventions, some aesthetic code, or a 'poetic' grammar. In other words, it is directed against any rule-model of literature. The only relevant norm for literature is the linguistic norm, and by this we mean not just the norms that can be found in a grammar book, but all the implicit but

---

4. The 'test' was performed four times between 1983–85 with about 330 participants: during lectures hand-outs showing the variations A-D were distributed among members of the audience, who expressed preference for the variants; the original was given the highest value by clear majorities, sometimes of 100 %. It should be added, however, that this was never meant as a rigorous test, but rather an exemplification of the theory, including a piece of 'learning by doing' for the audiences, nothing more.

valid rules that regulate linguistic communication. One may identify them by the fact that:

(1) Linguistic norms are obeyed in most cases;
(2) deviations from these norms are usually met with sanctions by other participants in the communication;
(3) these sanctions are usually accepted by those concerned, precisely because they form the basis of mutual interest and successful communication.

These rules apply to grammar and speech act conditions, to rules for inferencing and truth evaluation, or to writing conventions and turn taking, etc.

Poetry relates to the totality of these norms. In other words: in poetic works these norms are violated. Poets deviate from linguistic norms at all levels and in all forms. But not arbitrarily:random deviations do not constitute poeticality. A deviation becomes poetic by fulfilling a recognizable *function*. It is this function that creates a specific relation, absent in everyday linguistic usage.

The deviation has an INTERNAL FUNCTION when it creates (or allows the creation of) a relation within the text it occurs in. Concerning our hypothesis about evaluation, three types of relationship may be distinguished: (1) a relationship of similarity, as in rhyme, meter, or alliteration, all of which are deviations from linguistic norms; (2) a relationship of contrast, as in the patterning of oppositions in a poem; (3) a relationship of ordered sequencing, as in graded iteration, visual constellation, or climactic enumeration.

Next to internal functions, a poetic deviation can also have an EXTERNAL FUNCTION, in creating a relation between the text and a fact outside the text, e.g. political or ethical matters. In case the term 'external' may suggest something of less importance, I would like to emphasize that reference to extra-literary values may bear on the intra-literary value of a work. It may even come to bear on the question whether we are dealing with poetry or not – i.e. whether the deviations are artistically motivated. By this, it is understood that the external function may also consist in relating a text to other *texts*, for instance in the form of parody or allusion.

Literary history shows us how specific types of deviation and their functions become automatized parts of a literary tradition in the course of time. Like 'standard deviations' in empirical psychology, they become part and parcel of readers' expectations. However, they are not expected in a normative sense, as linguistic norms are, but in a kind of adaptable expectation: Here we are prepared to correct our expectations in case they are frustrated. This is fundamentally different from our behaviour in the case of non-poetic deviation. As we have seen, such instances result in the acceptance of sanctions. In other words, we stick to the norms in daily life, even when they are violated. At the same time, these expectations, grounded as they are in literary tradition, resemble those created by linguistic norms in that they have an effect of habituation, structuring our reading experiences. As such, they must be taken into account when studying literary judgement. I propose to study such processes under the name of (literary) quasi-norms, indicating that they resemble linguistic norms in their effects, while being different in terms of their commitment.

To these literary quasi-norms poets often react in ways comparable to their dealings with linguistic norms. This entails that the model of poetic deviation employed so far must be conceptualized in a dynamic way in order to potentially serve for the history of literary forms. A poet of some ambition, especially in the era of 'Modernism', will not simply get accustomed to and blindly follow the quasi-norms, but deviate from them, and thus re-invent the quasi-norms continually. This internalized protest against habituation, this tendency to write against the grain of literary automatization, can work at two distinct levels. On the one hand it may violate the historically developed quasi-norms of literary writing, such as poetic verse-forms or stanzaic composition and rhyme schemes, narrative strategies of presentation, or the standardized metaphors that are habitually employed, for instance in referring to one's beloved in terms of a rose or the sun. On the other hand, a quasi-norm may also be constructed within the confines of one text only. Such text-internal quasi-norms can be found in a metrical expectation, for instance, built up by the strict metrical beat of verse-lines, which is subsequently deviated from. An example can be found in Keats's poem Endymion (Keats 1982: 72–73):

> ... that all those gentle lispers
> May sigh my love unto her pitying!
> O charitable echo! hear, and sing
> This ditty to her! – tell her! – So I stay'd
> My foolish tongue ...

The (somewhat loose) iambic metrical pattern of the lines gets broken precisely at the moment when the subject is a ditty. Moreover, the enjambment effect after "stay'd is a powerful one, as it suggests a meaning (i.e. to remain in the same place) that turns out to be wrong in the following line, where it emerges that 'stay' is used as a transitive verb here, meaning 'to hold'. Again, it is not the deviation from the internal metrical or syntactic pattern as such which is of importance, but its ability to be functionalized. Plain violations of norms in themselves do not constitute poetic innovation.

In order for deviations to have an effect on readers, this functional requirement can be stated as a general principle of the theory. Empirical evidence for this may be found in Gibbs et al. (1991). Readers were presented with metaphorical, literal, and anomalous comparisons; some readers were told that these comparisons had been taken from the writings of famous twentieth century authors, whereas another group was told that the comparisons had been generated by a computer program. The latter group found the comparisons less meaningful, were slower in processing the metaphoric ones, and provided fewer interpretations of the statements. The differences in response between the two groups were statistically significant. Zwaan (1993: 33) sums up the results neatly when he writes: "It seems, therefore, that readers are more willing to invest cognitive effort in processing a given linguistic structure when they know it is intentionally constructed."

What consequences emerge from the application of these theoretical and historical insights to the study of modern poetry? Here we immediately run into the problem of free verse or 'prose-poetry', texts that seemingly do not deviate from any norm whatsoever. It would appear, then, that the model developed above is unable to describe and explain the poetic effects these texts may have. However, such 'free verse' can be understood only within the framework of a deviation model. First, texts of this kind deviate from the historically developed structures of versification, and their effects are in large part due to the fact that they play on this contrast with traditional expectations. Second, and more important still, in abandoning traditional literary quasi-norms, they do not return to the linguistic norms of everyday communication. For one thing, they incorporate quite strong deviations from typographical norms in the use of blanks: free verse lines do not run up to the right hand margin of the page, but present an irregular flow of enjambments. See Van Peer (1993) for an overview and analysis of such typographic norms and deviations. With respect to the problem of free verse the article concludes: "An inherent contradiction seems to be involved here: the revolutionary turn against traditional poetic devices which has occurred in our century has, paradoxically, caused a renewed interest in these structural principles of the poetic tradition. In other words, the maxim that poetry exists by deviation from everyday typographic norms and by repetitious uses of these and other arrangements remains fundamentally intact, even in the most avant-gardist experiments" (p. 51).

It has been pointed out that the typographic deviations typically associated with free verse may attain an almost arbitrary character. Although this criticism is generally not altogether false, it is not applicable to every concrete instance. As an example, let us look at one of the poems[5] by Emily Dickinson, illustrating the peculiarities of her verse.

> When Etna basks and purrs
> Naples is more afraid
> Than when she shows her Garnet Tooth
> Security is loud –

---

5.   Number 1161 in *The Poems of Emily Dickinson. Reading edition*, ed. R.W. Franklin. Cambridge, MA: The Belknap Press of Harvard University Press 1999.

There are a few metaphorical meanings involved which one must understand in order to experience the poem's force, notably 'basks and purrs' in line 1, where the volcano is metaphorized into a sleeping cat, and 'Garnet Tooth' in line 3, where the cat has awakened into a bloody-minded feline showing her teeth. But the crucial effect of the poem hinges on the final word, where, contrary to general expectations, it is asserted that loud noise creates a feeling of security. This deviates from the general notion held (I think) by most people that loud noise makes them afraid, whereas feelings of security are generally thought to be induced more easily by a quiet surrounding. Not so in the case of volcanoes, says Dickinson: better have them rumble and roar regularly. At least then we know what to expect (and feel secure). Now this meaning is extended in the last line, where it comes to relate to things generally. And again this clashes with our everyday concepts, which tell us that earthquakes, fires, explosions, and most calamities are accompanied with loud noise. Hence the poem defamiliarizes such concepts and makes the reader look at them in a new way, so that the deviation from the conceptual norm may function as a device to re-conceptualize the world. The result will be a cognitive re-shufflling of ideas and relations, while also producing some emotional gratification through the element of surprise. The way these deviational effects are created may be observed clearly through a test in which variations to the text are compared:

Variation E

> When Etna basks and purrs
> Naples is more afraid
> Than when she shows her Garnet Tooth
> Security is lax –

We have changed very little in the text: one word only. And its replacement is highly similar to the original: it is also an adjective, with the same number of phonemes, and beginning with the same consonant. Yet we observe that the whole poem now collapses. The reason is that everything now falls into the confines of our entrenched categories: the concept of 'lax security' exists in our minds independently of Dickinson's poem, and the text does not add anything to it. Nor does this version produce any surprising effect any more, for precisely the same reason. As predictable, version E will not be judged as good a poem, and has little chance of surviving in the literary canon. We see here that the first impression the poem creates, namely that (apart from the metaphors) it is written in rather straightforward, close to everyday diction, is highly misleading. Indeed, there is no rhyme and little meter, no significant alliteration or assonance, and the poem's syntax is so simple that it almost resembles some factual statement in a geography book. But the final word disrupts the expectations set up by the previous textual elements. Only, of course, when ignoring the two metaphors discussed above. There is no reason, however, why we could not take them into account when studying the poem's quality. One could test their significance, for instance, by replacing them by less metaphoric expressions, as has been done in the following version:

Variation F

> When Etna sleeps
> Naples is more afraid
> Than when she shows her fiery corona
> Security is loud –

While this version may be less poetic than the original in that the feline associations are no longer possible, the central device in the final line is kept intact. Predictably, its evaluation by readers will result in a middle position between the original and version E.

Furthermore, we may observe that in the original the verse structure coincides with syntactic units. One can investigate the effect of this arrangement on readers' judgement by presenting them a version that contains several deviations from the isomorphism between syntax and verse-line:

Variation G

> When Etna basks
> and purrs, Naples
> is more afraid than
> when she shows her
> Garnet Tooth – Security is
> loud –

Finally, we may conceive of a version in which the free verse technique has been implemented, but from which the crucial defamiliarizing device has been eliminated. Such a manipulation will result in something of the following kind:

Variation H

> When Etna basks
> and purrs, Naples
> is more afraid than
> when she shows her
> Garnet Tooth – Security is
> lax –

Our theoretical model predicts that this version will be judged slightly higher than version E, and far lower than either the original or version G. We now have a (predicted) hierarchy of quality, which runs (in decreasing order):

```
HIGH:    Version G
  .      Original

  .      Version F

  .      Version H
LOW:     Version E
```

And now to a second mainstream of modern poetry, which has also been criticized or even declared dead for a couple of years: 'concrete' or 'visual' poetry. As an example, we attempt to give an English version[6] of a German text by Burckhard Garbe from 1982:

```
        WHE
        NTH
        EPO
PESPEAKETHEXCA
THEDRACATHOLIC
        SHA
        VET
        OGI
        VEC
        REDIT
```

We picked out this rather simple text because its deviation from norms of typographic layout is legitimated by nothing but external functions - and this in no less than three ways. This, again, can be shown by testing some variants. As in version J, one could easily produce a poem in free verse with the identical text – but, without a doubt, the result would lack a motivation (by Internal or External functions) for the completely pointless segmentation of lines:

Variation J

> When the Pope
> Speaketh ex cathedra
> Catholics have
> To give credit

---

6.   In the German text, "Wenn der Papst ex cathedra spricht, müssen Katholiken dran glauben" (Burckhard Garbe: *sta(a)tus quo. ansichten zur lage*. Göttingen: Edition Herodot 1982:47), the pun on the double meaning of the idiom "müssen dran glauben" ('have to believe in it' as well as 'have to pay for it, perhaps even with their lives') is, of course, slightly different from the ambiguity of 'to give credit (to/for)'. But in this context it is not semantics, but the form of presentation that matters.

One could as well imagine this poem as a satirized epigram with traditional versification, for instance brought into the meter of a 'Chevy Chase' ballad stanza:

Variation K

> When speaks ex cathedra the Pope
> And tells them how to live,
> All catholics, in fear or hope,
> The credit have to give.

However, by bringing the words not into meter but into the visual 'constellation' of a crucifix, the author succeeds in creating three different 'external relations' for his poem: (1) to the object of reference – for the cross has always served as a sign and emblem especially of the Roman Catholic church; (2) to the rich literary tradition of cross-formed poems – but contrary to this medieval and baroque tradition, the structure of the cross does no longer work in an affirmative, i.e. redoubling way, but has a critical function instead; (3) to the symbolic (and no longer confession-bound) function of the cross as standing for human suffering in general – thus indicating that many a Christian soul in our days may literally be crucified by some papal encyclical or other.

All this is of importance when attempting to explain why most participants preferred (and perhaps all experienced readers will prefer) Ulla Hahn's original poem to the alternative versions we produced. It is now time to retrace our steps and provide the explanatory hypothesis for this fact. In order to explain the higher evaluation of the original poem over its rival versions, three conditions can be outlined. In general, this leads to the theoretical prediction that a poem will be experienced more poetic, i.e. as aesthetically more rewarding, the more it fulfills the fundamental poetic principle of functional deviation from linguistic norms and literary quasi-norms. The three conditions can be specified as follows:

(I)   A text containing a deviation B, which serves one internal function only, will be evaluated lower than that same text if it contains a deviation A serving more than one internal function.

For instance, in line 2 of version B, the term 'Strukturen' (structures) replaces 'Formen' (forms) of the original. Although the two terms are quasi-synonymous, the substitution has annihilated the line-initial rhyme with 'Normen' (norms) in line 4. The replacement of the original 'Poren' ('tears' in the English version) by 'Drüsen' (English 'glands') in line 8 destroyed a similar line-initial rhyme. Finally, substituting 'wohlauf' (well then) for 'wohlan' (come on) in line 10 has effaced the rhyme with 'getan' ('anon' in the English version) in the final line. (More about the importance of well-hidden rhymes in condition III.)

(II)   A text containing a deviation C, which serves an internal function only (e.g. producing an end rhyme), will be evaluated lower than that text if it contains a deviation A serving the very same internal function and an external function in addition (e.g. alluding to another famous text in literary history).

In version C this can be seen in the replacement of the final two lines of the original by a synonymous formulation, which, however, is no longer an exact echo of Heine's famous lines in his Loreley poem: "Und das hat mit ihrem Singen / Die Loreley getan." In other words, although the formulation is semantically almost identical and still contains a deviation from everyday linguistic norms (in the repetition) creating some measure of poeticity, it fails to establish an intimate link with Heine's celebrated poem. Where readers have the choice between two alternative texts, the one with the additional external function will be judged as having a higher value.

(III)   A text containing a deviation D, which serves traditional functions only (internal or external), will be evaluated lower than that text if it contains a deviation A which fulfills the same functions, and adds an innovative one (by functionally deviating from literary or text-internal quasi-norms).

This is precisely what we observe in Ulla Hahn's text. It deviates, first, from the traditional requirement that poems have end-rhyme, and secondly, from the modernist requirement that poems do not rhyme at all. These are two external deviations, but the poem also deviates from its own, internally established quasi-norms, for instance in avoiding both the end rhyme ('auf' / 'Hauf'; 'soll' / 'voll') in the final stanza and the line-initial rhymes ('Formen' / 'Normen'; 'Ohren' / 'Poren') of the first two stanzas. Version D, by contrast, has reproduced such rhyme pairs in the final stanza, thus taking out the internal deviation. It has also relegated all rhyme words to their traditional position at line ends, thus making this version more traditional, and less innovative. It is this lack of novelty in version D that makes readers rate it of lower quality than the original poem. (About novelty, see Martindale 1990.)

All this is not just a cry for novelty, but rather recognition of the important function that such deviations fulfill with respect to the theme of the poem. The explicitly stated thesis of the 'ars poetica' is implicitly disproved by the text itself; the old, traditional norms are not implemented, but their memory is kept intact precisely through their demonstrative transgression. Evidently, these are not 'proofs' that Ulla Hahn's poem 'is' of high quality (maybe they could be employed rhetorically in the debate over the status of her work). Instead, they are explanatory hypotheses that help us understand and explain the processes of evaluation and canonization as they take place in the reading process of individuals, and in the history of a culture. Indeed, what Ulla Hahn does here is yet another, contemporary exemplification of the old stratagem of presenting a poetics in a poem through a poem. This theme is announced in the title, a clear allusion to Horace's *Epistula ad Pisones*, but also to Archibald MacLeish's famous "Ars poetica,"[7] where it is said

> A poem should not mean
> But be.

That is precisely what Ulla Hahn's poem does (and it does so only in version A), namely that it *is* more than it *says*.

References

Doležel, L. 1990. *Occidental Poetics. Tradition and Progress*. Lincoln, NB: University of Nebraska Press.

Ellis, J. M. 1974. *The Theory of Literary Criticism. A Logical Analysis*. Berkeley, CA: University of California Press.

Erlich, V. 1955. *Russian Formalism: History – Doctrine*. The Hague: Mouton.

Franklin, R.W. 1999. *The Poems of Emily Dickinson. Reading edition*. Cambridge, MA: The Belknap Press of Harvard University Press.

Fricke, H. 1981. *Norm und Abweichung. Eine Philosophie der Literatur*. (Norm and Deviation. A philosophy of literature). Munich: C.H. Beck.

Fricke, H. 1991. *Literatur und Literaturwissenschaft. Beiträge zu Grundfragen einer verunsicherten Disziplin*. (Literature and Literary Studies. Contributions to the foundations of a despairing discipline). Paderborn: Ferdinand Schöningh.

Galan, F. W. 1985. *Historic Structures. The Prague School Project, 1928–1946*. Austin TX: University of Texas Press.

Gibbs, R. W., J.M. Kushner & W.R. Mills. 1991. Authorial Intentions and Metaphor Comprehension. *Journal of Psycholinguistic Research* 20: 11–30.

Hahn, U. 1981. *Herz über Kopf*. Stuttgart: Deutsche Verlags-Anstalt.

Hakemulder, J. 2004. Foregrounding and Its Effect on Readers' Perception. *Discourse Processes* 38: 193–218.

Hakemulder, J. 2007. Tracing foregrounding in responses to film. *Language and Literature* 16: 125–139.

Hansen-Löve, A. A. 1978. *Der russische Formalismus*. Wien: Verlag der Österreichischen Akademie der Wissenschaften.

Keats, J. 1982. *Poems*, Book I, G. Bullett (ed.). London: J. M. Dent.

Leech, G. N. 1969. *A Linguistic Guide to English Poetry*. London: Longman.

Martindale, C. 1990. *The Clockwork Muse. The predictability of artistic change*. New York NY: Basic Books.

Miall, D. S. & D. Kuiken. 1994. Beyond Text Theory: Understanding Literary Response. *Discourse Processes* 17: 337–352.

---

7.   Archibald MacLeish, *Collected Poems 1917–52*. Cambridge, MA.: Harvard University Press, s.d., p. 41.

Sopčák, P. 2007. 'Creation from nothing' – A foregrounding study of James Joyce's drafts for *Ulysses*. *Language and Literature* 16: 183–196.

Steiner, P. 1984. Russian Formalism. A MetaPoetics. Ithaca NY: Cornell University Press.

Striedter, J. 1989. *Literary Structure, Evolution, and Value. Russian Formalism and Czech Structuralism Reconsidered*. Cambridge MA: Harvard University Press.

van Peer, W. 1986. *Stylistics and Psychology. Investigations of Foregrounding*. London: Croom Helm.

van Peer, W. 1992. Literary Theory and Reader Response. *Reader Response to Literature. The Empirical Dimension*, E. F. Nardocchio. (ed.), 137–152. Berlin: Walter de Gruyter.

van Peer, W. 1993. Typographic Foregrounding. *Language and Literature* 2(1): 49–61.

van Peer, W., J. Hakemulder & S. Zyngier. 2007. Lines on feeling: Foregrounding, aesthetics, and meaning. *Language and Literature* 16: 197–213.

van Peer, W., S. Zyngier & J. Hakemulder. 2007. Foregrounding: Past, Present, Future. In *Prospect and Retrospect. Papers from the Poetics and Linguistics Association International Conference, New York, 2004*. D. Hoover (ed.) Amsterdam: Rodopi.

Weimar, K. 1986. On Traps for Theory and How to Circumvent Them. *Stanford Literature Review* 3: 13–30.

Zwaan, R. 1993. *Aspects of Literary Comprehension*. Amsterdam: John Benjamins.

Zyngier, S., van Peer, W. and Hakemulder, F. 2007. Love in Literature. Complexity, Foregrounding, and Evaluation. *Poetics Today* 28: 4.

CHAPTER 12

Philosophical perspectives on literary value

Paisley Livingston

Meta-axiological distinctions introduced here include cognitivism and non-cognitivism on the status of evaluative discourse, as well as revisionary and non-revisionary positions. I argue that anti-realist and error-theoretical views of evaluative claims tend to be revisionary in ways that conflict with the realist orientation of much evaluative discourse, yet I contend that this does not provide a decisive reason in favor of cognitivism. While categorical aesthetic imperatives are hard to justify, some relevant hypothetical imperatives or 'oughts' follow from prevalent commitments and preferences, and some of these hypothetical imperatives have important implications in arguments over literary value. Dispositional accounts of value and 'ideal judge' conditions are also canvassed.

In what follows I shall take up some central issues in meta-axiology, the branch of philosophy that engages in second-order reflection over values and evaluative discourse (for background, Darwall et al. 1993; Sinnott-Armstrong & Timmons 1996). My highly selective survey will be conducted with an eye to the implications of key philosophical strategies for questions pertaining to the topic of literary value. I propose no systematic theory of the latter, but do schematically indicate what I take to be some cogent basic assumptions and lines for future enquiry.

1. Contrasts and options

A schematic map of main positions in meta-axiology can be drawn in terms of two basic contrasts. The first contrast amounts to a familiar distinction between cognitivist and non-cognitivist approaches, where the former affirms, while the latter denies, that evaluative utterances are made true or false by relations between their contents and relevant non-subjective, extra-discursive referents. The cognitivist option further divides into realist and error-theoretical sub-options, the basic tenets of which will be set forth below.

A second distinction contrasts revisionist and non-revisionist positions. According to the latter, although evaluative practice is far from perfect, no fundamental revision is to be recommended. (Revisionist projects may be rejected for various reasons, such as the idea that they are simply unnecessary, or desirable, yet unlikely to succeed.) A different type of account finds, on the contrary, that evaluative discourse is so basically flawed as to warrant a thoroughgoing revision, and various proposals along these lines are then made. One option calls for the revision of significant aspects of our first-order evaluative attitudes and utterances; a second option deems the latter in order, while promoting a thoroughgoing revision of higher-order assessments of first-order evaluations. A third option urges both revisions.

For the sake of clarity, we may point out that a 'first-order' evaluative statement is one that makes some claim about the value of something, such as a literary work. A 'second-order' discourse takes such statements as its object, claiming, for example, to say something about the status or justification of first-order statements. Some theorists contend that there are no logically necessary relations between first-order axiological positions and second-order, meta-axiological ones, but that is far from obvious.

Conjoined, these two contrasts allow us to identify four important types of positions as well as some of the characteristic reasonings motivating them. I begin with a fairly quick survey of these positions before moving on in the following section to assess arguments surrounding them.

A. Non-revisionary cognitivism

Although realism has been defined in increasingly sophisticated ways in recent debates, there is still a large consensus to the effect that a core realist idea is that evaluative discourse is assertoric and tends to be spontaneously understood as such. What makes an evaluative judgement true is not the making of the judgement or its psychological constituents, but features of what the judgement is about; what is more, at least some of our evaluations are correct in that they refer successfully to actual qualities of their objects. Realists tend to hold, then, that evaluative discourse is basically in order as it stands (which does not mean that there are no outstanding questions about valuable properties or features and their status).

For example, when we read a literary work and admire it, we are hardly likely to think that the only reason we have for this feeling is that we have the feeling: there seems, on the contrary, to be something *in* the work to which one responds, something of value that is neither invented nor 'projected' by one's experience of the work, in short, the objects and qualities that we find ourselves to be experiencing. For example, the language of the work is witty, intriguing, fresh, probing, innovative, well-organised, etc. We may also have grounds to believe that when combined in the right sort of way, such qualities can suffice to make a work a good work (perhaps because it is thereby apt to fulfil various functions characteristic of literary value). What kind of experience of the qualities of a poetic work can I have if I cannot believe that my positive and negative responses are in some important way responses to, and assessments of features of the work itself, such as its stylistic qualities and special use of the language? None at all, the realist responds, adding that at least some readers are in fact capable of responding sensitively to the values of literary works. In short, Dante's lines are not admirable because the reader admires them; the informed, competent reader admires them because they are admirable and have great literary value.

B. Revisionary cognitivism

The error theorist (Mackie 1977; Joyce 2001) agrees with the realist that evaluative discourse is assertoric, but holds that moral discourse, for example, is in fact false because it postulates entities that do not exist. For reasons that the error theorist tries to identify, people are simply inclined to believe falsely that their value judgements are about an external, existing reality; they consistently make the error of believing their is some objective requirement that puts them under the obligation of doing 'the right thing'. The error theorist may allow that there is ultimately nothing to do be done about this, since people will go on believing in false, objective claims about the external reality of Value. What can be revised, however, is the erroneous, second-order understanding of value promulgated by realist philosophers.

In the case of moral philosophy, the non-existent category of entities postulated by evaluative discourse is a matter of what John Leslie Mackie (1977) called 'objective prescriptions' – imaginary properties that are 'queer' or out of place in a naturalist framework. These are properties the very identification or recognition of which is supposed to have necessary implications for what people should do, or in other words, cases where a prescriptive 'ought' follows form a descriptive 'is'.

Similarly, when readers and critics reflect on judgements of value and try to ponder the place of such a thing as literary value in the physical universe, they can easily locate the evaluatings and preferences of readers, but not any real Value (such as an ontically independent substance). Yet it is this Value that realism posits as existing independently of psychological events, and it is Value that is supposed to function as a truth-maker for evaluative utterances. Error theory instructs us to conclude, then, on these and other grounds, that literary merit is entirely relative to our contingent capacities and backgrounds. Change the background, and the evaluative result changes, sometimes quite radically. And if the right sort of preferences and 'cognitive stock' are not in place, preaching is of no use: there is nothing in nature that can *require* anyone to prefer reading one sort of work over another. It is at least coherent to imagine an informed person who grasps the reasons why a canonised work is said to be great literature, but does not agree that this work has any real value, and this without error or irrationality (cf. Miller 1992).

C. Revisionary non-cognitivism

According to this family of doctrines, in its current condition evaluative discourse is often wrongly thought to have assertoric force, yet this erroneous second-order conception of evaluative utterances can and should be replaced by a non-cognitivist theory and practice. Thus utterances of the form 'X is good or right' should be recast as expressions of approval or as exhortations. What 'X is good' really means is 'we like X', or 'I like X', the suggestion being that the addressee should like X as well. So when Henry James (1984:614) called Elizabeth Stoddard's *The Morgensons* 'a thoroughly bad novel', he could not have rationally being doing more than expressing his own sentiments about the book or recommending that others respond to it in a manner similar to his own. Lucidly translated, what James said was 'Respond with disapproval to *The Morgensons*' or 'I disapprove of *The Morgensons* ', or 'Down with *The Morgensons*' (or some combination of such exclamations). Future utterances in this vein should be recast in light of this corrective, second-order understanding of the discourse.

D. Non-revisionary non-cognitivism

One species of emotivism claims that as it currently exists, evaluative discourse in fact makes no assertions and hence commits no cognitive error. Although there may be superficial linguistic features of our evaluative utterances that makes them appear to be assertions, this is misleading, since all that is really going on is exhortation or the expression of feelings. One can express one's feelings insincerely or incorrectly, of course, but if the expression is a veridical indication of one's state of mind, there is no error involved. The task to be performed by second-order theory is to replace faulty cognitivist accounts defended by philosophers; the latter are not, however, deemed to be central to evaluative practice.

Application of the distinction between revisionary and non-revisionary stances is not always as straightforward as I have implied. Given ongoing disputes about the current status of evaluative discourse, one theorist's desired revision is the other's thesis about the *status quo*. Also, although a theorist may claim that his or her account is non-revisionary, this may be misleading. Non-cognitivists who present their proposals as simple elucidations of evaluative discourse may in fact be excising those aspects of the discourse that a cognitivist finds essential.

2.   Assessing the options

Support for non-revisionary cognitivism (as well as for revisionary non-cognitivism) is derived from salient and pervasive features of the phenomenology of evaluative or valenced experience, which finds – or seems to find–value and disvalue 'in its objects'. As long as we persist in having preferences and making reasoned decisions (or in the illusion of so doing), a first-order phenomenological 'realism' of some sort exerts a strong, intuitive pull. If the truth of the antecedent ('As long as we persist ...') is a biologically necessary condition of agency, a consistent, lived nihilism is not an option. Try to imagine how one could deliberate over what to do and make effective decisions and commitments if each and every reason motivating any possible choice was understood as having no genuine advantages or any form of goodness.

Whether realism or error theory is correct as a second-order generalisation about the status of all such valenced experiences is, however, a separate issue, as long as we assume that the necessity of our holding a belief does not entail its truth. (It will not do to reason backwards, from the practical difficulty of living with error theory, to the falsehood of the latter.)

Is such a claim about the phenomenology of valuation sufficiently justified? Here one can appeal to the reader's experience – for example, the experience of reading. Is it reasonable to doubt that many experiences have valences situated on a spectrum extending from extremely positive to highly negative? Hardly, as long as we allow for overall ambivalence and uncertainty as to how various, local and specific valences and aspects are to be weighted and compared. Thus, although it is reasonable to doubt the accuracy of global, comparative assessments of the literary achievements of major figures in the canon (Shakespeare vs. Goethe, etc.), recognition of the valenced properties of works, such as the wittiness of a given passage, is a matter of a more immediate appreciative response arising from a basically realist orientation. Thus it is not controversial to say that the valences in question pertain to the content of the experience, that is, to the qualities of what is experienced, the experienced qualities of objects. The canonical phrase is 'This text I am reading is brilliant!' and not 'It is brilliant that I am reading this text!', or 'My reading of this text is brilliant!'

This empirical claim about the realist orientation of evaluative experience and discourse supports a dilemma argument against *non-revisionary* non-cognitivism: either the philosopher's restatement of the thrust of evaluative discourse respects its realist orientation, or it betrays or vitiates the very content of valenced experience. The former horn amounts to giving up on anti-cognitivism, since the second-order theory mirrors the intrinsically realistic orientation of first-order evaluative attitudes. Yet the latter horn, with its insistence on the inadequacy of a realist orientation, amounts to a slide from non-revisionism to revisionism. For example, either literary evaluators are described as (rightly or wrongly) making claims about the inherent merits and demerits of literary performances and works, or these evaluators are described as only reflecting features of their education or background. The latter is clearly a revisionary conclusion. A quietist cannot translate 'Dante's language is superb!' as 'I was raised to believe that Dante's language has a superb quality'.

Arguments surrounding *revisionary* non-cognitivist proposals are quite complex. Key disputes centre on such issues as: (a) Is the revision sufficiently warranted by actual flaws in the discourse as currently practised? Do we really have decisive grounds to favour non-cognitivism over cognitivism? (b) How thoroughgoing must the revision be? Is it, for example, only a matter of a global shift in second-order theory, or must 'concrete practice' also be significantly revamped? For example, is it really cogent to propose that we can keep the first-order discourse the same, while being agnostic or anti-realist about second-order, metaphysical questions? (c) Would the benefits of the proposed revision justify the costs? (d) Given outstanding uncertainty and disagreement with regard to answers to the above questions, how should the risks be summed up in an overall judgement? How likely is it, for example, that fallible grounds for favouring a fundamental revision of the discourse could actually motivate sweeping reform? (e) Given that the revisionist proposal itself rests upon some form of evaluative utterance, what are the implications, for that proposal, of the proposed revision of evaluative discourse? Is the proposal itself based on a suitably revised instance of evaluative discourse? If the revisionist urges a significant weakening of the status and force of evaluative discourse, and if the revisionist's own discourse is evaluative, consistency requires a corresponding weakening of the revisionist's own urgings.

As the questions just evoked should indicate, revisionist proposals lead us into a tangle of issues and contentions. A systematic treatment of these matters cannot be attempted in this essay, so I shall limit myself to what I take to be a few key points.

First of all, proposals for a massive and sweeping reworking of the fabric of evaluative discourse are hardly promising. The track record on this topic is uncontroversially dismal, in part for technical reasons (Dreier 1999). But we can understand this point without delving into the intricacies of contemporary philosophical semantics. Just think what it means to read a literary work and experience its language as having various specific, valenced, qualities. For example, one finds the lexical patterns repetitive and cloying. Can you get yourself to believe that this is just a subjective illusion, and at the same time stop experiencing the words of the work, and more generally, of all works, in a valenced way? And if you were to do so, what would be left of your evaluative experience of literary works?

Thus questions (c)–(e) come to the fore. Given the fallible nature of the sort of theorizing that is supposed to motivate such an enormous undertaking, is it reasonable to opt for any such scheme, or to think it likely of success? A negative response seems well warranted.

In light of the serious problems surrounding the viability and adequacy of proposed revisions of actual, realist theory and practice, arguments pertaining to the question of the soundness of basic cognitivist assumptions would appear to be a privileged topic for further deliberation. Two questions in particular have a central position given the dialectical situation as I have described it: (1) just what are the error theorist's best reasons and arguments against realism?; and (2) given those arguments, is there a way to elucidate and justify a given evaluative discourse?

3. Cognitivism and non-cognitivism about literary value

One of the central tenets of the non-cognitivist critique of moral realism is Mackie's 'queerness' objection to the effect that morality essentially and implausibly involves the postulation of a strong, categorical imperative, or a commitment to the existence of something like an 'objective prescriptivity' standing outside anyone's *contingent* interests or desires. As we can read in stories by the Marquis de Sade, the libertine has grown up hearing that wantonly cruel actions are evil, and he can competently recapitulate the moral arguments others find compelling. Yet the libertine is unmoved by such reasonings. He lacks any desire to behave morally and so 'has no reason' to inhibit his lust for cruel actions (unless he has prudential or purely instrumental reasons, such as fear of punishment). The error theorist reasons that there are no natural, moral properties of actions that could give the libertine reason to refrain from acting as he wants or chooses. The motivation to behave morally cannot be derived from epistemic or prudential rationality.

To concoct a rough analogue in the domain of literary evaluation, the libertine knows perfectly well that the obscene literature he enjoys reading has no genuine literary value, yet lacks any motivation to alter his ways, and so lacks any reason to admire and appreciate great literary works. The naturalist's assessment of this situation is that there is no Reason in nature that gives the libertine any reason to change his ways. Other persons having different interests and desires will, of course, have reason to oppose the libertine's will, but they can give no non-circular argument why the libertine should change his preferences.

One might protest here that the implied assimilation of literary and moral judgements is misleading: judgements of literary taste are really quite unlike distinctions between good and evil actions, precisely because they lack the strong, prescriptive dimension characteristic of the latter. The proposed example is misleading, one might add, precisely because it incorporates what many people would consider a moral element – obscenity. Consider, then, a somewhat different case: suppose someone has a good grasp of the reasons why Marguerite Duras (amongst many others) is generally considered a far better writer than Françoise Sagan, but remains unmoved, and always prefers reading Sagan's novels and others of this ilk. Does such a reader have any reason to try to get his or her readerly practice and evaluative statements in line with what is recognised as 'expert opinion'? Where is the compelling, non-circular argument that this reader 'ought' to do so? Do we not need a value judgement to get us from literary facts to a literary 'ought'?

The latter, Humean point about the gap between factual and prescriptive utterances is notoriously hard to overturn. Yet even if it is granted, it does not follow that there are no tenable evaluative claims, or that all forms of realism are incorrect (Brink 1989). Many if not most readers as a matter of fact do have interests and potential motives which, if reflected over and rationally articulated, turn out to have direct or indirect implications for evaluative judgements. The needed 'ought' falls out of various other 'oughts' (prudential, moral and aesthetic) to which the person is already in principle, if not always in practice, committed. The logic of this situation is simple: if you already grant that some goal is one that you ought to realise, and if I point out to you that some other goal follows directly and necessarily from that goal, then I do not need to get you to accept some other, independent goal in order to make my argument. Instead, I point out to you what follows from a position you already accept. And there may be such commitments that can provide a good basis for arguments about literary value. A bit more specifically, I have in mind such widely accepted *prima facie* duties as gratitude, self-improvement, and beneficence, or the importance of contributing to others' well-being (Ross 1930; Audi 2004). Commitment to these and other standards has implications for one's literary judgements and related activities. For example, the duty of self-improvement can militate against repetitive consumption of what is generally recognized as inferior fiction. Someone who is genuinely persuaded that expert opinion favours one kind of literature over another may have a prior commitment to the basic duty of self-development, and thus have independent grounds or motivation to try to get his or her own, spontaneous inclinations in line with expert judgements.

Thus, even if we were to accept error theory's doubts about judgements based on a categorical imperative or duty, hypothetical judgements based on contingently accepted duties and standards remain cogent. In other words, the argumentative task may not be the daunting one of proving to someone that it is his duty to read the forbidding but great classics; instead, the contention would be that a given programme of reading follows from goals that a person already has.

Setting various sweeping theoretical proclamations aside, there is actually a great deal of agreement on this score amongst literary theorists and critics. Little doubt is expressed about the existence of evil or politically hateful literary works – assuming agreement over 'correct' moral and political standards. The genuinely controversial topic in literary theory is not the status of evaluative discourse *per se*, but that of judgements pertaining to what might be labelled specifically literary value of an artistic or belletrist variety. The deeply contentious issue is whether there is any such thing as truly great literature, as opposed to literary works classified as such by persons enjoying social distinction and power. Such classifications are said to be deceptive in that their real motivation and function has nothing to do with specifically literary value.

Thus another error-theoretical claim, distinct from the worry about objective prescriptions, becomes pertinent. I have in mind the so-called queerness objection that the error theorist raises against realism. Realists, the contention runs, postulate the existence of entities that are really quite odd within a naturalist ontological framework: objective requirements that put people under an obligation even if they have no subjective reasons for recognising any such duty. The thought is this: there simply are no objective states of affairs that can make global assessments of specifically literary (artistic) merit correct or incorrect. Such entities are but reifications of readers' contingent preferences with regard to rather different states of affairs, and so claims about them are false. Here another one of Mackie's error-theoretical arguments reveals its relevance: the fact of at least apparent, widespread disagreement over particular value judgements is taken as casting reasonable doubt over realists' claims that there really are values 'out there' to be discovered. If there were, why do lucid and informed investigators continue to disagree (or at least to think that they are disagreeing as they dispute each other's contentions about 'the same' non-existent values)? Why is it easier to explain people's evaluative disagreements in terms of their divergent backgrounds, interests, and socialisation?

How might realists about specifically literary evaluations respond to such a challenge? They can rejoin that nothing crucial follows from the failure to achieve universal or near-universal agreement. The same situation holds, after all, for even the most banal, well-entrenched factual beliefs as well as the most successful scientific explanations. The more interesting question is whether there is not a significant amount of reasoned agreement amongst informed parties, and if so, what plausible basis for that agreement there might be.

A first task is that of assessing statements of the form: 'An artistically or aesthetically valuable quality or feature of work W is ____', where the blank is filled in by such terms as 'wittiness', 'elegance', and the like. Is it reasonable to be a sceptic about any and all statements in this vein on the grounds that there is nothing in the world that could make them true? One's response to such a question need not hinge on a dispute over the success or adequacy of some particular, explicit definition of literature or of the art of literature. Instead, the debate can be centred on putative qualities that would be covered by any plausible notion of specifically literary value. For example, 'hackneyed' refers to stylistic features which, *ceteris paribus*, count against a work's having a positive literary value, while 'elegant' and 'insightful' name properties that tend to make a positive contribution to a work's specifically literary merits. What, then, is the status of the referents of such terms? Are there really such features of works, or are these just readerly projections?

Dispositional theories of value are a relevant resource in this regard (Lewis, D. 2000; Lewis, C. I. 1946; Pettit 1991; Railton 2003; Wiggins 1987, 1998). Very generally, such dispositional analyses take the following basic form:

> *W is Q just in case agents respond to W in way q under condition C.*

In other words, Q is taken to be a disposition that manifests itself under certain conditions. A paradigmatic example would be such properties as colour or sweetness: something is red, or sweet, just in case it looks or tastes the right sort of way to the right sort of observers under certain conditions. On the (moderately) optimistic assumption that dispositions can be successfully analysed in terms of conditionals, this amounts to the following type of thesis:

> *W is Q just in case: if agents encounter W under condition C, response q obtains.*

In the case of judgements of literary value, a first take on how the formula could be filled in reads as follows:

> *(Literary Value, or LV) Work W has a valuable literary quality, Q, just in case readers who experience the work under the right conditions experience it as manifesting q-ness.*

Such analyses have apparent virtues and vices, over which philosophers continue to puzzle (Johnston 1998; Koons 2003; Holland 2001; Vallentyne 1996). An apparent virtue is that this kind of analysis promises to take on board the idea that the reader's response is indicative of the work's value. Yet this latter fact does not reduce the value of the work to the response, as in the hopeless thought that what one values in the work is nothing more than one's own evaluative response. That disastrous conclusion is ruled out, according to this analysis, because the work/reader relation is essential to the disposition, where this disposition is taken to be the basis of the work's having the valued quality. The claim is not, then, that it is a priori that anyone who values a work thereby deems his or her own response constitutive of the work's value; the idea, rather, is the empirical claim that responses of a certain kind are indicative of the work's have a valued disposition, relative to certain kinds of readers or responses. This thought need not violate evaluators' basic realist orientation.

On the other hand, an apparent vice of dispositional analyses of value is that they may be hopelessly circular because the puzzling value property, Q, figures on both sides of the analysis (Blackburn, 'Circles'). For example, what does the following sort of phrase really tell us?

Woolf's *Orlando* is giddy and probing if and only if readers who read it under the right circumstances find that it manifests a giddy, probing quality.

If we do not know what manifesting Q-ness (the giddy and probing quality) is all about, we can hardly find such an account informative, no matter what other terms appear between the first and second appearances of 'Q'.

One way to go here is to try to find a way to avoid the circularity. For example, the response may be further explicated in terms of notions that neither contain nor depend upon Q. The problem with this line of thought is that the circularity creeps back in if the terms employed are sufficiently synonymous to be convincing stand-ins for the target response. It will not do merely to shift from 'giddy and probing' to some synonyms. And if they are not sufficient stand-ins, the analysis is inadequate.

Another option is to acknowledge circularity while contending that it does not matter given the particular objectives with which the analysis – or more broadly, the elucidation or account – is framed. For example, one points out that the goal is not to explain elegance, vivacity, giddiness, etc. to someone who has never experienced an utterance as manifesting such qualities. Yet the account can still be informative, provided that condition C establishes a significant constraint on the work-response pairs recognised as constitutive of the disposition. Here is where the tradition brings in various idealisations or refinements that help to bridge the gap between haphazard and spurious responses, on the one hand, and those that accurately limn, reveal, and manifest the work's artistically relevant capacities. The idealisation, then, must be a matter of a specification of the conditions under which the correct or appropriate responses – that is, the responses revelatory of the work's relevant, valued disposition – occurs. The dispositional analysis is not, in other words, an empty ratification of any and every response as a 'discovery' of the work's dispositions.

Here is where Humean considerations regarding the virtues of true or ideal judges become relevant (Levinson 2002). Such a judge is unprejudiced and has broad, comparative experience of works of the relevant sorts, as well as the requisite background knowledge, fine sensibility and perceptual, emotive, and cognitive capacities. If, then, the style of the utterance is cloying, repetitive, derivative, hackneyed, plodding, etc., such a judge will tend to take note of these features; if, on the contrary, the style is energetic, vivid, fresh, probing, innovative, etc., these features will also be noted, as long as the judge's appreciative abilities have not been impeded. The manifestation of the work's value-relevant capacities depends, then, upon the traits and activities of observers, but is not adequately characterised as an arbitrary projection of the observer's emotions or sensibility. Thus the broad formula labelled (LV) above must be revised. The responses are not those of any and all possible readers, but those of actual, expert readers and idealisations of same.

The framework I have just sketched can be developed by means of empirical investigations into the extent to which there is broad agreement amongst informed readers regarding the specific valued qualities of particular literary works, as well as about more general, valued literary functions. It may well be that such research can show that much apparent disagreement is spurious (a matter of a *dialogue de sourds*), and that on various particular issues there is more agreement amongst the informed than relativist theory acknowledges. A separate line of investigation concerns the grounds and capacities involved in specific judgements: to what extent have actual evaluators performed as 'true judges' in their appreciations of particular works? On some cynical accounts in literary theory, the response is 'not at all', but such a sweeping claim has yet to be given any solid, factual basis. It may well turn out that a closer look will support the hypothesis that in a range of central cases, readers' first-order, realist orientation is well-warranted: the expert reader's response is indicative of the work's inherent value, that is, its capacity to give rise to this very response.

In sum, one way of synthesizing and extending my argument in this paper runs as follows: specifically literary value, and the various aesthetic artistic qualities that contribute to it, are primarily a matter of an utterance's capacity to give rise to intrinsically valued experiences amongst evaluators who themselves have the requisite capacities. Thus two sorts of capacities contribute to the actualisation of literary value: those of the evaluator and those of the work. Yet this is not a matter of affirming an 'order of determination' whereby it is the reader's activity that is somehow constitutive of the work's qualities and value in a strong, causal sense. The relevant readerly or evaluative capacities are a matter of sensitivity, attunement, and knowledge, and more generally, of the ability to gauge and realise the work's dispositional value – what C. I. Lewis labelled 'inherent value' (Lewis 1946; cf. Livingston 2004). Such a conclusion, unlike other main strategies in meta-axiology, squares with the basic, realist orientation of our evaluative experience. Yet it does not rest upon the two implausible postulations that fuel anti-realistic intuitions – the thesis of an objective 'imperative' to prefer a given type of literature (namely, excellent works of literary art), and the thesis that everyone's literary judgements must agree if any of them are to have any measure of rightness or justification.[1]

References

Audi, R. 2004. *The Good in the Right: A Theory of Intuition and Intrinsic Value.* Princeton NJ: Princeton University Press.

Blackburn, S. 1993. Circles, Finks, Smells and Biconditionals. *Philosophical Perspectives* 7: 331–51.

Blackburn, S. 1993. *Realism, Quasi or Queasy?* In *Reality, Representation, and Projection,* J. Haldane & C. Wright (eds), 365–84. Oxford: OUP.

Brink, D. O. 1989. *Moral Realism and the Foundations of Ethics.* New York NY: CUP.

Darwall, S., Gibbard, A. & Railton, P. (eds). 1997. *Moral Discourse and Practice: Some Philosophical Approaches.* New York NY: OUP.

Dreier, J. 1999. Transforming Expressivism. *Noûs* 33: 558–72.

Haldane, J. & C. Wright (eds). 1993. *Reality, Representation, and Projection.* Oxford: OUP.

1.   Many thanks to Willie van Peer for helpful editorial suggestions on drafts of this paper.

Holland, S. 2001. Dispositional Theories of Value Meet Moral Twin Earth. *American Philosophical Quarterly* 38: 177–95.

James, H. 1984. *Literary Criticism*, ed. Leon Edel. New York NY: Library of America.

Johnston, M. 1998. Are Manifest Qualities Response Dependent? *The Monist* 81: 3–43.

Joyce, R. 2001. *The Myth of Morality*. Cambridge: CUP.

Koons, J. R. 2003. Why Response-Dependence Theories of Morality are False. *Ethical Theory and Moral Practice* 6: 275–94.

Levinson, J. 2002. Hume's Standard of Taste: The Real Problem. *Journal of Aesthetics and Art Criticism* 60: 227–38.

Lewis, C. I. 1946. *An Analysis of Knowledge and Valuation*. LaSalle IL: Open Court.

Lewis, D. K. 2000. Dispositional theories of value. In *Papers in Ethics and Social Philosophy*, D.K. Lewis (ed), 68–94. Cambridge: CUP.

Livingston, P. 2004. C. I. Lewis and the Outlines of Aesthetic Experience. *British Journal of Aesthetics* 44: 378–92.

Mackie, J. L. 1977. *Ethics: Inventing Right and Wrong*. Harmondsworth: Penguin.

Miller, R. M. 1992. *Moral Differences*. Princeton NJ: Princeton University Press.

Pettit, P. 1991. Realism and Response-Dependence. *Mind* 100: 587–626.

Railton, P. 2003. *Facts, Values, and Norms*. Cambridge: CUP.

Ross, W. D. 1930. *The Right and the Good*. Oxford: OUP.

Sinnott-Armstrong, W. & M. Timmons (eds). 1996. *Moral Knowledge? New Readings in Moral Epistemology*. New York NY: OUP.

Vallentyne, P. 1996. Response-Dependence, Rigidification and Objectivity. *Erkenntnis* 44 : 101–112.

Wiggins, D. 1987. *Needs, Values, Truth: Essays in the Philosophy of Value*. Oxford: Basil Blackwell.

Wiggins, D. 1998. In a Subjectivist Framework, Categorial Requirements and Real Practical Reasons. In *Preferences*, C. Fehige & U. Wessels (eds), 212–32. Berlin: Walter de Gruyter.

CHAPTER 13

The qualities of literatures

A concept of literary evaluation in pluralistic societies

Renate von Heydebrand and Simone Winko

In this article we outline our conception of literary evaluation in pluralistic societies building on recent theories of values and the canon and on the results of empirical research, especially in social psychology and the psychology of cognition. We argue that the evaluation of literature has to be considered in social terms, not merely as an individual act. Our model is designed to facilitate the analysis of evaluation. Its advantage, in our view, lies in abandoning the notion of literary quality as a property intrinsic to the text, without denying that there have to be textual properties corresponding to the value expectations which people bring to literature. It also provides a basis for a pluralistic evaluation of literature, going beyond the convention of aesthetic autonomy and taking into account the entire spectrum of social functions associated with literature.

The situation is one with which we are all familiar. A neighbour asks us, as an 'expert', to recommend a 'good' book. Should we really suggest one of the texts we love and continually re-read – Shakespeare's sonnets, *Don Quixote*, Goethe's *Elective Affinities* or Kleist's *Marquise von O.*, or indeed Proust's *Recherche*, Joyce's *Ulysses*, Kafka's *The Trial*, Beckett's *Endgame*? Or perhaps something contemporary, by Herta Müller or García Marquez? If we follow our own preferences, we know that the book is likely to go unread. Our professional reputation as judges of literature may remain intact, but for the person soliciting our opinion, the text is still not 'good'.

The example, as far as it goes, merely shows that readers' preferences differ – a very basic empirical fact, yet one that still continues to exercise literary scholars. This has been apparent in the often tumultuous debate on the literary 'canon' at the end of the twentieth century. On the one hand, there have been repeated calls by cultural conservatives to restore the (Western) canon as a corpus of privileged texts which define a universal standard of literary quality. On the other, this position has been fiercely contested by a range of critics, including Leslie A. Fiedler (1981), Barbara Herrnstein Smith (1988), John Guillory (1993) and the exponents of deconstruction (Jacques Derrida, Paul de Man), who have marshalled strong arguments against the very notion of a single canon of texts or legitimate ways of reading. In a more overtly radical vein, the notorious charge has been brought – by among others, feminists, practitioners of Colonial Studies and the initiators of the Western Culture debate at Stanford University – that the canon is limited to "dead white middle-class males".[1]

The idea, based on the canons of scripture, of a restricted category of authors and literary works that have a binding exemplary status and serve as a general measure of quality, corresponds to a hierarchically stratified society which is now firmly consigned to the past: a society whose upper echelons defined a stable order of values that was cemented by institutions and supposedly endorsed by the entire community (see Hahn 1987). We, however, are living in a pluralistic society, differentiated by function instead of rank, which has few values in common. The values associated with literature are not part of this limited consensus. It is time that the academic study of literary evaluation accepted this fundamental reality and began to take it seriously.

In our study of literary evaluation, completed some years ago, von Heydebrand & Winko (1996), henceforth H/W, we tried to explore some of the implications of this insight.[2] Our conclusions are summarized in the following essay. Our aim was to model and analyze the processes of literary evaluation in such a way as to facilitate historical and empirical studies on the foundations of literary quality in the various areas of our culture. These analyses were necessary in order to address two problems which have not been satisfactorily resolved in the recent debates on the canon. Using our model of literary evaluation it is possible, on the one hand, to reconstruct the conditions of justification for the controversial 'Western' canon,[3] and on the other, to give proper academic consideration to the alternative canons proposed by those who, for varying reasons, are foreign or hostile to the writings of 'dead white middle-class males'.

---

1. See, from a general perspective, Renate von Heydebrand and Simone Winko, "Geschlechterdifferenz und literarischer Kanon. Historische Beobachtungen und systematische Überlegungen", *Internationales Archiv für Sozialgeschichte der deutschen Literatur* 19(2) (1994), pp. 96–172, especially pp. 145–157.

2. Since then very few substantial studies on the processes of literary evaluation have been published; an outstanding exception is the excellent work of Friederike Worthmann 2004.

3. In his impassioned yet poorly argued defence of the 'Western' canon, Harold Bloom attempts but signally fails to deliver such an analysis; see Bloom 1994.

1.   A model of literary evaluation

A starting point for our model was an observation generally ignored by theories of literary evaluation. 'Literary evaluation' is by no means limited to professional judgements on literary texts, since evaluations play an important part in all areas of the 'literary system',[4] in a wide variety of guises, and in professional and non-professional contexts alike. A few examples may help to clarify this.

In the *production* of literary texts, evaluations can influence the act of writing either beforehand – for example, in the choice of subject-matter or the conception of certain characters – or during the writing process – e.g. in the use of particular stylistic devices, such as emphasising the significance of a piece of information by metaphor or repetition or by putting the information in a position where the reader is bound to notice it. Evaluations are also made by literary *mediators*, such as publishers and editors, who decide on the appearance and presentation of literary texts; by television and radio producers, who supervise the adaptation of texts for other media; and literary critics, scholars and teachers, who interpret texts and make them accessible to a wider audience. As well as making explicit value judgements, all these individuals evaluate literature implicitly by selecting particular texts considered worthy of attention. The same applies to the two types of literary *reception*: on the one hand, reading, and on the other, the various forms of secondary reception by interpretation, translation, screen adaptation, rewriting, criticism, etc.[5] Both types of reception offer instances of evaluation via selection. In the primary sphere, for example, a reader chooses a certain text from the multitude of new publications. In the secondary sphere, the critic or interpreter decides to give the text more or less space; other works whose value has already been defined are used as points of comparison; special efforts are made, or not, to recruit a good translator, and so forth.

As this brief sketch already indicates, literary evaluation takes two distinct forms: on the one hand, explicit linguistic utterances, well known; and on the other, frequently overlooked, non-linguistic acts of selection whose evaluative significance may not be apparent to the actor. Our model of evaluation takes account of both these aspects.

---

4.   The concept refers to the literature-related system of action which in Germany can be seen to constitute itself at the beginning of the nineteenth century as an 'autonomous' social subsystem; see Pfau and Schönert (1988). For important critical remarks, see Günter 2005.

5.   A wide variety of meanings have been attached to these terms in literary studies. S. J. Schmidt (1980:274–92), for example, defines 'reception' purely as the 'understanding' of a text, and uses the term 'processing' (*Verarbeitung*) for all the remaining operations carried out on texts, including interpretation and criticism.

1.1   Basic concepts

In view of the variety of areas involved, and the range of guises which literary evaluation can take, we have to choose an axiological framework theory which is broad enough to accommodate the social and individual aspects of evaluation, to deal with evaluation as an act of selection and also to consider it as a linguistic act. Such a theory has to offer scope for combining the perspectives of three different disciplines – sociology, psychology and linguistics. It therefore has to move beyond the bounds of specifically literary theory, and to eschew the essentialism of traditional theories of value. In our case, the necessary framework was found in the theory of value proposed by analytical philosophy.[6]

Since the concepts used in the debate on evaluation are neither adequately defined nor used at all consistently, we carried out a number of explications[7] with a view to establishing clarity. In this paper, a certain insistence on terminological precision is therefore essential; see H/W, pp. 37–48 for a comprehensive definition. The concept of 'evaluation', as used by us, denotes a complex social act by which a subject attributes value to an object, in a concrete situation and on the basis of certain *standards of value* and certain *categorizing assumptions* (see below). The attribution can be carried out by verbal means, or it can take the form of a non-linguistic act.

The *subject*, i.e. the instance which carries out the evaluation, can be an individual, a group or an institution. The *object* can be a literary text or a mental representation thereof, but the range of possible objects of evaluation also includes the impact of a text or part of a text, the author as an individual, a concrete object (e.g. a book), or an event, institution or constellation of factors in literary life or even in society as a whole. The model needs to be capable of accommodating all *literature-related* acts of evaluation, since the latter are closely connected with the evaluation of the actual *texts*.

One of the reasons why so much substantive and conceptual confusion arises in discussions of literary evaluation is that the concept of 'value' can be understood as pertaining to a criterion or standard on which an evaluation is based, and also to a characteristic of the object itself. We therefore consider it necessary to distinguish between *standards of value* in the subjective realm and *attributive values* in the domain of the object. Subjective standards of value cause an object or a property thereof to seem valuable or worthless; their validity is context-dependent

---

6. Our theoretical and terminological starting point here is Zdislaw Najder's *Values and Evaluations*, Oxford 1975, which gives a systematic and lucid exposition of the discussion on these issues in linguistic philosophy; see H/W, pp. 38f.

7. An 'explication' analyzes the actual uses of a concept but also includes suggestions as to how it may be used more clearly; see Pawlowski (1980, Chapters I and V).

and historically variable. This means that an object is not *intrinsically* valuable or worthless, regardless of context; instead, it only acquires an (attributive) value in relation to a standard of value. The impression that objects have an intrinsic value depends entirely on the stability of standards and contexts.

But how does a person making an evaluation come to relate the properties of an object – which in themselves are neutral – to a standard of value, and thereby to judge them valuable or worthless? In our model, this act of relating properties to standards is explained in pragmatic terms; specifically, on the basis of what we have called the *categorizing assumptions* involved in evaluation. This term refers to a phenomenon which has been overlooked in previous models of literary evaluation, i.e., the fact that two people with a common standard of value can still have differing opinions about how an object has to be constituted for that standard to be applied to it. The term therefore denotes the conditions which have to be met, in the view of an evaluator, in order that properties may be related to values. Categorizing assumptions of this type include, for example, assumptions founded in poetics about the properties a text must display in order to count as 'beautiful', or assumptions based on genre theory about the characteristics that distinguish a 'good' sonnet from an inferior one. Like criteria of value, these assumptions are partly conventionalized, and their validity is a matter of social or group-specific agreement, but they are also partly influenced by individual factors. While the social element of evaluation lies in group consensus, individual deviation from the assumptional norm is a main reason for the frequent controversies in the evaluation of literature.

1.2 Types of evaluative action

The connection between verbal and non-verbal evaluation, as distinguished above, consists in the fact that, for both aspects, reference to a standard of value is constitutive, though such reference is generally no more than implicit. *Linguistic* evaluations require a standard of value – as well as certain categorizing assumptions – in order to progress from the description of a text to its evaluation; these criteria therefore form the basis for justifying linguistic evaluations. The type of literary evaluation associated with this is the *judgement*. In *acts* of evaluation, values represent the basis of motivation, which is why we also call these values *'motivational'*. They manifest themselves in various types of *selection*.

If we look at motivational evaluations, standards of value correspond to the 'value orientations' in theories of social psychology. Value orientations are acquired through the process of social learning, and assume a central position in the personality structure of an individual, to the extent that they influence his perceptions of reality and of his own self. They are actualized in situations requiring some form of decision, and give rise to actions or influence the way in which actions are carried out. From this, their relevance to selection is obvious, not only with regard to non-verbal acts of choice, such as a decision whether or not to buy, or to review, a certain book, but also where these acts of choice are the subject of retrospective verbal comment – for example, when a literary historian explains why he has decided to exclude a particular set of texts from his narrative. Value orientations can also influence a further type of action – the act of 'preconscious selection' – which plays a significant but not always clearly definable role in our encounters with literature. This type of preference action has a particular importance for reading, or 'text processing' (i.e., recognition and understanding). It exemplifies the point that value-governed selections can steer our dealings with literature in a particular direction long before any reasoned evaluation has been formulated, a point well made by Worthmann (1998, especially p. 29).

Referring to a model of *text processing* which is now broadly accepted, we regard the understanding of a text as an interaction between processes which originate in both text and reader, leading eventually to a certain representation of the text in the reader's mind.[8] Crucial to our concept of literary evaluation is the idea that value orientations can influence – via the schemata of text processing – the perception and understanding of texts.[9] Textual schemata are generally seen as having two functions. First, they are used by readers to create textual coherence, by filling the gaps in the text and creatively supplementing the 'blank spaces'. Second, they have a selective effect, in so far as they ensure that a reader can only realize a part of the wide range of possible meanings in any given text passage. Schemata provide the interface at which value orientations can impact on text processing, since although they are consensual (i.e., determined by group conventions) they also depend on individual factors – namely on what the reader knows, on his emotions, intentions and motivations, and therefore on his value orientations. This can manifest itself in various ways in the business of reading and understanding. If, for example, an author reading a poem by another writer fills the 'blank spaces' with meanings that depend on his personal theory of poetic form, then his understanding of the text will be influenced by the values that apply to 'good' poetry in the context of that theory. Another example: the value orientations of a reader may colour his perceptions of the text to such an extent that he completely, albeit unwittingly, ignores certain of its properties. One could cite many everyday instances of this; a historical example is to be found in the reception of Charlotte Perkins

---

8.   See, on this issue, Kintsch & van Dijk (1978) and Rumelhart, (1980). See also the concise survey by Viehoff (1988).

9.   See also Mary Crawford and Roger Chaffin, "The Reader's Construction of Meaning: Cognitive Research on Gender and Comprehension", in Elizabeth A. Flynn and Patrocinio P. Schweickart (eds.), *Gender and Reading*, Baltimore 1986: 3–30.

Gilman's *The Yellow Wallpaper* (1892), a novel dealing with the incarceration and madness of its central female character. Today, it is evident that this text can be read according to the genre schema defined by Edgar Allan Poe, and if the publishers of the 1890s had seen it in this light, they would have been bound to find it interesting. However, since it was written by a woman known for her authorship of 'women's books', the Poe schema was not used, and various significant features of the text went unnoticed.[10]

For the concept of 'literary evaluation' in the narrower sense of passing explicit linguistic judgements on literary texts, the above considerations mean that the very basis of evaluation, the literary text-object as a mental representation, can be shaped by previous evaluations; in other words, that the text has already been evaluated prior to the 'real', linguistically manifest act of evaluation (see Worthmann 2004: 91–101).

These linguistically manifest evaluations in the form of judgements are the type of evaluation that has been investigated most often; see, for example, Smith (1988, Note 1), Kienecker (1989), Furbank (1995) and Piecha (2002).

In our model, it represents the third type of evaluation as a social act, after preconscious and conscious selection. Value judgements have the form of statements[11] with which an attributive value is ascribed to an object on the basis of a criterion of value. The bindingness or validity of such a judgement can vary: a speaker may use exactly the same form of words when giving an informal opinion or passing a carefully considered judgement. The crucial factors here are, on the one hand, the institutional conditions of the context of utterance, and on the other, the speaker's intentions. When expressing a general opinion, for example, he will underpin his verdict by reference to his own feelings, or to what others supposedly feel, whereas a formal judgement has to be backed by explicit reasons which are open to inter-subjective scrutiny. However, value judgements of this kind can only be justified by reference to a context, i.e. in relation to a situation of utterance and a value system in which the validity of standards and the appropriateness of categorizing assumptions are firmly established.

1.3 Collective dimensions of evaluation

As we have already indicated, the evaluation of literature has to be considered in *social* terms, not merely as an individual act. The value orientations in which standards of value criteria and categorizing assumptions are anchored, are acquired

---

10.   This intriguing case is dealt with in more detail by Kolodny (1980, especially 455–460.)

11.   Instead of being articulated as explicit judgements, most verbal evaluations are implicit; see H/W, pp. 60–73.

through a social learning process; indeed, socially mediated schemata play a part in determining the most basic perception of texts, let alone the way in which they are understood. And, as a rule, the contexts of utterance in which evaluation takes place can also be identified as areas of social, literature-related action. In our description of this collective dimension of evaluation we have used the sociological concepts of 'norm' and 'role' (H/W, p. 89–105)

Norms are generally based on values and regulate the actions of individuals in standard situations; they are accepted by society as a whole or by certain groups, and their observance or non-observance is subject to positive or negative sanction. The *validity of norms* in a society or group can be assessed in two ways: either by statistical description of the regularities of actions – in this case, the 'norm' is the 'normal' action, that which is most often observed – or by reference to prescriptive, programmatic statements – in which case the 'norm' is a model or paragon, a goal that will not always be achieved. In the first case, a literary scholar would derive the norms of literary quality from best-seller lists; in the second case, the norms would be taken from the canon of world literature and its accompanying 'master discourse'. Norms are also distinguished by the *strength of the relevant sanctions*. Compliance with 'consensual' norms is voluntary and positively sanctioned within their field of application (e.g. the 'normal' opposition of avant-garde literature to the 'classical' canon[12]). 'Conventionalized' norms, of which the actors are scarcely aware, are also subject to weak sanctions only (an example of this would be a breach of the convention, adopted by the literary 'social system', that didactic literature must be viewed as inferior). However, 'imperative' norms, which are not necessarily accepted by those concerned, are enforced with a degree of rigour by the sanctioning mechanisms such as state censorship or the educational system (for example, in the condemnation of literature that is considered offensive on religious, moral or political grounds).

The assessment of literary quality is governed by norms from two main social spheres – the economic and the cultural. These are the norms of, on the one hand, 'economic capital', which relate supply (by authors and publishers) to demand (from potential readers), and of the 'symbolic' or 'cultural capital'[13] which in each case regulates the possible gains in terms of knowledge, action orientation, gratification, prestige, etc. Among these norms of 'cultural capital', the ones which dominate the awareness of literary scholars are those associated with the conven-

---

12.   See Schulz-Buschhaus (1988, especially pp. 46ff).

13.   The distinction between 'economic' and 'symbolic' or 'cultural capital' is drawn by Pierre Bourdieu (1984).

tion of aesthetic autonomy[14] which emerged towards the end of the eighteenth century. According to this convention, the task of literature is neither to instruct nor merely to entertain, and it should not be read with expectations of these kinds. Texts which resist 'autonomous' reception are subject to negative sanction; readers who try to interpret such literature in referential terms and relate it directly to their own experience are marked down as naive. However, in other areas where literature is produced and/or consumed, such as the entertainment industry or the 'therapy' milieu, these norms find very little support.

Roles, to the sociologist, are institutionalized cultural schemata: their function is to ensure that people's scope for action in a group or society remains sufficiently restricted to be manageable. They are linked even more closely than norms to social situations and functions. Thus an individual can assume a variety of roles in different situations and in respect of different literary functions, and can therefore also evaluate texts in different ways; the resultant potential role conflict was illustrated above by the example of the university teacher asked to make literary recommendations for the lay reader.

The most important roles in the literary social system were cited in our enumeration of the areas in which literature-related acts of evaluation occur: the roles of the professional mediator and processor, and those of the 'normal' reader and the author. *Mediators* evaluate partly under the influence of economic norms, and partly also on the basis of norms of social prestige and political relevance. Nonorthodox evaluation, applying the wrong norms, can incur strict sanctions and cost the mediator his job. The interpretative and evaluative actions of the *processors* are similarly conditioned by the profiles and the internal – cultural and economic – norms of the institutions in which they are employed. Here, too, certain sanctions exist, mainly affecting the individual's position in the hierarchy. The weakest set of norms is that associated with the acts of reading and evaluation performed by the 'normal', *non-professional* reader. However, the decision to read and evaluate purely on the basis of personal preference – the most common form of this is 'identificatory' reading, in which readers empathize with the characters and problems portrayed in the text – means a loss of prestige within the literary 'social system' and is therefore subject to negative sanction. The action of *authors*, creating literature as the material basis for evaluation by others, can also be seen as a form of role-governed evaluation, a response to literature-related norms in the field of shifting tensions between economic and symbolic capital, and to norms of writing which have established themselves in literary tradition such as 'deviance'

---

14.   A 'convention', in the established sense, is identical with a 'norm' in the sense employed by us.

or 'originality'. Sanctions have a very direct impact in terms of success or failure, though their eventual effect may change considerably with the passing of time.

The quality of literature, therefore, is invariably defined in relation to the collective normative spheres in which the judgement applies and the selection is to be accepted. In each case the task then remains of analyzing how a particular evaluation actually takes place, in the context of interaction between collective and individual norms and values and, where applicable, of the conflict between different roles.

2.   Advantages of the model

Our model is designed to facilitate the analysis of evaluation. Its most important advantage, in our view, consists in abandoning the notion of literary quality as a property intrinsic to the text. For this reason, the model is particularly well suited to investigate the questions of why and how even 'canonic' texts can be subjected to widely differing evaluations – in the course of history, or at one and the same time in different spheres of communication about literature. It also provides a basis for a pluralistic evaluation of literature, going beyond the convention of aesthetic autonomy and taking into account the entire spectrum of social functions associated with literature.

However, equal importance must be accorded to the realization that there have to be textual properties corresponding to the value expectations which people bring to literature, and that these properties can be tailored to match the relevant expectations more or less exactly. This applies to all the normative areas in which literature is evaluated – not only to the literary system, but also to all the less prestigious literary sub-systems which have a direct relationship to everyday concerns and a practical function in supplying entertainment, religious, ethical or political guidance, therapeutic solace, and so forth. For 'aesthetic' literature, the nature of these properties has still not been sufficiently investigated, and in other areas the question has hardly been studied at all.

For this reason, the second part of our book is devoted to historical examples of evaluation and changes in evaluation. Various explanations are offered, in the light of the model, for the existence of a literary canon. In the third section, we try to sketch a framework for the evaluation of literature from all functional areas, and to identify, on the basis of exemplary evaluations, some of the textual properties which currently appear to confer particular value on two specific types of literature: the 'literary' text and the crime novel.

2.1 Model-based analyses of historical examples

Using historical examples, we have attempted to show how the factors in our model of evaluation have influenced acts of evaluation in the past. This affords a number of insights into the history of literary taste, although for reasons of space, the conclusions are limited to Germany.

In the first example, dealing with attitudes to Baroque literature (H/W, pp. 134–62), we analyze what is probably the most dramatic single shift in the history of evaluation, leading almost inexorably to the emergence of the literary system and the theory of aesthetic autonomy. Here, it also becomes apparent for the first time how prevailing notions of poetic form can influence the evaluation of literature by acting as perceptual schemata and 'categorizing assumptions'; thus, writings which are highly prized when literature is dominated by rhetoric are dismissed as empty bombast by the proponents of aesthetic autonomy. The second example (H/W 163–85) discusses this historic shift, occurring around the year 1770, in the context of the transition from oral to written culture, with the rise of reading as a new mode of reception which transformed the character of evaluation; at the same time, the example of the *Volkslied*, as a genre burdened with ideological meanings, is used to elucidate the significance of literary genres as schemata in the process of evaluation. In the third example, we employ evaluations of Goethe's *Wilhelm Meister* (H/W 186–221) to illustrate in some depth the connection between reading and evaluation in various literature-related roles. This work was used by the literary luminaries of Weimar and Jena to school themselves in the 'aesthetic' approach to literature, thereby elaborating the distinction between professional, 'autonomous' evaluation and the 'heteronomous' judgement of the lay reader. It is also shown that the evaluations of writers are generally shaped – as one might expect – by the theories that inform their own literary production. The fourth example focuses on the significance of mediating institutions as factors in evaluation and especially in the process of canon-formation. The material for this section is supplied by the comprehensively documented history of the reception of Annette von Droste-Hülshoff, (H/W 222–50) a writer whose sex and regional orientation have continually served as – highly reductive – schemata for the perception and evaluation of her literary achievements. Example number five, which is a contribution in its own right to the history of literary theory, shows how, in the main academic theories of literature and literary value after 1945, evaluation depends largely on the critic's own theory of literature (H/W 251–306). Looking at the objects of evaluation, the methods, criteria of value and categorizing assumptions, and bearing in mind the involvement of other theoretical and historical contexts, we systematically compare the following theories and theorists:

- traditional hermeneutic evaluation, of the purely phenomenological type practised by Wolfgang Kayser, and in the form as extended by Friedrich Sengle and Walter Müller-Seidel to include elements of intellectual history;
- hermeneutic evaluation combined with elements of Marxism (Theodor W. Adorno and the various manifestations of *Ideologiekritik*);
- evaluation on the basis of semiotic theory in structuralism (Mukarovsky) and reception theory (Hans Robert Jauss);
- the questioning of evaluation in post-structuralism and deconstruction (Roland Barthes, Paul de Man);
- and finally, evaluation in feminist literary studies (drawing on deconstruction and the critique of ideology).

By extending the enquiry, in this section of the study, to the theoretical and historical context of the ideas concerned, we have also tried to grasp the development and selection of conceptions of evaluation in 'motivational' terms, against the background of political and social factors and in relation also to the institutional pressures of the academy.

2.2 Canon formation: Perspectives of explanation and normative considerations

Our model focuses attention on those individual and collective factors on the 'subject' side which are necessary in order to convert specific properties on the 'object' side – the literary work – into 'values'. An approach of this kind inevitably faces the charge of relativism. But surely, some critics will say, there is a durable, if variable, corpus of texts, the so-called canon of world literature, in which literary 'quality' is objectively embodied and which can and must be a basis for analyzing these 'objective' values? We address this question in a final sketch of the history of evaluation, going beyond the examples previously cited and exploring several different perspectives for explaining the relative stability of a canon of world literature (H/W 311–21). According to the first perspective, the canonic works embody eternal aesthetic values which elicit a consistent response from an aesthetic sensibility which is part of a fixed human nature, outside time and space. Disagreement among evaluators and changes in the canon can therefore only arise from a lack of evaluative competence and the application of inappropriate criteria. However, this argument already implies that literary quality is in some measure connected with the evaluator's normative socialization. The second perspective, based on a philosophy of history, accepts from the outset that canon-formation is shaped by philosophical and aesthetic assumptions and their historical evolution. In their interpretive history, or 'interpretive canon',[15] canonical works can be seen to exemplify the historical decay of metaphysics. The durability of the works, according to this view, is explained by the ease with which their formal aspects can be used as a convenient peg on which to hang the central discourses of beauty, goodness and truth. For this, textual properties such as complexity and polyvalence are necessary but not sufficient conditions. With the third, (macro-)sociological perspective, the evolving interests of groups or entire societies are considered in their significance for literary canon-formation and canonic change. John Guillory (1993, espially The Preface and Part I) sees the previous canons as an instrument, in the first place, of social differentiation. We agree with the argument of Joachim Küpper (1997, especially pp. 57 ff.), and also of Pierre Bourdieu (1984), that the canonic stability of a small number of literary works cannot be explained primarily by their intrinsic properties; instead, one must look at their long-term usefulness for the historically evolving models by which social elites define their relationship to the world. However, polyvalence and complexity tend to enhance this kind of usefulness, although these qualities themselves do not suffice to establish canonicity. Thus the dominance of the 'subject' side persists in all three perspectives.

The criteria of quality derived from the canon of world literature – i.e. 'representing the history of metaphysics' or 'usefulness to social elites' – also signal that the canon in question is one that lays a comprehensive, though perennially controversial, claim to validity. But this does not exclude proposing a variety of discrete canons, with differing ranges, for the various functions of literature and contexts of utterance (H/W 326–40). Even in the relatively distant past there were already several, partly conflicting canons: a 'canonic' example is furnished by Mikhail Bakhtin's opposition between literature and carnival. Bourdieu's model of cultural stratification is a further, contemporary, instance. Looking at the present, pluralistic societies specifically assume the coexistence of a large number of cultural and literary canons, each having its own internal criteria, and its own patterns of context-dependent behaviour and interpretation. What remains is the task of re-evaluating these differences and investigating them more closely. Our model, which relates literary value to subjects and contexts, establishes the basis for this; however, the fine detail of the superstructure has yet to be worked out.[16]

---

15.   This concept, now firmly established, takes account of the fact that, although a canon is made up of 'material' works (or, in many cases, a series of authors' names used metonymically), the values on which the claim to canonicity is based are defined only via interpretations of the works in question. See the initial discussion of this problem in von Heydebrand (1991, especially p. 5f.)

16.   Our specimen evaluations of modern texts from the spheres of 'literature' and the crime novel (H/W 341–376) offer only a few very general hints as to how this task could be approached.

Deciding on a hierarchy between the canons of 'elite' and 'popular' culture, or even between different genres within these cultural fields, would be a matter for meta-evaluation. How, under today's conditions, is a cultural elite to establish its legitimacy and justify its canon vis-à-vis its popular or ethnically different competitors? And does a novel, for example, have a greater a priori value than an aphorism? Is a poem with a 'message' automatically better than one which relies on the free play of language? These questions are probably couched in the wrong terms: democratic pluralism inherently challenges us to accept functional differentiation and to withhold approval from all hierarchies, whether social or genre-related. Yet as individuals, we still have to make decisions, in situations such as that of a university teacher who can only deal with a limited number of literary texts. Here, too, our model can offer a framework for identifying an individual point of view and reflecting, within a social perspective, on one's personal standards of value, as well as those of others.

3.   Issues for further study

Our conception of literary evaluation in pluralistic societies incorporates, on the one hand, theories and questions from the debates on values and the canon, and on the other, the results of empirical research, especially in social psychology and the psychology of cognition. The last section of our essay summarizes these points of connection with empirical literary studies and points to some of the issues that require further investigation.

Some of our assumptions have the status of hypotheses which could be verified by empirical research:

(1) Our own experience, as empirically minded literary historians and in our dealings with students, has taught us how useful it is to apply the concept of 'categorizing assumptions' and to look at the function of such assumptions in the evaluation of literature. In our model, this concept offers a basis for explaining situations where differences in evaluation arise even though the criteria of value remain the same. Further empirical work would be necessary to specify ways of identifying these assumptions and reconstructing their impact on the process of evaluation, and to assess the relative significance of individual and collective factors.

(2) In theory, the approach of professional readers should be less subjective, but in practice their perceptions of texts are selective and evaluative. What, then, is the role of 'intrinsic' textual properties in evaluation, and to what extent can such properties 'resist' the evaluator's selective reading? A meaningful answer to these questions would require careful empirical study of the behaviour of

professional readers, exploring how they read, interpret and evaluate texts in their various roles (see Andringa 1994).

(3) According to our model, texts which are themselves value-laden tend, to a greater extent than texts of a more neutral, descriptive type, to increase the impact of value orientations on the constitution of meaning, since texts of this kind either have a suggestive effect and invite the reader to accept the evaluations exemplified in the text, or they activate the reader's own values and encourage him to think about them. These hypotheses are based purely on our own experience, and would have to be tested systematically.

However, more important than testing these assumptions would be the empirical investigation of evaluative acts and processes of canon formation in a range of contemporary literature-related areas. Here, there is a major research gap waiting to be filled. Among the many issues that spring to mind are two specific problems which urgently require analysis.

The first such problem concerns group-specific ways of perceiving 'canonic' texts. This arises, for example, in connection with the fact that many students find themselves completely 'turned off' by texts from the canons of academia and traditional middle-class culture. It is necessary to clarify whether canonized texts (a) have common or similar properties, to which (b) certain groups of readers react more positively than others. One could then ask whether the problem in fact has anything to do with the texts themselves, or, instead, with value orientations which determine the perception of the texts. Some hypotheses have already been formulated here,[17] but they need to be tested. In doing so, it would be essential to break down the sample according to the readers' level of education and previous acquaintance with literature, and also by factors such as political and moral convictions. In our experience, to cite one example, the textual properties seen by feminists seem to differ from those identified by other readers, male or female.

The second problem concerns the influence of literary media on the formation of standards of value. A current example which would repay closer study is that of hyperfiction, as a new type of text. Here, two distinct approaches would seem necessary. From a descriptive point of view, one could analyze actual evaluations in respect of the standards of value underpinning them. It would be necessary to enquire whether, or how, the standards of value are affected by the fact that the texts are no longer sequentially structured, the plot being variable so that readers can generate their own stories. One would have to consider the mechanisms that organize the text and also the various modes of reception, in order to explain the differences in value judgements, which apparently correspond, at least

---

17.   See, for example, Küpper (1997, especially pp. 57–61).

in part, to different strategies of reading and patterns of expectation.[18] However, adopting a normative approach, one would also need to investigate the extent to which the characteristics and conditions of the new medium *must* be considered in developing appropriate criteria by which to evaluate the texts (see Simanowski 2002: 23–26).

The dual functionality of our model, as described above, qualifies it as a theoretical basis for both these research perspectives. On the one hand, it offers points of connection for descriptive analysis or reconstruction in empirical and historical studies, and on the other, it provides a conceptual framework for normative projects such as the development or justification of criteria.

References

Andringa, E. (ed.). 1994. *Wandel der Interpretation. Kafkas Vor dem Gesetz im Spiegel der Literaturwissenschaft.* Frankfurt: Westdeutscher Verlag.

Bloom, H. 1994. *The Western Canon. The Books and School of the Ages.* London: MacMillan.

Bourdieu, P. 1984. *Distinction: A Social Critique of the Judgement of Taste.* Cambridge, MA: Harvard University Press.

Crawford, M. & Chaffin, R. 1986. The Reader's Construction of Meaning: Cognitive Research on Gender and Comprehension. In *Gender and Reading,* E. A. Flynn & P. P. Schweickart (eds), 3–30. Baltimore, MD: Johns Hopkins University Press.

Fiedler, L. A. 1981. Literature as an Institution: The View from 1980. In *English Literature: Opening Up the Canon,* L.A. Fiedler and H. A. Baker, Jr. (eds), 73–91. Baltimore, MD: Johns Hopkins University Press.

Foltz, P. W. 1996. Comprehension, Coherence, and Strategies in Hypertext and Linear Text. In *Hypertext and Cognition,* J-F. Rouet et al. (eds), 109–136. Mahwah, NJ: Lawrence Erlbaum.

Furbank, P. N. 1995. On Criticism as Value-Judgement. *The Iowa Review* 25(3): 162–65.

Gilman, C. P. 2000. *The Yellow Wall-Paper and Other Writings.* New York, NY: The Modern Library. (Orig. 1982).

Günter, M. 2005. 'Ermanne dich, oder vielmehr erweibe dich einmal!' Gender Trouble in der Literatur nach der Kunstperiode. *Internationales Archiv für Sozialgeschichte der deutschen Literatur* 30: 38–61.

Guillory, J. 1993. *Cultural Capital: The Problem of Literary Canon Formation.* Chicago, IL: University of Chicago Press.

Hahn, A. 1987. Kanonisierungsstile. In *Kanon und Zensur,* A. Assmann & J. Assmann (eds), 28–37. Munich: Wilhelm Fink.

von Heydebrand, R. 1991. Probleme des 'Kanons' – Probleme der Kultur- und Bildungspolitik. In *Methodenkonkurrenz in der germanistischen Praxis. Vorträge des Augsburger Germanistentages,* J. Janota (ed.), 3–22. Tübingen: Niemeyer.

von Heydebrand, R. & S. Winko. 1996. *Einführung in die Wertung von Literatur. Systematik – Geschichte – Legitimation.* Stuttgart: UTB.

---

18.   It is interesting to compare, for example, the various reactions to Michael Joyce's *Afternoon. A Story*; see Foltz (1996) and Wingert (1996).

Kienecker, M. 1989. *Prinzipien literarischer Wertung. Sprachanalytische und historische Untersuchungen.* Göttingen: Vandenhoeck.

Kintsch, W. & T.A. van Dijk. 1978. Toward a Model of Text Comprehension and Production. *Psychological Review* 85: 363–394.

Kolodny, A. 1980. A Map for Rereading: Or, Gender and the Interpretation of Literary Texts. *New Literary History* 11: 451–467.

Küpper, J. 1997. Kanon als Historiographie. In *Kanon und Theorie,* M. Moog-Grünewald (Ed.), 41–64. Heidelberg: Universitätsverlag C. Winter.

Najder, Z. 1975. *Values and Evaluations.* Oxford: Clarendon Press.

Pawlowski, T. 1980. *Begriffsbildung und Definition.* Berlin: Walter de Gruyter.

Piecha, A. 2002. *Die Begründbarkeit ästhetischer Werturteile.* Paderborn: Mentis.

Pfau, D. & J. Schönert. 1988. Probleme und Perspektiven einer theoretisch-systematischen Grundlegung für eine 'Sozialgeschichte der Literatur'. In *Zur theoretischen Grundlegung einer Sozialgeschichte der Literatur. Ein struktural-funktionaler Entwurf* (Toward a Theoretical Foundation of a Social History of Literature). R. von Heydebrand, D. Pfau and J. Schönert (eds), 1–26. Tübingen: Niemeyer.

Rumelhart, D. E. 1980. Schemata. The Building Blocks of Cognition. In *Theoretical Issues in Reading Comprehension,* R. J. Spiro, B. Bruce & W. Brewer (eds), 33–58. Hillsdale, NJ: Lawrence Erlbaum.

Schmidt, S. J. 1980. *Grundriss der Empirischen Literaturwissenschaf* [Outline of an Empirical Science of Literature], vol 1: *Der gesellschaftliche Handlungsbereich Literatur.* [The Realm of Literature's Social Action]. Wiesbaden: Vieweg.

Simanowski, R. 2002. *Interfictions. Vom Schreiben im Netz.* Frankfurt: Suhrkamp.

Smith, B. H. 1988. *Contingencies of Value: Alternative Perspectives for Critical Theory.* Cambridge, MA: Harvard University Press.

Schulz-Buschhaus, U. 1988. Kanonbildung in Europa. In *Literarische Klassik,* H. J. Simm (Ed.), 45–68. Frankfurt: Suhrkamp.

Viehoff, R. 1988. Literarisches Verstehen. Neuere Ansätze und Ergebnisse empirischer Forschung. *Internationales Archiv für Sozialgeschichte der deutschen Literatur* 13: 1–29.

Wingert, B. 1996. Kann man Hypertexte lesen? In *Literatur im Informationszeitalter,* D. Matejovski & F. Kittler (eds), 185–218. Frankfurt: Campus.

Worthmann, F. 1998. Literarische Kanones als Lektüremacht. Systematische Überlegungen zum Verhältnis von Kanon(isierung) und Wert(ung). In *Kanon Macht Kultur. Theoretische, historische und soziale Aspekte ästhetischer Kanonbildung. DFG-Symposion 1996,* (Canon Power Culture. Theoretical, historical and social aspects of aesthetic canonization). R. von Heydebrand (ed.), 9–29. Stuttgart: Metzler.

Worthmann, F. 2004. *Literarische Wertungen. Vorschläge für ein deskriptives Modell.* Wiesbaden: Deutscher Universitätsverlag.

Author index

Subject index

In the series *Linguistic Approaches to Literature* the following titles have been published thus far or are scheduled for publication: